D0192806

The Commandos at Dieppe:
Rehearsal for D-Day

Allies at War – The book of the TV series
Simon Berthon
ISBN 0-00-711622-5

By Sea, By Land: The Royal Marines 1919-1997,
An Authorised History
James D. Ladd
ISBN 0-00-472366-X

For Five Shillings A Day, Personal Histories of World War II
Dr Richard Campbell Begg and Dr Peter Liddle
ISBN 0-00-713720-6

And forthcoming from HarperCollins*Publishers*

Falklands Commando
Hugh McManners
ISBN 0-00-714175-0

> "The spirit of the dead will survive
> in the memory of the living"
> *The Mission*

The Commandos
at Dieppe:
Rehearsal for D-Day

Operation Cauldron,
No 4 Commando attack
on the Hess Battery
August 19th, 1942

Will Fowler

Collins

HarperCollins*Publishers*
77–85 Fulham Palace Road
Hammersmith
London W6 8JB

everything clicks at www.collins.co.uk

First published in Great Britain by HarperCollins*Publishers* 2002
This edition published by HarperCollins*Publishers* 2003

1 3 5 7 9 10 8 6 4 2

ISBN: 0–00–711126–6

Printed in Great Britain by Clays Ltd, St Ives plc

A catalogue record for this book is available from the British Library

Contents

"Be on guard! Eyes and ears alert!
Kick the Anglo-American and his helpers in the snout!"

Colonel General Curt Haase,
CO 302nd Infantry Division, Dieppe

"Commandos are made up from murderers, gangsters,
and the like...
Cold steel is the only way to deal with them"

Order of the Day,
302nd Infantry Division, Dieppe

Commandos -"Churchill's rats who kill by night"

German propaganda slogan

"A raid was launched in the early hours of to-day on
the DIEPPE area of enemy-occupied FRANCE"

Communiqué 06.00 hours August 19, 1942

"At daybreak No. 4 Commando, consisting of
252 all ranks, including Allied personnel, assaulted the
six gun battery covering the West approaches
to the port of Dieppe"

Communiqué August 19, 1942

"My task was fundamental:
in and out – smash and grab"

Lt Colonel The Lord Lovat,
Commanding Officer No 4 Commando

"It was luck, nothing more than luck...
Probably the luckiest mortar shot of World War II"

Troop Sergeant Major James Dunning
C Troop No 4 Commando

" It had been a rough party
with no quarter asked or given"

Major Derek Mills-Roberts
Second-in-Command No 4 Commando

"Set them on fire. Burn the lot"

Lt Colonel The Lord Lovat,
CO No 4 Commando 07.15, August 19, 1942

"813 Battery has been destroyed by men
with blackened faces"

Report to HQ 302nd Division
12.00, August 19, 1942

"The last survivors, like all the enemy encountered,
fought well"

Notes from Theatres of War No 11

"The success of the operation was
chiefly due to the excellence of junior leading
and superior weapon training"

Lt Colonel The Lord Lovat, CO No 4 Commando
quoted in Notes from *Theatres of War No 11*

"Sweat saves blood, but this fact is not
appreciated until the battle is over"

Major Derek Mills-Roberts
Second in Command No 4 Commando

I extend to all Commanding Officers and troops who
have taken part in the action my praise and my thanks.
Today I have been able to report
"The troops have fought well"

C-in-C West von Rundstedt,
Field Marshal

"This is one of the things the peacemakers will have to
think about after this war –
happiness in fighting men.
I saw men go into action and out of it with a happy
eagerness on their faces. I felt the touch of it myself –
reprehensible, perhaps, but there it was"

A.B. Austin
War Correspondent attached to No 4 Commando

Foreword

"Who carries the 2-inch Mortar?"

"The platoon commander" chorused the classroom of Riflemen.

"No" replied my successor in his lecture on the structure and weapons of an infantry platoon "the Platoon Sergeant".

"Mr Fowler always carried it".

He was right, but the young Territorial Army soldiers of 9 Ptn, C Coy, 4th Bn The Royal Green Jackets, the platoon that until recently I had had the privilege to command, had seen me carry it on exercises. The Platoon Sergeant was probably delighted by my tactically unsound and rather eccentric behaviour, as picking up my rifle I also slung the 3.3kg mortar over my shoulder.

In training I found that, with practice, the smoke bombs could be placed to screen targets at ranges up to 300 metres. At night the instant light from the illumination bombs was very effective in defensive actions and springing ambushes.

It was also great fun to fire.

In a television programme about the attack on Dieppe, Pat Porteous VC, standing on the site of a German coastal battery, described how the Troop Sergeant Major (TSM) of C Troop No 4 Commando with a 2-inch mortar crew, had landed HE bombs with great accuracy on the position. One had hit stored ammunition and triggered a huge secondary explosion effectively destroying the battery.

Subsequently writing an article about light mortars, now often called Commando Mortars, I alluded to personal experience and cited the dramatic success of this weapon at Dieppe.

Some years later at a military dining club, the brainchild of the writer and historian Donald Featherstone, I discovered one of the members had been an Army Commando in World War II.

It was only later that I realised that Jimmy Dunning had been the young TSM commanding the 2-inch Mortar crew at Dieppe. With characteristic modesty he explained that he had little part in the success which was the result of hard training by the mortar crew of Privates J. "Jock" Dale and F.J. Horne.

Jimmy was then working on his very successful book *"It Had To Be Tough"* about Commando training in World War II. It was to be published in 2000 on the 60th anniversary of the establishment of the Commandos.

Realising that 2002 would be the 60th anniversary of Operation JUBILEE fired my interest in the No 4 Commando action. Though numerous books had been written about the larger operation, which remains overwhelmingly a tale of courage and tragedy, none had focussed on No 4 Commando.

At dawn the Commando had attacked and destroyed the coastal battery, code-named HESS, at Varengeville to the west of Dieppe. In books about Dieppe the attack, code named CAULDRON, was normally covered in a chapter, that often began with sentences like "However on the right flank the operation went according to plan..."

CAULDRON was more than an operation that went according to plan – it was a victory, a triumph of planning, training, leadership and courage.

"Have you contacted Emyr Jones?" asked Jimmy Dunning when I discussed the idea of writing a book about CAULDRON.

Veterans and researchers agree that Emyr Jones is the unofficial archivist of the No 4 Commando action. He has trawled the war diaries, notes and reports at the Public Records Office, Kew and interviewed or corresponded with British, French, German and American veterans. After three years of advertisements and sending over 5,000 letters he had by 1990 assembled the nominal role of the officers and men of the Commando who fought in CAULDRON.

His photographic collection is remarkable. I am grateful to him not only for the use of photographs, but also the unique account by Gerard Cadot and the documents accessed from the PRO.

On August 18, 2000 I went to Dieppe with Jimmy, Jane his wife and Emyr. We drove out from the town, past the honey coloured limestone houses of Varengeville west to the little hamlet of Le Mesnil.

"Well here it is" said Jimmy as we looked out across some rough pasture towards a wood. With holiday bungalows and cows quietly grazing, it was initially hard to imagine that this was the location of the Commando attack.

With Jimmy and Emyr as guides however the history in the countryside came alive.

"This was where Dickie Mann took up his position," said Emyr as, walking north towards Vasterival, we passed a gap in the hedge. Here a camouflaged Commando sniper had picked off the German gunners.

It was then into the woods to look at the site of the battery from the viewpoint of the 2-inch Mortar crew and C Troop.

Turning right down the road past the Hotel de la Terrasse we made the hazardous descent down the Port de Vasterival, the gully leading to the sea. Stepping off the concrete steps onto the sand and pebbles we were on Orange Beach 1. It was low tide – the conditions in which the Commandos had departed after the attack.

Returning we paused at the church at Ste Marguerite in the "Place du No 4è Commando" where the human cost of the action is remembered by the names of 16 Commandos on the memorial on the wall.

Down the hill to the mouth of the River Saâne and we were on Orange Beach 2. A fine rain was falling and there was an onshore breeze, the sea, the shingle beach and the river looked uninviting.

Prior to the visit to France, I had contacted one of the two surviving US Rangers who had been attached to the Commando. Alex Szima proved a lively and knowledgeable correspondent who had never succumbed to the temptation to "throw out that old stuff from the war". His archive of cuttings, letters and reports was informative not only about the establishment and history of the Rangers, but also US reaction to Dieppe.

Returning to Dieppe I dodged the rainsqualls to visit the plaque commemorating the Ranger dead on the site of the casino at the seafront. They were the first American soldiers to be killed in action on European soil in World War II.

Back in Hampshire as work progressed Jimmy was generous with the loan of books, documents and photographs. Without these and his advice and guidance, much of the detail in this book could not have been included.

He put me in touch with two Commando veterans, Bren gunner George Jones and demolition expert John Skerry. I am grateful to John for details of the make up of the charges used to destroy the guns and his recollections of the operation and fellow Commandos.

Hampshire military historian and antiquarian book dealer, Ken Ford generously supplied me with books and other references from his extensive collection.

The Imperial War Museum Sound Archive provided a unique record of interviews with the men who fought at the HESS battery. To listen to the tapes is to hear not only first hand accounts, but also to receive a lesson in a non-intrusive but effective interview technique.

The busy staff at Romsey Public Library, a branch of the Hampshire County Library Service, were a great help, tracking down titles long out of print and checking publication dates.

Dr Alistair Massie of the National Army Museum who produced from the archives the papers of No 4 Commando's Intelligence Officer Lt Tony Smith gave me an added insight into the operation.

I am grateful to Andrew Salanson and the team at Avalon Design + Print who took my scribbles and rough references and turned them into the excellent and authoritative maps within the text.

My thanks to Tim Stenkis of the Royal Signals Museum who provided the technical data for the radio sets used by No 4 Commando.

Former comrade in arms Dr Simon Chapman TD provided a valuable insight into European practices in orthopaedic medicine.

It was as I worked through this mass of information, autobiographies and accounts that I realised that I had encountered No 4 Commando before.

As a 12-year-old curled up in my school dormitory I had read *The Raid at Dieppe*, a book that had definitely not come from the school library. The account of JUBILEE by the American correspondent Quentin Reynolds originally published in 1943 as *Dress Rehearsal the Story of Dieppe*, had come out in paperback after the war with an eye catching cover and a new and grammatically questionable title.

In the book Reynolds quoted US Rangers who reported seeing British Commandos picking and eating apples as they moved through an orchard exchanging fire with the Germans.

To a schoolboy this was gripping and memorable stuff.

Forty years on the schoolboy had finished the first draft of this book about the Commando action at Dieppe and Jimmy, Alex and Emyr generously then read it and offered advice and corrections.

Any oversights or errors that appear within the finished text are mine alone. To critical veterans of No 4 Commando and informed readers I can only offer the plea in mitigation of the American historian Professor Stephen Ambrose, "Military historians do the best they can".

All of the people who helped with the book were in effect occasional visitors to it, one person lived with it from the beginning. Throughout the months of writing and research I enjoyed the love, support and encouragement of Carol my wife. Without her it would have been impossible.

In the days of the manual typewriter, authors would sometimes grandly thank their wives "for turning my scrappy typing and corrections into a readable manuscript". Thankfully typewriter ribbons, carbons and correcting fluid are now history.

Carol has done a far greater professional service, expertly and painstakingly editing the manuscript.

Thank you for everything.

Will Fowler
Romsey, Hampshire
September 2001

Introduction

At dawn on August 19, 1942 the training and planning for Operation JUBILEE became a bloody reality.

The operation was an Anglo Canadian attack against the German held French coastal town of Dieppe that in the planning had been assigned the code name JUBILEE. In the attack the bulk of the force, some 4,963 men of the 2nd Canadian Division, was committed to frontal assaults on the town and adjoining coast.

The head of Combined Operations, Admiral Lord Louis Mountbatten, who had overall command of the operation, would emphasise that JUBILEE was not a raid but a reconnaissance in force. The landings, supported by 28 Churchill tanks of the Calgary Regiment, took place on eight beaches and the troops were tasked with destroying batteries and other installations in the town before making their withdrawal.

In addition to the 2nd Canadian Division about 1,000 British Commandos from No 3 and No 4 Commandos and A Commando RM (formed in early 1942 and subsequently designated 40 Cdo, RM) were involved in supporting the main attack.

Despite awesome bravery the landing on the shingle beaches in front of Dieppe was stopped almost before the Canadian soldiers had left their landing craft. On that one day the 2nd Canadian Division lost 3,164 men and 215 officers as well as all its tanks and other vehicles. These were losses as bad as or worse than the blood baths of the Western Front in World War I.

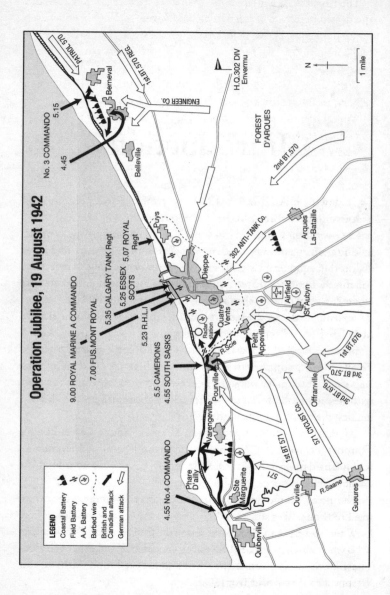

Operation Jubilee, 19 August 1942

LEGEND
Coastal Battery
Field Battery
A.A. Battery
Barbed wire
British and
Canadian attack
German attack

9.00 ROYAL MARINE A COMMANDO

7.00 FUS. MONT ROYAL

5.35 CALGARY TANK Regt

5.25 ESSEX
5.07 ROYAL
SCOTS Regt

5.23 R.H.L.I

5.5 CAMERONS

4.55 SOUTH SASKS

4.55 No.4 COMMANDO

Phare
D'ailly

Quiberville

Ste
Marguerite

571

571 CYCLIST CO.

1st BT 571

Ouville

R.Saane

Gueures

Offranville

3rd BT 676

3rd BT 570

1st BT 676

Petit
Appeville

R.Scie

Pourville

Varengeville

Radar
Station

Quatre
Vents

St Aubyn

Airfield

302 ANTI-TANK CO.

Arques
La-Bataille

2nd BT 570

FOREST
D'ARQUES

H.Q.302 DIV
Envermu

ENGINEER Co.

1st BT 570 REG.

Berneval

5.15

4.45

No. 3 COMMANDO

Belleville

Puys

Dieppe

PATROL 570

N

1 mile

16

The Royal Navy suffered 550 casualties, lost 33 landing craft and the destroyer HMS *Berkley*, torpedoed after she had been severely bomb damaged. The RAF lost 106 aircraft, while the Luftwaffe who had committed 945 aircraft to attacking the Allied beachhead, lost only 48.

With some justification the Germans could claim Dieppe as a victory, their casualties on land totalled only 591.

As part of this operation No 4 Commando, a largely British force but which also included French Commandos, American Rangers and Canadian signallers, attacked and neutralised the six 155 mm guns of No 813 Battery close to Varengeville-sur-Mer. This battery on the right flank of the main beaches had been given the code name HESS.

The story of the No 4 Commando attack, given the separate code name Operation CAULDRON, is a model of sound planning, intensive training and the tactics of "fire and movement".

The plan was the brainchild of Lieutenant Colonel The Lord Lovat the commanding officer of No 4 Commando. He trained and led this force that defeated a roughly equal number of Germans who were dug in behind barbed wire, protected by interlocked machine gun positions and anti-aircraft guns that could be used in a ground role.

In the fighting Captain Pat Porteous RA was hit in the hand and thigh but led the assault by F Troop, part of the "movement" group, and finally collapsed weakened by loss of blood when the objective had been secured. He was awarded the British and Commonwealth's highest decoration for gallantry the Victoria Cross.

Of the four US Rangers attached to Number 4 Commando, Corporal Franklin D. "Zip" Koons became the first US serviceman to kill a German on land in World War II – Koons was awarded the Military Medal by the British.

The operation would also mark the first return to France by men of the Free French Forces.

When the press in USA picked up the story of the 50 US Rangers who were attached to JUBILEE they gave it the biggest headlines since Pearl Harbor. The *New York Daily News* splashed "Yanks in 9-hr Dieppe Raid" across its front page.

CAULDRON was the only success of the disastrous and tragic Operation JUBILEE. This is the story of the men who fought and won at the HESS Battery that summer morning.

CHAPTER 1

1942

It was a year that had begun badly and month by month was getting worse.

In the Far East the Imperial Japanese Army and Navy were enjoying a run of successes against the United States, Britain and such European colonial powers as The Netherlands and France – themselves occupied in Europe by Nazi Germany for nearly two years.

On January 11 the Japanese 5th Division entered Kuala Lumpur in Malaya and on February 15 Singapore fell to the Japanese and 80,000 British and Commonwealth soldiers were marched into brutal captivity. On February 19 Japanese bombers attacked Darwin on the Australian mainland causing panic, they would strike again on March 22. Between February 27 and 29 the Allies had lost five cruisers and six destroyers in action against the Imperial Navy in the battle of the Java Sea. Fear gripped Australia as it braced itself for a Japanese invasion.

On March 8 Rangoon, the capital of Burma fell and by early May the Japanese had pushed into most of Burma and were advancing towards the eastern borders of the huge British colony of India. On August 10 following the arrest by the British of the Indian Congress Party leader Mahatma Gandhi, rioting broke out in the cities of Bombay, Poona and Ahmedabad.

On March 11 General Douglas MacArthur, who commanded US and Filipino soldiers, escaped to Australia from Luzon in the Philippines. On April 5 five Japanese aircraft carriers sailed into the

Indian Ocean and attacked Colombo, Ceylon (Sri Lanka) and sank two British cruisers as well as other warships. Two days later they hit Tricomalee and sank the carrier HMS *Hermes*. On the same day 78,000 US and Filipino troops surrendered on Bataan – the largest capitulation in US military history. A day later they set off on the notorious "Death March" in which about 16,000 died or were killed. On May 6 on the island fortress of Corregidor, General Jonathan Wainwright surrendered his surviving force of 15,000 soldiers to 1,000 Japanese commanded by General Masaharu Homma.

In Britain the strategic importance of the Battle of Midway fought that year between June 3 and 6 had not been comprehended despite some bold headlines in the British papers. The naval action between the US Pacific Fleet and Japanese Combined Fleet was a tactical victory for the Americans who, though they lost the carrier USS *Yorktown*, managed to sink four Japanese carriers. Though no one realised at the time it was a victory that pushed Japan onto the defensive in the Pacific.

In Europe too the news was bad. The German Army that invaded the USSR on June 22, 1941 had been held at Moscow in the winter of 1941-42 but now on May 8, 1942 in the rolling wheat fields of the Ukraine they launched their new summer offensive, *Unternehmen Blau* – Operation BLUE.

In savage fighting at Kharkov between May 12 and 28 they defeated a planned Soviet Spring offensive and then rolled eastwards. The offensive by General Malinovsky's South Front crushed in *Unternehmen Fredericus 1* cost the Germans 20,000 men, but the Soviet losses were staggering, 214,000 men, 1,200 tanks and 2,000 guns.

The Soviet Black Sea naval base of Sevastopol fell on July 2 after a prolonged siege. Following fierce street fighting, in which artillery was used at point blank range against strong points in apartment blocks, Rostov on the Don fell on July 23. The northern city of Leningrad struggled to survive surrounded by German and Finnish troops, in a siege that would last from the autumn of 1941 to January 1944. During this time over 600,000 citizens would die of starvation and some would stay alive only through cannibalism.

In the hot summer months of 1942 the 6th Army, part of Army Group A under Field Marshal Siegmund List reached the outskirts of the industrial city of Stalingrad, on the Volga. To the south east the critical oil fields of the Caucasus were within reach and Maikop fell on August 9, though its installations had been torched or demolished.

In *Werwolf* – Werewolf, the grandiloquent name for his headquarters established for the summer offensive of 1942 at Vinnitsa in the Ukraine, Germany's Leader – *Führer* Adolf Hitler followed the campaign with febrile fascination.

For the British the news from the Far East was consistently bad. For Churchill and the Allied planners in London it was vital that the USSR remained in the war. The vast distances of the Eastern Front and the almost limitless strength of the Red Army would absorb the bulk of Nazi Germany's troops and equipment. For Britain Germany remained the main enemy. On February 20 the government of President Franklin Roosevelt granted the USSR a $1,000 million loan. On May 26 Britain and the USSR signed a 20 year mutual assistance treaty in London. At the signing Vlachislav Molotov, the Soviet Commissar for Foreign Affairs, urged the British Prime Minister Winston Churchill to launch a landing in Europe, a second front, to take the pressure off the USSR.

Britain had been sending supplies to the USSR in convoys of merchant ships that had since September 1941 sailed north skirted the North Cape of Norway and docked at Murmansk. During the following year 60 ships had been lost out of 14 Arctic Convoys, losses deemed acceptable for the political and material assistance that was being rendered to the USSR.

On July 4, 1942 the British Admiralty ordered the 34 ship Convoy PQ17 to scatter after it had received intelligence that the German battleship KMS *Tirpitz* was about to attack. The information was incorrect, but the ships, now unprotected by escorts, were easy prey for U Boats and Ju 88 bombers of *Kampfgeschwader* (KG) 30 and He 111H-6 torpedo aircraft of 1/KG26 which attacked it for five long days in the Arctic summer. On July 10 some 13 ships limped into Murmansk. Convoy operations to the USSR were subsequently cancelled and not resumed until September.

To Joseph Stalin these losses seemed small compared to those suffered by the USSR in men and equipment as well as huge areas of its industrial and agricultural heartland. If Stalin decided to cut his losses and conclude a separate peace with Germany, huge resources would be released to fight the Anglo American armies in the west. It was a threat that Stalin, a brutal pragmatist, was quite capable of carrying out. The USSR had even made secret contacts with Germany to explore the possibility of calling a cease-fire to be followed by peace negotiations. Stalin was on record as saying,

"In war I would deal with the Devil and his grandmother."

An operation to relieve the pressure on Russia was therefore vital. In Britain the Imperial General Staff were horrified when Churchill suggested Operation JUPITER, a plan to seize areas of northern Norway to reduce the threat to Arctic Convoys. It was an attempt to head off these and other unrealistic schemes proposed by Churchill, that made operation JUBILEE, the attack on Dieppe, seem like the least worst option.

In Britain where Communism had many followers people saw the Soviet Union as the only country making an effective stand against Nazism, a popular slogan among Left Wing activists was "Second Front Now!" In *Unauthorised Action*, the trenchant study of the origins and responsibility for Operation JUBILEE, the Canadian academic Brian Loring Villa includes a powerful account of this.

"At one of the Second Front Now meetings in Trafalgar Square early in April 1942, a speaker in Home Guard uniform tried to quiet down the Second Front agitation by asking whether it was right for the uninformed public to tell the Government and the Imperial General Staff what operations they should be undertaking. The crowd roared 'YES' until it reverberated across the square and down to Whitehall."

Churchill and the Chiefs of the Imperial General Staff were acutely aware that a full scale invasion of northern Europe was not viable and they looked for other European theatres in which pressure could be brought to bear on Nazi Germany.

One option seemed to be air attacks. On February 19, 49 year old Air Marshal A.T. "Bomber" or "Butch", Harris was appointed as Commander-in-Chief, Bomber Command. On May 31/June 1 on the

1,001st day of the war RAF Bomber Command struck Cologne in the first "Thousand Bomber Raid". It was a spectacular attack and in a filmed interview Harris grimly prophesied, "They sowed the wind. They will reap the whirlwind. Luebeck, Rostock, Cologne – they are just the beginning." Saturation bombing against major conurbations represented a change in tactics and Churchill noted, "This proof of the growing power of Britain's bomber force is also a herald of what Germany will receive, city by city, from now on."

In the Mediterranean theatre British and Commonwealth forces had initially enjoyed military successes against the Italians in 1940-41. However in Greece and Crete they had been defeated by German armour, dive bombers and paratroops and forced to withdraw, with costly losses in ships, men and equipment. On February 12, 1941 a German force, that would become famous as the *Deutsches Afrika Korps* commanded by the hard driving General Erwin Rommel, had landed in Tripoli to assist the Italians in North Africa. He immediately went onto the offensive driving back the exhausted British and Commonwealth forces. Attacks and counter attacks followed and at the start of February 1942 the British 8th Army, which had dug itself into positions in Gazala was outmanoeuvred and heavily defeated. It retreated from Cyrenaica and Rommel captured the port of Tobruk on June 21 and with it 35,000 prisoners and vast stocks of supplies.

The *Afrika Korps* pushed on towards Egypt and when it arrived at the Alamein area on June 30 there was panic in Cairo and moves to evacuate the city and redeploy the headquarters to Palestine. Clearly North Africa was not a theatre in which pressure could be brought to bear on Nazi Germany.

Shocked by the loss of Tobruk, that had held out under siege in 1941 and the huge losses in the Far East, there was a call in the House of Commons for a motion of no confidence in Prime Minister Winston Churchill's leadership. The debate on July 3 in which 50 MPs spoke lasted 19 hours, 50 minutes. The attack on the Prime Minister was defeated by 475 votes to 25, with 30 abstentions and 75 members either ill or serving abroad.

On the home front the Cathedral City of Exeter was hit three times in ten nights in May in "Baedeker" raids, Luftwaffe attacks directed against cultural targets. New civilian food rationing restrictions including a ban on the production of ice cream and white bread. Some sort of local victory was needed to raise domestic morale as well as assisting the USSR.

Only occupied northwest Europe seemed to offer a possible area for such an operation, albeit on a modest scale.

In 1942 the German international illustrated propaganda magazine *Signal* featured a map of Europe and North Africa in which only the neutral Sweden, Spain, Portugal and Switzerland and the enemy Britain were not coloured red as either an ally or a conquest of the Third Reich.

Two years earlier, immediately after the defeat of France and the British evacuation at Dunkirk on June 4, 1940, Churchill had urged that volunteer raiding forces should be formed to take the war back to newly occupied Europe.

For many British servicemen the withdrawal from France and evacuation at Dunkirk had been a humiliation that was compounded by the subsequent Luftwaffe air attacks on Britain between 1940 and 1941, and there was a real desire to take some kind of offensive action.

Churchill proposed that these raiding formations be called "Commandos" a name he took from his experiences in the South African War.

In the South African war of 1899 – 1902 between Afrikaans speaking Boers and British and Imperial forces, both sides used cavalry and mounted infantry for patrolling and raids. Boer militia forces were grouped into "Commandos", a word taken from the Portuguese, and as the weight of numbers and improved British tactics forced the Boers onto the defensive, their Commandos adopted guerrilla tactics. The hardy Boers, who were excellent shots and good horsemen, sustained the war despite terrible hardships. The Boer civilian population who had provided support were moved into concentration camps by the British, who used a system of block houses and barbed wire fences along railway tracks to restrict the movement of the Commandos. By May 1902 these tactics had worked and the Boers sued for peace.

The young Winston Churchill, working as a war correspondent had been captured by the Boers in 1899 and subsequently escaped. His admiration for his tough adversaries included a lasting friendship with a former Boer Commando leader, soldier and South African statesman, General Jan Smuts.

The Director of Military Operations and Plans, Major General R.H. Dewing drafted the memorandum that would set the style for the new Commandos. They would be largely based on the military regional administrative areas in the UK known as Commands. "One or two officers in each Command will be selected as commando Leaders. They will be instructed to select from their own Commands a number of Troop Leaders to serve under them. The Troop Leaders will in turn select the officers and men to form their own Troop."

Though many men in the pre-war Regular Army had lived by the adage "Keep your eyes open, mouth shut and never volunteer for anything" they were among the first volunteers for the new force. Clifford Leach who would later serve with F Troop No 4 Commando admitted that after volunteering "I didn't quite know what I had let myself in for". Ken Phillot a soldier with the Gloucestershire Regiment (Glosters) saw on battalion orders that "Volunteers were wanted for Special Duties".

"This seemed to offer something different, although I had no idea what these Special Duties would be. I informed my Company Commander that I wished to volunteer."

At the same time that Commandos were being raised, there was a drive to break down the barriers between the Royal Navy, Army and Royal Air Force and to conduct Combined Operations (Combined Ops). A Combined Operations Headquarters was established under the dynamic leadership of 69 year old Admiral Sir Roger Keyes the hero of the Zeebrugge raid of World War I. He held the post from July 1940 to October 1941 when, following a disagreement with the British Chiefs of Staff, he was replaced by the 41 year old Admiral Lord Louis Mountbatten.

Sir Roger Keyes stands out as the champion of the Commandos in the face of War Office hostility at a very difficult period in the war and so is in effect the father of British Special Forces. "Time spent in his company made one feel twice one's size; and that, of course is what

Combined Operations Command 1942

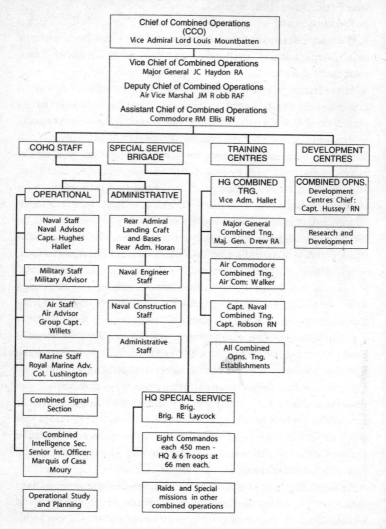

Chief of Combined Operations
(CCO)
Vice Admiral Lord Louis Mountbatten

Vice Chief of Combined Operations
Major General JC Haydon RA

Deputy Chief of Combined Operations
Air Vice Marshal JM R obb RAF

Assistant Chief of Combined Operations
Commodore RM Ellis RN

COHQ STAFF

SPECIAL SERVICE BRIGADE

TRAINING CENTRES

DEVELOPMENT CENTRES

OPERATIONAL

ADMINISTRATIVE

HG COMBINED TRG.
Vice Adm. Hallet

COMBINED OPNS.
Development
Centres Chief:
Capt. Hussey RN

Naval Staff
Naval Advisor
Capt. Hughes Hallet

Rear Admiral
Landing Craft
and Bases
Rear Adm. Horan

Major General
Combined Tng.
Maj. Gen. Drew RA

Research and
Development

Military Staff
Military Advisor

Naval Engineer
Staff

Air Commodore
Combined Tng.
Air Com: Walker

Air Staff
Air Advisor
Group Capt. Willets

Naval Construction
Staff

Capt. Naval
Combined Tng.
Capt. Robson RN

Marine Staff
Royal Marine Adv.
Col. Lushington

Administrative
Staff

All Combined
Opns. Tng.
Establishments

Combined Signal
Section

Combined
Intelligence Sec.
Senior Int. Officer:
Marquis of Casa Moury

HQ SPECIAL SERVICE
Brig.
Brig. RE Laycock

Operational Study
and Planning

Eight Commandos
each 450 men -
HQ & 6 Troops at
66 men each.

Raids and Special
missions in other
combined operations

leadership is all about" wrote Lord Lovat. "He was, like most genuine people, a very uncomplicated man, with straightforward beliefs and simple views on life. Old Sir Roger had none of the devious ways which can pass for cleverness today. To let him down was unthinkable."

Mountbatten who had served in the Royal Navy in World War I was a charismatic and ambitious officer and the great-grandson of Queen Victoria.

At the outbreak of the war he had commanded the 5th Destroyer Flotilla and took part in the evacuation of Norway. As captain of the destroyer HMS *Kelly* he had brought the severely damaged vessel back to England at the end of the campaign. In April 1941 he was sent to Malta and saw action off Crete; *Kelly* was finally sunk in air attacks in May 23, 1941 to the south of the island. Churchill then appointed him Advisor on Combined Operations and he undertook the preliminary planning of the invasion of Europe. In March 1942 Churchill made him a member of the Chiefs of Staff Committee.

Mountbatten's exploits as the captain of the destroyer were the basis of Noël Coward's film *In Which We Serve* which was in production in England in the summer of 1942. Royal connections and his exploits as a destroyer captain had helped to make Mountbatten a familiar name in the USA, a country that had entered the war following the Japanese attack on Pearl Harbor on December 7, 1941. Though he had charm and diplomatic skills and General Dwight Eisenhower was among his admirers, he also had his critics during the war amongst senior officers and afterwards amongst historians.

Nigel Hamilton in his three volume authorised biography of Field Marshal Montgomery would later say of Mountbatten, "as Chief of Combined Operations he was a master of intrigue, jealousy, and ineptitude. Like a spoilt child he toyed with men's lives with an indifference to casualties that can only be explained by his insatiable, even psychopathic ambition ... a man whose mind was an abundance of brilliant and insane ideas often without coherence or consistent 'doctrine'. Allied to the equally undisciplined, wildly imaginative Churchill – with whom Mountbatten would often stay for weekends – the two made a formidable and dangerous pair."

Writing when Mountbatten was still alive Lovat, who at Dieppe would command Number 4 Commando with distinction, said of the Chief of Combined Operations, "Mountbatten was the cheerful extrovert who had been lucky at sea".

To reinforce the spirit of co-operation in Combined Operations, a distinctive red and dark blue flash had been designed. It featured the anchor for the RN, the recently introduced Thompson sub-machine gun for the Army and the RAF eagle. Both the Army and the Royal Marines had formed Commandos which were the permanent ground forces of Combined Operations.

The Commando units that were eventually raised were numbered No1 to 9, 11 and 12. A No 13 Commando was never formed.

They were later joined by a unique force with the same title. Number 10 Inter-Allied (IA) Commando a formation including anti-Nazi German personnel and other troops drawn from German occupied countries. It had a British staffed HQ and eight troops, No's 1 and 8 were French, No 2 Dutch, No 3 German, Austrian, Hungarian and Czech – mostly Jews who had been given Anglicised names, No 6 was Polish and No 7 Yugoslav.

The origins of No 10 Commando are shrouded in some mystery. It was officially formed in January 1942 and its first CO fresh from commanding 4 Commando was the colourful Lt Col Dudley Lister.

The French troops in No 10 Commando were under the Alsace born Marine Captain Philippe Kieffer and made up No 1 and No 8 Troops and a K-gun (.303 gas operated light machine gun) Section of No 9 Troop. Fifteen French Marines and officers, all originally from *1er Bataillon Fusilier Marine*, from the original soldiers of No 10 Commando would play a significant part in the Dieppe operation, four would provide invaluable assistance for No 4 Commando.

No 30 Commando was an inter-service intelligence gathering formation. In 1942 the three Royal Marine Commandos were formed, numbering 40, 41 and 48. All Army and Marine Commandos were part of four Special Service Brigades that were in turn controlled by a Special Service Group. (The title Special Service would be changed to Commando in 1944)

By 1942 a Commando consisted of between 460 and 500 men,

about half the size of a modern British Army Infantry Battalion commanded by a Lieutenant Colonel and divided into six troops. Five were fighting troops of about 60 men backed by a headquarters troop with attached heavy weapons. Weapons were largely those found within a British Infantry Battalion, though there was a wider distribution of automatic and specialised weapons and equipment issued for specific operations.

The size and structure of the Commandos and their role was not the only thing that set them apart from the Army.

George Cook, who served in F Troop of No 4 Commando in an interview for the Imperial War Museum (IWM) recalled the different style of discipline and leadership.

"You'd volunteered for the Commandos, they realised that you were human beings and you had a bit of sense, that you didn't need to be roared at and shouted at, screamed at all the time. Not only that, if you did anything, even in training, everything was explained to you. If you'd a different idea, even as a lowly Private, you could say "Well, sir, don't you think if we went that way instead of this way it would be easier?" If you were right that was the method that was adopted."

John Price one of a 3-inch Mortar crew in the Commando remarked in his IWM interview "What I liked about the Commandos after the ordinary infantry, we were allowed to have some common sense. We were allowed to show initiative. We were briefed before we went into action, not herded like sheep."

No 4 Commando was formed in Weymouth in July 1940 and its first commanding officer was Lt Colonel D.P.D. "Percy" The Legard (The 5th Inniskilling Dragoon Guards). The first Commanding Officer's parade was held in the town's old Pavilion on July 22, 1940. Fifty years later the veterans of No 4 Commando unveiled a plaque at the Pavilion, commemorating the establishment of the Commando and its service in Europe in World War II.

Sir Roger Keyes called No 4 his "Cavalry Commando" partly because some of the officers and men had been recruited from Yeomanry cavalry regiments, but also because to provide it mobility in an anti-invasion role they had been equipped with 500 bicycles.

One of the first volunteers, Ken Phillot, as a Private soldier was surprised to be interviewed in person by Colonel Legard. Phillot recalled that:

"He then started to ask me questions such as:

'I see you have already seen active service. Tell me, can you swim at least 500 yards in full kit?' I replied that I was a good swimmer and thought I could do so.

'Can you drive a car and ride a motorcycle?' I replied I could. He then asked what my pre-war hobbies had been to which I replied swimming, boxing and motor-cycling. I was asked if I had done any climbing and satisfied him when I said that I was born and lived on the edge of Exmoor where there was nothing but hills and moorland. He then asked :

'Can you stand plenty of bloodshed?' I laughed and replied:

'Well, if anyone else can, I am sure I can!'

'Good' he replied 'wait outside'."

At the close of the interviews Phillot, along with five or six other men was called back and the Colonel asked:

"Do you know what you are volunteering for?" The men replied that they did not and after being told that they were "A lot of bloody fools (for) … not knowing" the Colonel explained the role of the force. Phillot recalled that when his Company Commander, a big rugby playing South African, learned about the Commandos he too volunteered.

In *It Had To Be Tough* James Dunning, soon to be the youthful 22 year old Troop Sergeant Major (TSM) of C Troop at Dieppe, recalls that though the majority of volunteers were men in their twenties, there were also some "old sweats" Regular soldiers, some of whom were nearing forty.

Amongst the youngsters were Gunners J. Halliday and H.J. Pike who when they joined the Commando were barely out of their teenage "boy" service in the Army. They would both rise to the rank of Sergeant before being commissioned. "Spike" Pike would later serve with distinction with the Glosters in Korea on the Imjin River.

"Two 'oldies'", recalls Dunning were G.'Chalky' Blunden and H.Donkin, "Both were hardened pre-war regulars, well into their thirties when they volunteered. Normally quiet and well-disciplined soldiers they were virtual tigers when roused, and most outspoken if they reckoned the task in hand was pointless, unprofessional or just 'a load of bull...' On such occasions they didn't mince their words and the fact that they had not been promoted beyond acting lance corporal was evidence of their refusal to be 'Yes' men or 'creepers'. Notwithstanding in a tight corner or desperate situation they didn't question or flinch, they 'got stuck in...'." Blunden would win the Military Medal during the fighting at Dieppe in August 1942. Donkin having survived Dieppe and D Day would be killed in action during the No 4 Commando attack on Flushing in November 1944. John Skerry and Fred Gooch who had fought with the 1st Battalion The East Surrey Regiment in the BEF in France in 1940 joined No 4 Commando at Winchester.

The unspecified challenge of Special Duties also attracted regular warrant officers and senior NCOs. Bill 'Jumbo' Morris of the Royal Tank Regiment was in his thirties when he joined No 4 Commando. He would become its Regimental Sergeant Major (RSM) and be remembered by Dunning as having a "quiet but decisive manner – 'firm but fair' summed up his philosophy as RSM. Men knew where they stood with him and he gained the respect of all ranks by providing a good example of guts and determination. No one sweated and struggled more than RSM Morris on the gruelling speed and cross-country marches that he hated, but never dodged."

Sergeant 'Timber' Woodcock joined from the South Staffordshire Regiment and was promoted to TSM in No 4 Commando. After Dieppe Lovat recommended him for a commission but he declined and became the first RSM at CBTC Achnacarry. He returned to No 6 Commando under Lt Col Derek Mills-Roberts and landed at D Day.

The Commando also had men who had fought against Franco in the Spanish Civil War. In 1940 veterans of the International Brigade enjoyed something of a reputation as experts in low level tactics and were lionised in popular publications like *Picture Post*. Tom Wintringham's *New Ways of War*, published by Penguin in 1940 typified a new style of military evangelism propounded by former members of the International Brigade. However Lou Chattaway a Spanish Civil War veteran who joined B Troop in Weymouth as a private soldier was a modest and able soldier who rose steadily through the ranks and four years later went ashore at D Day as a Troop Sergeant Major. His pre-war experiences had in fact been quite colourful, during the Spanish Civil War Chattaway had been captured by Nationalist troops but managed to escape.

Of the officers Dunning, an acute observer, notes: "Among the original Troop Leaders and junior officers were several who were destined to become Commanding Officers of their own, or another Commando. They included regular, TA and Emergency Commission officers with differing backgrounds, personalities and physical attributes, yet regardless of such differences they all shared one common quality – leadership. It was the application of this priceless intangible quality that made them outstanding and inspiring Commando leaders".

The establishment of the Commandos was in its way very typically British. Improvised, slightly eccentric and under resourced. Nothing typifies this more than the accommodation arrangements for officers and men.

In a conventional regiment or battery housed in a barracks there would be buildings allocated for soldiers, NCOs and officers, with other related buildings like stores and an armoury for weapons. The Commandos had none of these conveniences but relied on billeting soldiers with local families in the area in which they were training. The landladies received £1.10s or "Thirty Bob" – £1.50 a week for housing and feeding the Commando soldier. Wages in 1940 were about £5 a week, so a Commando could be a useful supplement to a family's income. The officers often opted to be housed in a local hotel.

It may have been improvised, but because of the commitment of dedicated and courageous men to make it work – it did, beyond the expectations of some of its most enthusiastic champions or pessimistic antagonists.

Under the command of Lt Col Lister, the Commando saw action in 1941 in Operation CLAYMORE, the attack on the Lofoten Islands. At about this time it was joined by an officer who would change the Commando profoundly.

Captain The Lord Lovat was initially a supernumerary Captain attached to B Troop. For Lovat the raid had many lessons including the most basic tactical one, "That morning No.4 Commando wore steel helmets – useless impedimenta of a forgotten age – for the last time as a raiding force."

Following the Lofoten raids the Commando was based at Troon a coastal town in Ayrshire in north-west Scotland. Relations were good with the local population and on June 13, 1942 at St Nivan Church, Lt David Style, who would play a significant role in Operation CAULDRON, married Mary Balfour. Fred Gooch and John Skerry had the good fortune to be billeted with Mrs Campbell. With her two sons away in the RAF Mrs Campbell was delighted to have the two young Commandos as lodgers and they were just as pleased to be in a house with her three attractive daughters. Soon Fred was walking out with Rachel the oldest daughter and soon Ray' as she was known to all had become Fred's steady girlfriend.

The future commanding officer of No 4 Commando the 31 year old Simon Fraser, The Lord Lovat, had served in the Scots Guards before the war and later the Lovat Scouts[1] the Yeomanry Regiment that his father had founded.

Simon Fraser the 24th Chief of Clan Fraser of Lovat, was known universally as "Shimi" from the traditional medieval Gaelic title he inherited in 1933 of "Mac Shimidh" – Son of Simon after Simon Fraser founder of the Clan. Even the officers in No 4 Commando would know their commanding officer by this abbreviated traditional title. Under Lovat No 4 Commando would enjoy a sense of loyalty akin to that of a fighting Clan and its chief.

Tall, with striking good looks, Lovat was the heir to a Scottish and world wide clan that could trace its origins back to the 12th Century.[2] The first impression of Lovat recalled by A.B. Austin, the journalist who was attached to the Commando for Operation CAULDRON, was of "a tallish Commando officer with slightly wavy brown hair, a small Guards moustache, a full, youngish face, and a pleasant, speculative, slightly quizzical smile."

The American journalist H.R. Knickerbocker of *The Chicago Sun*, who interviewed some of the Commandos at Newhaven, after they had returned from Dieppe in August, 1942 was more fulsome. He described Lovat as "a tall, curly-haired, blue-eyed, radiantly handsome, wealthy young nobleman, whose behaviour in this war refutes those critics who believe the British "upper class" isn't pulling its weight."

Knickerbocker added with something of a journalistic flourish " 'Shimi' is in this war for the purpose of killing Germans and among the toughest Commandos, he is known as the most refined and efficient killer of them all. His men would follow him on the most forlorn hope, such was their task at Dieppe."

Later in the war when Lovat was part of an Allied mission to Moscow, Churchill contacted Stalin and, quoting the poet Lord Byron, said of Lovat. "He is the mildest-mannered man that ever scuttled ship or cut a throat".

Lovat had other admirers. In *Love is Blue*, the colourful diary of her wartime experiences, Joan Wyndham, then a young officer in the Women's Auxiliary Air Force (WAAF) gives her impressions of Lovat. In the autumn of 1942 she had been posted to Scotland and was invited to a dance at the Royal Engineers Officers' Mess that had been at established at Beaufort Castle the home of Lord Lovat. She confided to her diary, "There is not a girl in our Mess who doesn't secretly lust after him – including me! – and the very thought of visiting his home and maybe catching a glimpse of him thrills me to the marrow."

On a later visit Wyndham met the family and household who in her description emerge as slightly eccentric, hospitable and entirely democratic. Lovat she decided did not look like a Commando dressed in "pin-striped trousers, green tweed jacket and an orange suede waistcoat.

Our first impression was that he was quite fiendishly good-looking. He has a terrific figure and carries himself well. But when you get close to him you notice he has rather small eyes and an inclination to put on flesh under the chin – not *quite* my *Daily Mirror* hero!"

Months before he was subject to this detailed scrutiny Lovat had been promoted to Second in Command of No 4 Commando and led it on Operation ABERCROMBIE. The operation by a joint Commando and Canadian force drawn from the *Fusiliers Mont Royal* was a raid on the French seaside resort area of Hardelot near Boulogne on the night of April 21-22, 1942. Deep sand dunes and thick barbed wire prevented the force from penetrating far inland and though there was a brief firefight they did not take prisoners or conduct reconnaissance.

Lovat recalled that "Boulogne boosted morale but two men could have been more usefully employed in a stealthy reconnaissance of the Dieppe shore by Kayak canoe: indeed, plotting beaches and supplying a mapped description of coastal defences before stirring up the hornet's nest will always save lives."

Commando raids against Europe and North Africa were inevitably constrained by the number of suitable targets that were not too heavily defended and were close to the coast.

The first had been launched against the French coast near Le Touquet and Boulogne on the night of June 23-24, 1940. Two groups landed and for one minor injury killed two German sentries and grenaded an enemy held building. On July 14-15, No 3 Commando raided the German occupied British island of Guernsey. These small inauspicious beginnings, were the pointer for greater schemes. *Combined Operations 1940-1942* the publication produced in 1943 by His Majesty's Stationery Office (HMSO) compared these small scale raids to the trench raids of World War I. Like the raids from this previous World War they gathered intelligence and took the war to the enemy.

Significant successes were chalked up with attacks on March 4, and December 27, 1941 against the Lofoten Islands in Norway. In Operation CLAYMORE the first raid, about 300 British and 50 Norwegian troops commanded by Brigadier J.C. Haydon made a surprise landing. They destroyed 800,000 gallons of fish oil that could be used to produce glycerine, an ingredient in explosives production, as well as 18 fish oil factories. Some 250 prisoners were taken and 314 Norwegian volunteers returned with the raiders. What was not made public was that the current settings for Enigma the German encryption machine were captured from the KMS *Krebs*, an armed trawler, by a boarding party from the destroyer HMS *Somali*. The captured codes and equipment were passed to the top secret ULTRA signals decryption operation at the Government Code and Cypher School at Bletchley Park.

The island of Vaagso 100 miles north of Bergen was raided on December 27, 1941.

The attack, code named ARCHERY, was conducted by No 3 Commando with attached troops including Norwegians. It was a tougher fight than the Lofotens, the Commandos suffered 70 casualties including 17 killed and the Royal Navy two killed and six wounded. They returned with 98 prisoners, a number of Norwegian volunteers and left behind widespread destruction. The German armed trawlers KMS *Föhn* and KMS *Donner* were captured respectively by HMS *Onslow* and HMS *Offa* during the operation and yielded further valuable Enigma intelligence.

Operation ANKLET a diversionary raid on the Lofoten islands to support the Vaagso operation enjoyed considerable success. Some 300 men of No 12 Commando caught the garrison off their guard after Christmas dinner and remained on the islands for two days. The destroyer HMS *Ashanti* captured the trawler KMS *Geier* adding further to the haul of Enigma intelligence.

Raids by the British Special Forces on occupied France and Norway, now increasing in intensity, kept pressure on the Germans. Some senior servicemen and government ministers saw them as a way in which Britain could demonstrate support for the USSR and show its determination to pull its weight in the war to its new and powerful ally the USA.

On January 15, 1942 only months after the United States had entered the war the US Army 34th Infantry Division commanded by Major General Russell P. Hartle sailed from New York bound for Belfast, in Northern Ireland and so were among the first US troops to land in Britain.

In Washington General George C. Marshall Chief of Staff of the US Army had tasked Brigadier General L.K. Truscott with the mission of learning about the techniques of British Combined Operations and the US Army general was attached to Mountbatten's headquarters. With Marshal's authorisation Truscott wrote to Hartle instructing him to set in train the organisation of an American commando style unit.

Hartle had in his aide Major William (Bill) Darby the man who would change the character of the US Army forever.[3]

Like Lovat's first cousin David Stirling, who in World War II would be the driving force that formed the Special Air Service Regiment (SAS), Darby would be the man who established the US Rangers. Darby however enjoyed support from the highest quarters. After the war both formations would become élite special forces within their respective armies.

By May 1942 before all of the 34th Infantry Division had landed in Northern Ireland Darby was becoming frustrated by the lack of activity. On June 8, he was instructed by Hartle to form the unit that Truscott had decided would be known as Rangers. The historic name recalled the force of American Colonists that had been formed in the 18th Century with the formal title of His Majesty's Independent Company of American Rangers.[4]

It would be structured as an HQ Company of eight officers and 69 men and six Ranger Companies each of three officers and 63 men. It would have an authorised strength of 26 officers and 447 men.

The 1st Ranger Battalion was activated at Carrickfergus near Belfast in Northern Ireland on June 19, 1942. It was formed from 2,000 volunteers mainly drawn from the V Corps US Army who were whittled down through a basic selection course.

Officers and Non Commissioned Officers (NCOs) Darby stated, "should possess leadership qualities of a high order with particular emphasis on initiative and common sense. All officers and men were to possess natural athletic ability and physical stamina and, insofar as possible, be without physical defect".

First Sergeant Alex J. Szima, a Regular Army soldier and one of the original Rangers, explained that the initial selection "was by defective feet mechanics. The men were marched in groups of thirty or forty…, followed by a lorry. As one fell out; he was processed for return to his unit … we took the last bunch on the largest convoy imaginable, this took us three days to complete. The route was from Belfast to Londonderry."

At his medical examination another original volunteer Private Franklin Koons realised that the minor hernia that he had managed to conceal during his initial service in the Army would be discovered. He was concerned that the Medical Officer (MO) would insist that he have corrective surgery that would probably mean he would not pass the Ranger course.

"You know you have a hernia," said the MO.

"Yes sir!"

The MO told him he was not fit for service.

"So I did a couple of strenuous exercises" said Koons in an interview with Pat O'Donnell in June 1998, "I bent over touching my hands to the floor to prove it wouldn't affect me and I did this a couple of times until the doctor said,

"Fine! You don't have a problem!""

The age range of the successful volunteers was between 17 and 35. The 34th Infantry Division had produced 281 of these men, the 1st Armored Div 104, Anti- Aircraft Artillery Troops 43, V Corps Special Troops 48 and Northern Ireland Base Section 44. With the exception of Darby none of the Ranger officers were from the Regular Army but were either National Guardsmen or Reservists. The majority of the enlisted men in the Rangers were draftees who had volunteered, Szima recalled that only 25 or 30 men were from the Regular Army. Among the volunteers it was reported were a former lion tamer and a full-blooded Sioux.

The officers and men who had been selected were posted to the Commando Basic Training Centre (CBTC) at Achnacarry Castle in Scotland. Ten per cent had been added to the strength of the Ranger Battalion to cover for men who would injured or even killed in training. Major Darby, known to his men as "El Darbo", recalled the training programme run by Lt Colonel Charles Vaughan a 50 year old, six foot two inch Guardsman and veteran of World War I.

"The British Commandos did all in their power to test us to find out what sort of men we were. Then, apparently liking us, they did all in their power to prepare us for battle."

Donald Gilchrist who would serve as a Lieutenant with No 4 Commando at Dieppe remembered Vaughan with respect. He "came through the First World War … and remembered that many men had been sent to the Western Front without sufficient training. Many had no idea of the conditions of war, especially in the winter months…

Training was never stopped because of the weather or on Sunday. He said "Hitler didn't stop the war because it was Sunday.""

This drive for realism included live firing exercises with incoming small arms fire and the controlled detonation of TNT charges to encourage men across obstacles or off the beach during amphibious training.

Sergeant Irving "Bill" Portman of F Troop No 4 Commando who would later become one of the staff at Achnacarry, remembered one instructor firing a Bren Light Machine Gun (LMG) so that the rounds impacted extremely close to a group of French Commandos. The men were on the famous "Opposed Landing", the amphibious exercise that marked the climax of the course at CBTC. As the assault boat neared the shore a bullet passed through one of the paddles.

Once they had landed, "These bloody Frenchmen, they opened fire right back at us. They all carried live ammunition on training exercises… These Froggies weren't so damn particular as we were. When they came ashore they were looking around for targets. We had to take cover."

James Ladd in *Commandos and Rangers of World War II* explains that the original training programme often lasted three months, though this was later reduced to six weeks. To infantry soldiers some of the training was familiar, what was a novelty was the intensity and realism. To many men demolition techniques, unarmed combat, living in the field and amphibious operations and cliff assaults were both exciting and challenging skills that they were keen to master.

Dunning who was an instructor at Achnacarry notes in *"It Had to be Tough"* that the time in the training programme was allocated as follows:

Weapon training, including foreign arms	19%
Fieldcraft, Movement and Tactics	13%
Firing of Weapons/Grenades/Field Firing	11%
PT incl Ropework and Unarmed Combat	10%
Boating	9%
Map reading	8%
Speed marches	6%

Night training	5%
Mines and demolitions	4%
Drill	4%
Climbing	3%
Set-Piece Exercises (incl Opposed Landing)	3%
Training films	3%
Medical Lectures and First Aid	3%

Plus Final 36 hours scheme and Final Day Activities

One of the first lessons that new intakes at the depot learned was from the row of well kept "graves" they encountered as they marched past the Guard Room. On the grass verge of the drive to the Castle were wooden headstones and in place of an epitaph was the cause of the fictional victim's death.

"This man failed to keep his rifle clean"

"This man looked over cover not round it"

"This man stood on the skyline"…

When the first Rangers arrived at Achnacarry after the speed march from the railway station one of them is reported to have gasped

"Jesus, the sons of bitches, they kill us on the march from the railroad, and when we get here they bury us."

Darby insisted that the US officers and men train together with no distinction in rank. Among the toughest parts of the training as they had already discovered were the speed marches that increased in length during the time at Achnacarry. The ability to march, even run, at speed, carrying weapons and equipment would play a significant part in the No 4 Commando attack at Dieppe.

The course made demands not only on physical stamina, but also on emotional strength. Gilchrist remembered the assault course – more of a cross-country run with seriously challenging obstacles. At the end of the course, at the top of a hill, were frames rather like gallows from which hung sand bag bayonet targets. Giving the requisite wordless yell of rage he bayoneted his target and then with a sigh of relief sat down. An instructor watching his performance walked over and said quietly.

"Gilchrist you'll have to do better than that. Have a rest and go back and do it again."

By August 1, 1942 the US Ranger Battalion had completed its training at Achnacarry and was undertaking amphibious warfare training with the Royal Navy at the shore station HMS *Dorlin*. It was while the men were here that 50 of their number were selected to accompany British and Canadian forces to Dieppe. The Rangers would thus have the distinction of being the first US soldiers to see action on land in the European Theatre of Operations (ETO) in World War II and sadly some would be the first to be killed.

For Szima, fearful that his earlier training as a clerk in the US Army would trap him in the offices of the Ranger HQ Company, being selected for operation CAULDRON "was like escaping".

Far from CBTC the British Commando operations against Norway were beginning to convince Hitler and the *Oberkommando des Wehrmacht* (High Command of the Armed Forces) OKW, that the northern flank was a potential target for a large-scale invasion. He ordered the building of extensive coastal defences and by 1944 the garrison stood at over 350,000 troops – men who might otherwise have been available to fight in Normandy on D Day.

Probably the finest example of Combined Operations that had taken place to date was Operation BITING in France on the night of February 27, 1942. RAF aerial reconnaissance photographs of the coast showed a German *Würzburg* early warning and fire control radar in a remote location on the cliffs at Bruneval near Le Havre. This sophisticated 560 MHz radar had a range of 30 km (18.5 miles). A Company strength force drawn from the newly formed 2nd Bn The Parachute Regiment and 1st Parachute Squadron Royal Engineers with Flight Lieutenant Cox, an RAF radar technician, was assembled under command of Major John Frost. (The battalion had been formed from men from the original No 2 Commando who had initiated military parachute training and so became the first British Army parachute unit).

That night, under cover of a local bombing raid, they parachuted from 12 modified Whitley bombers, landing a few miles inland from Bruneval. They quickly made their way to the site and dividing into two groups neutralised the crew and garrison, while the Royal Engineers and RAF expert dismantled components from the radar.

At 02.15 the raiders moved down a gully to the beach and waited for Royal Navy small vessels to evacuate them. There was a nerve-wracking delay as the RN craft avoided a German destroyer. By dawn the men and their radar booty were safely back in Portsmouth harbour. The operation had cost two killed, six wounded who were evacuated, and six missing, but it had netted equipment yielding invaluable technical intelligence for the radar war.

In early 1942 the scale of operations changed dramatically with Operation CHARIOT an attack on the French port of St Nazaire, now a German naval and U-boat base. The aim was to destroy the lock gates of the huge dry dock, the *Forme Ecluse* built for the French Atlantic liners, and thus deny the port facilities to the Germans and major warships like the KMS *Tirpitz* then in Norway and the KMS *Bismarck*.

The raid in the early hours of the morning of March 28 was conducted by volunteers from No 2 Commando, commanded by the pipe smoking Lt Col Charles Newman of the Essex Regiment. Commander Robert Ryder RN, a former Antarctic Explorer and winner of the Polar Medal, commanded the naval element of 18 small coastal assault craft and the ex-US Navy 1,090 ton "flush deck" destroyer the former USS *Buchanan*. The ship had been passed to the Royal Navy as part of the Lend Lease agreement between the USA and Great Britain and renamed HMS *Cambeltown* she would be commanded by Lieutenant Commander S.H. Beattie.

The destroyer had her funnels cut down and was altered to look like a *Möwe* Class German destroyer. As part of the attack HMS *Cambeltown* with her bows packed with explosives, would ram the dock gates at full steam. This was scheduled for 01.30, she hit them at 01.34, and the Commandos on board raced ashore to destroy the winding gear for the gates and attempted to neutralise the U-boat pens. It was a violent and costly night in which only three assault craft escaped, 169 Commandos were killed and 200 taken prisoner.

Beattie and Newman learned later in Prisoner-of-War (PoW) camp, that along with Ryder who had escaped, they had been awarded the Victoria Cross (VC), Britain's highest award for gallantry. The VC also went to Able Seaman Savage who had manned his 20mm Oerlikon gun throughout the operation silencing German guns, until he was mortally wounded. The second Commando VC of the war was awarded to Sgt Thomas Durrant R.E. of No 1 Commando who had been attached to No 2 and who was in charge of the Bren gun on Motor Launch 206. Badly wounded he continued firing until the launch was boarded and he was taken prisoner. He died the following day.

In the morning, as senior German officers were inspecting the wreck of HMS *Cambletown*, three tons of Amatol high explosive in the bows detonated. The Germans were killed, as were two Commando officers who had been captured and taken back to the ship – though aware of the charge in the bows of the destroyer, they remained silent. The lock gates were shattered and the remains of the destroyer were carried half way down the dock. KMS *Tirpitz* never left Norway and remained there to be finally bombed to destruction by RAF Lancasters on November 12, 1944.

The St Nazaire raiders were awarded a total of 83 decorations for an operation that shocked the Germans and inspired the public in Great Britain and the United States.

Operation RUTTER a joint Army and Commando raid on the French port of Dieppe had been planned for July. It was a logical development in these bigger and more ambitious attacks on the coast of Occupied Europe, which would involve even larger numbers of troops and because of a potential threat from German tanks based in the vicinity of the coast would be supported by armoured vehicles.

The planning was undertaken by the Combined Operations Headquarters and General Headquarters (GHQ) Home Forces which delegated its authority to Lt General Bernard Montgomery, then Commander-in-Chief (C-in-C) South Eastern Command. Under Montgomery's chairmanship the proposed raid grew into a frontal assault without a heavy preliminary air bombardment.

The 2nd Canadian Division commanded by Maj-General J. Hamilton "Ham" Roberts was nominated to undertake the major part of the attack. There had been political pressure from Ottawa for the Canadian division, which had been in training in the UK since 1940, to be given a major mission. Men had been assembled on the Isle of Wight and were thoroughly trained, briefed and ready to go when on July 7, 1942 bad weather caused the operation to be cancelled. Montgomery then recommended that the cancellation should be "for all time" and shortly afterwards left to command the 8th Army in the Western Desert.

Meanwhile in the United States the US Army Commander-in-Chief General George C Marshal was pressing for a rapid build up of US troops in the United Kingdom to implement operation SLEDGEHAMMER. This would be the invasion of Europe to support the USSR if the Soviet Union showed signs of collapsing under the weight of German attacks. With huge optimism it envisaged a quick defeat of Nazi Germany that would then allow the USA to concentrate its military resources on the war against Japan. Churchill was adamantly against SLEDGEHAMMER and favoured a longer more indirect approach that would begin in North Africa by defeating the *Afrika Korps*. A major operation in northern Europe that kept up the impetus of earlier Commando raids would show a commitment to a full invasion in the future and would mollify public opinion in the USSR and the USA. The Dieppe plan, modified and renamed JUBILEE, was revived by the Chief of Combined Operations, Vice-Admiral Mountbatten.

British Intelligence in the Second World War Vol 2 notes, "The Chiefs of Staff gave their approval to *Jubilee* on 12 August, only a week before it was carried out… It has been suggested that the case for reviving the operation came from Combined Operations HQ whose amour propre had suffered from the cancellation (of RUTTER)."

To ensure greater security JUBILEE was mounted from five separate English ports between Southampton and Newhaven with a force of 4,963 Canadians, 1,075 British and Allied personnel and as a significant political gesture the 50 US Army Rangers.

No 4 Commando would have four Rangers attached from the 1st American Ranger Battalion, Sgt Kenneth D Stempson and Sgt Alex J Szima from HQ Coy, Cpl William R Brady from C Coy and Cpl Franklin M Koons from D Coy. For planners with a sense of history the presence of the Rangers had parallels with the part played by the small detachment of Rogers Rangers in General Wolfe's assault on Quebec on September 13, 1759.

In July the RUTTER naval force had been concentrated off the Isle of Wight and this obvious group of ships was seen by planning staff as a potential security risk since there were suspicions that it had been located by *Luftwaffe* reconnaissance aircraft.

The JUBILEE naval force, organised into 13 groups totalled 237 warships, gunboats and landing craft including 24 valuable Tank Landing Craft (LCT). The force was protected by six anti-aircraft landing craft and eight destroyers HMS *Calpe*, *Fernie*, *Brocklesby*, *Garth*, *Albrighton*, *Berkeley*, *Bleasdale*, and the Polish ORP *Slazak* which with their 4-inch guns were tasked with fire support missions.

The Royal Navy, smarting from the recent loss of the battleship HMS *Prince of Wales* and battlecruiser HMS *Repulse* sunk off Malaya by Japanese bombers on December 10, 1941, was reluctant to commit a cruiser to fire support missions. They feared that it might be damaged or lost in air attacks by the aggressive *Luftwaffe* in the narrow confines of the Channel. The terse words of the First Sea Lord Sir Dudley Pound to Lord Mountbatten summed up their reluctance during discussions about naval support for RUTTER.

"Battleships by daylight off the French coast? You must be mad, Dickie."

RAF Bomber Command had been requested by the air commander Air Vice-Marshal Leigh-Mallory to detach 300 heavy bombers to attack German positions at Dieppe.

However Harris was reluctant to divert his squadrons from their campaign against the German heartland to attack German defences at Dieppe. "The request, it must be remembered", writes John Terraine in *The Right of the Line*, "was for a precision night attack, regardless of weather conditions, on buildings facing the sea-front, while taking all possible care not to hit the town behind. Harris could make no guarantee of such accuracy, and faced with the prospect of a blazing town, its narrow streets choked with débris and impassable to tanks, the Canadian Land Force Commander accepted the withdrawal of the bombers."

The RAF did however commit 67 squadrons from nine Allied nations to the operation. Leigh-Mallory in overall command had deliberately chosen to make it a fighter heavy force, in the hope that the Luftwaffe would be drawn into action. The aggressive proponent of "big wing" operations was not to be disappointed.

The full force consisted of three squadrons of Douglas DB-7B Boston (Havoc) and two Bristol Blenheim light bombers, two squadrons of Hawker Hurricane IIC ground attack fighters armed with two 227 kg (500 lb) bombs. Of the 60 fighter squadrons, 42 were equipped with the Supermarine Spitfire Mark V, two with the Mark VI, four with the Mark IX, there were four with North American Mustang III operating as tactical reconnaissance fighters, six with Hurricanes and two Hawker Typhoon 1A squadrons. In addition the USAAF committed four squadrons of B17 Flying Fortresses and three squadrons of fighters to attack the *Luftwaffe* airfield at Abbeville.

RAF photo reconnaissance allowed the planners to build up what seemed to be a very detailed picture of the enemy defences. However the imagery and models produced for JUBILEE did not show all the defences, particularly those sited in the cliffs at the western end of the main Dieppe beach, and this would prove fatal for the operation. Major Reginald Unwin a Canadian intelligence officer attached to the planning staff warned of the potential threat from weapons sited in these caves, but his views were dismissed as unduly pessimistic.[5] Unwin felt so strongly that he refused to sign the final intelligence appreciation of German defences submitted for inclusion in the Combined Operations plan.

Intelligence from human resources was poor, little was known about the strength of the positions or location of German command posts. It was still believed that Dieppe was held by the 110th Infantry Division, a force that had in fact been transferred to the Eastern Front in Russia over twelve months earlier and been replaced by the 302nd Division. The 110th was described as battle weary from its time on the Eastern Front. Officers from the 302nd were surprised that British planners knew so little about Dieppe and its garrison since the local French population mingled easily with the soldiers in the town and adjoining countryside and would have been a useful source of human intelligence.

Among the range of intelligence sources examined in Great Britain were postcards and holiday photographs of Dieppe taken from the turn of the century to the 1930s. The gradient of the shingle beach was calculated from a post card of the sea front at Dieppe.

On the day of JUBILEE only No 4 Commando would be spared the high price in human lives that the Canadians and some British forces would pay for their optimism, enthusiasm to get into action and lack of adequate intelligence about their enemy and the ground over which they were to fight.

Notes

1 The Lovat Scouts were raised by the 14th Lord Lovat during the South African War of 1899 – 1902. The initial proposal was for a force of volunteers made up of 150 stalkers and ghillies from the Scottish estates. By late January 1900 the War Office had announced that the force would be two companies one of which would be mounted made up of 12 officers and 230 other ranks. The first company arrived in Cape Town on April 17. Eventually the Lovat Scouts reached a strength of six companies. The Scouts undertook reconnaissance and patrolling missions using skills learned in the Highlands of Scotland. The one serious action fought by the Lovat Scouts was on September 19 – 20, 1901 when in a night attack on their camp they suffered serious casualties in hand-to-hand fighting.

They survived the period up to World War I and entered the war as two regiments of the Territorial Army the 1st and 2nd Lovat Scouts. During the war both regiments served in a dismounted role at Gallipoli as the 10th (Lovat Scouts) Battalion, The Queen's Own Cameron Highlanders and fought in Macedonia and France from late 1916.

In World War II the Lovat Scouts were trained in mountain warfare by the Commando Mountain Warfare Centre; after further training in Canada they served as a mountain reconnaissance regiment in Italy.

Changes to the Territorial Army led to the Lovat Scouts being disbanded in 1967 but the title was retained by D Company (Gordon Highlanders and Lovat Scouts) and Support Group, 2nd Battalion, 51st Highland Volunteers.

2 The Lovat clan history is not without controversy. In 1715 Simon Fraser 11th Lord Lovat, "The Old Fox", supported the government against the First Jacobite Rebellion. However in 1745 in the Second Jacobite Rebellion he backed the Young Pretender, Prince Charles Edward and so found himself on the losing side. He was not actually in command of the Scottish army at Culloden but despite this the 11th Lord Lovat was found guilty of rebellion and beheaded on Tower Hill, London in 1747. He thus became the last nobleman to die under the axe.

Awaiting his execution he saw one of the stands erected for spectators, collapse as they crowded forwarded for a better view. Many were killed, crushed beneath the crude timber structure. With a sang-froid that would continue to run in the family veins he remarked coolly.

"The more the mischief, the better the sport."

Then granting the axeman his forgiveness, he made his peace with God and knelt to accept his execution.

The man who escaped the block, and who was in command at Culloden was the son of the "Old Fox". He was pardoned for his actions and went on to raise 1,500 Frasers for service in America.

The title was attained and the estates forfeit to the Crown. It would take nearly 100 years before the title was re-established.

3 Major William O. Darby was a young artillery officer from the Class of 1933 at West Point. He had experience in both pack and mechanised artillery as well as with cavalry and infantry and had undertaken amphibious training with one of the US Army divisions in the USA. General Lucien Truscott remembered him as "outstanding in appearance, possessed of a most attractive personality, and he was keen intelligent, and filled with enthusiasm... Darby's career both with the Rangers and subsequently, up to the time of his death in battle during the last days of the war, was to be a most distinguished one".

It is one of the tragic ironies of war that Darby was killed at the age of 34, serving as assistant division commander with the 10th Mountain Division in Italy on April 30, 1945, just a few days before the end of the war in Europe.

4 The US Rangers have a proud history. They trace their origin to 1670 when Captain Benjamin Church organised a company of troops designated Rangers. They fought with distinction during King Philip's War with the frontier Indians from 1670 to the end of the war in 1675.

However it was during the French and Indian Wars of 1754 to 1763 when nine companies of Rangers were organised under the command of Major Robert Rogers to fight for the British that the name became established. Rogers was an innovative leader and his Standing Orders drafted between 1756 and 1759 are as tactically relevant to Special Forces and infantry today as they were almost 250 years ago.

Rogers Rangers Standing Orders

1. Don't forget anything.
2. Have your musket clean as a whistle, hatchet scoured, sixty rounds powder and ball, and be ready to march at a minute's warning.
3. When you're on the march, act the way you would if you were sneaking up on a deer. See the enemy first.
4. Tell the truth about what you see and what you do. There is an army depending

on us for correct information. You can lie all you please when you tell other folks about the Rangers, but never lie to a Ranger or officer.

5. Never take a chance you don't have to.

6. When we're on the march we march single file, far enough apart so one shot can't go through two men.

7. If we strike swamps, or soft ground, we spread out abreast, so it's hard to track us.

8. When we march, we keep moving till dark, so as to give the enemy the least possible chance at us.

9. When we camp, half the party stays awake while the other half sleeps.

10. If we take prisoners, we keep them separate till we have had time to examine them, so they can't cook up a story between them.

11. Never march home the same way. Take a different route so you won't be ambushed.

12. No matter whether we travel in big parties or little ones, each party has to keep a scout 20 yards ahead, 20 yards on each flank and 20 yards to the rear, so the main body can't be surprised and wiped out.

13. Every night you'll be told where to meet if surrounded by a superior force.

14. Don't sit down to eat without posting sentries.

15. Don't sleep beyond dawn. Dawn is when the French and Indians attack.

16. Don't cross a river by a regular ford.

17. If somebody's trailing you, make a circle, come back onto your own tracks, and ambush the folks that aim to ambush you.

18. Don't stand up when the enemy's coming against you. Kneel down. Hide behind a tree.

19. Let the enemy come till he's almost close enough to touch. Then let him have it and jump out and finish him off with your hatchet.

Other Ranger formations followed, but Rogers' are regarded as the true originals.

Rogers was born in Methuen, Massachusetts Bay Colony on November 18, 1731. Besides the Indian and French Wars his military career included raising a force of Rangers to fight for the King during the Revolutionary War. His life ended in tragedy with debts and divorce and he died in England in a cheap lodging house in London May 18, 1795.

In 1775 the Continental Congress authorised that ten companies of expert riflemen be raised and equipped for the coming Revolution. In 1777 these soldiers were placed under the command of Dan Morgan and identified as "The Corps of Rangers". A separate force of 150 men under Thomas Knowlton were used for reconnaissance and designated the Connecticut Rangers.

Ranger units fought in the war with Mexico and the Civil War. In a classic Special Forces operation a formation known as Mean's Rangers attacked the ammunition train of General Longstreet and destroyed valuable stores.

When US special forces were to be established in World War II General Dwight

D. Eisenhower had pressed for a distinctive name for the American force because he asserted "the glamour of that name (Commando) will always remain and properly so – British".

General Truscott recalled that many names had been suggested but he favoured the title Ranger because, "Some of the oldest units in the Regular Army were originally organized as Rangers, and have carried the tradition into every war in which the nation has been engaged. On every frontier, the name has been one of hope for those who have required protection, of fear for those who have lived outside the law."

Hollywood may however have played a part in the choice of name for this new force. In 1940 MGM released in Technicolor *Northwest Passage* the film of the book by Kenneth Roberts. Directed by King Vidor it was a tale of adventure set in America prior to the Revolution during the wars with the French and Indians.

The lead character played by Spencer Tracy was no other than Major Robert Rogers, whose Rangers dressed in olive green buckskins fought their way through 125 minutes of rugged endurance and combat in the forests, swamps and lakes.

Their curious Glengarry style caps were the result of a Hollywood costume researcher's error. Many of the Rogers Rangers, as first or second generation Scotsmen wore the traditional wide beret commonly known as a "bonnet", to Americans this would have seemed distinctly incongruous since a bonnet was women's wear. So the Hollywood Rangers were kitted out in Glengarrys.

Northwest Passage remains a classic study of leadership and small unit tactics and as such was shown to all Commandos at Achnacarry as part of a "make do and mend" rest day during their initial training.

5 Two years later, with the strategic situation dramatically different another intelligence officer, the 25 year old Major Brian Urquhart, would have similar reservations dismissed because of an enthusiasm to get into action. This time the operation was the airborne operation code-named MARKET the plan to outflank the West Wall on Germany's western border in September 1944 by airborne landings to capture bridges. It would be followed up promptly by overland attacks code named GARDEN. Urquhart who commanded the intelligence cell at General "Boy" Browning's 1st British Airborne Corps HQ had seen aerial photographs of the Arnhem area that showed the presence of the armoured vehicles of the II *Waffen-SS Panzer Korps*, intelligence that had already been confirmed by the Dutch underground forces. Urquhart would recall later that his fears were dismissed because of "the desperate desire on everybody's part to get the airborne into action" – a desire that would result in over 7,000 airborne soldiers out of a force of 10,005 being killed, wounded or taken prisoner. Before the ill-fated operation Urquhart, who after the war would enjoy a distinguished career in the United Nations, suffered the humiliation of being sent on sick leave because he was told he was suffering from stress.

CHAPTER 2

Planning

Dieppe, in the *département* of Seine-Maritime on the often wet and windy Channel coast has the distinction of being France's oldest seaside resort, established long before Biarritz or Saint-Tropez in the south.

The town that would become known as "the poor man's Monte Carlo" was originally a fishing and trading port, sheltered from east and west winds by steep chalk cliffs that reach 92 metres (300 feet) and topped by the church of Notre-Dame de Bon-Secours. Protected by the cliffs is a safe deep anchorage carved out by the mouth of the river D'Arques.

The Norse navigators working along the northern French coast in their long boats had discovered it around AD 100 and called the harbour *djupa* – deep, the name stuck and in time it became Dieppe.

It had a violent history long before the events of 1942. Between 1420 and 1435 the town was occupied by the English during the Hundred Years' War. The castle at the western end of the town was built in 1435, the year that the inhabitants drove out their English occupiers. It was modified by German forces in World War II.

The largely Protestant Huguenot population of the port suffered greatly in the Wars of Religion. By the 16th Century Dieppe had become the principle port for the kingdom of France. Corsairs and privateers operated from Dieppe attacking British and Portuguese shipping. On the proceeds of this piracy one sea captain Jean Ango built an elegant manor house in the town of Varengeville-sur-Mer to the west of the port.

In 1524 the Florentine Giovanni Verrazano sailed from Dieppe to establish the community on the east coast of North America that he called Terre de Angoulème. Under the Dutch the community would become known as New Amsterdam and then under the British – New York. Verrazano is still remembered by New York's Verrazano Narrows Bridge.

In 1524 a French fleet based at Dieppe crossed the Channel to bombard the English port of Brighthelmstone – the future Brighton.

However relations between France and Britain improved enough for a 36 year old engineer, the Dieppe born Solomon de Caus to be appointed mathematical tutor to the Prince of Wales in 1612. In two books published in 1615 Caus (or Caux) describes the operating principles of a steam engine.

Dieppe expanded in the 17th Century both as a fishing and commercial port handling luxury merchandise like spices and ivory. However in 1668 almost 10,000 of its people died during a plague. In 1685 the Protestants in the town were persecuted after the revocation of the Edict of Nantes. In 1694 an Anglo Dutch fleet under Lord Berkeley bombarded the port for three days and the resulting fires destroyed many of the timber built houses in the old town.

Louis XIII ordered that the town be rebuilt in the classic style, with buildings faced in white limestone; the buildings and narrow streets around the churches of St Rémy and St Jacques are the result of the reconstruction.

Following the defeat of Napoleon in 1815 regular ferry services were set up with Newhaven and an English quarter was established in Dieppe.

Between 1824 and 1830 the Duchesse de Berry popularised Dieppe by establishing a summer season there and the wealthy and fashionable set in Paris began to visit the town. In the course of the 19th Century the railway linked Dieppe with Paris which was only 169 km (105 miles) away and the town prospered. In 1826 the English artist Turner painted *The Harbour of Dieppe*, one of three large exhibition pieces representing northern Continental ports.

Dieppe enjoyed a building boom as sea front hotels, casinos and baths were constructed. By the late 1880s visitors included Louis-

Phillipe, Napoleon III, the painter Eugène Delacroix, composer Camille Saint-Saëns, writer Alexandre Dumas and, following his release from prison in Britain, the writer Oscar Wilde. The English painter Richard Sickert lived in Dieppe from 1885 to 1905 and produced paintings of the area in distinctive dark, rich tones. Sickert returned to England in 1905 and died in London in 1942.

In the late 19th Century the wealthy begun to build holiday villas and among the members of the French artistic community who discovered the area was Claude Monet who in 1882 painted *Cliff Walk at Pourville* and *The Church at Varengeville*.

At Varengeville to the west of Dieppe the woods run down to chalk cliffs that drop precipitously to a sandy and rocky shore. The rocks support a healthy crop of the popular French delicacy *moules* – mussels. Varengeville is surrounded by a series of hamlets like the community of le Mesnil, they are linked by deep narrow roads, many of which run through dense woodland. Outside Dieppe, but with access to the sea through a few narrow valleys or gullies like the Petit Ailly, Port des Moutiers and the Port de Vasterival, the area became a popular location for holiday villas. For children the beach at Vasterival was a paradise of rock pools and shallow sandy beaches. For adults the Hotel de la Terrasse, at a bend in the path at the top of a flight of steps leading up from the beach, offered refreshment. Local residents were probably less pleased when further up the path a three storey building called "La Volière" was built as a holiday home for disadvantaged children from the Rouen area. Adjoining it was a small barn. Towards the end of the 19th Century the English architect Sir Edwin Lutyens built a distinctive country house to the east of Vasterival at the Parc Floral du Bois des Moutiers, the garden was laid out by the distinguished English garden designer Gertrude Jekyl.

It was in this historic and tranquil area that on August 19, 1942 Operation JUBILEE would be launched with landings by tanks and infantry along a ten-mile front. To the east of Dieppe the coastal battery at Berneval would be attacked and neutralised by No 3 Commando, who would land at two points on the coast, code named Yellow Beach 1 and 2.

At the western end of the beach head the battery at the hamlet of le

Mesnil close to Varengeville was the task of No 4 Commando who would also land at two points Orange Beach 1 and 2.

The batteries in these locations were respectively code named GOEBBELS and HESS after the Nazi Minister of Propaganda and the Deputy Führer.

The orders for the two Commandos were to destroy the batteries, or if this proved impossible, neutralise them by fire for the duration of the main landings and the subsequent withdrawal, until ordered to withdraw by the Military Force Commander.

If the No 4 Commando transport was sunk, but the Commandos were able to launch their landing craft they were to continue with the operation. The destruction or neutralisation of the GOEBBELS and HESS batteries was critical for the success of the main JUBILEE action since the guns on high ground to the east and west of Dieppe could deliver interlocking fire on ships and landing craft approaching the port. The commanding officers were however given the freedom to plan how they would attack these objectives.

In the plans originally prepared by Montgomery's staff for RUTTER these attacks would have been undertaken by airborne forces.

It was fortunate that in JUBILEE the two Commandos tasked for this mission would make an amphibious landing. It was a mode of delivery that had a better chance of ensuring that the force arrived intact and on time at its objective.[1]

Under the firm leadership of Lt Col Lord Lovat who had been promoted and assumed command on St George's Day in March 1942, "No.4 Commando (had)" in his words in his autobiography *March Past* "emerged from being a rabble in arms to turn slowly into a polished weapon. At Troon every man learnt he had to work to keep his place in the team. If we were not experts in the arts of war, it could be said that No.4 Commando measured up to what Churchill described as 'the canine virtues of vigilance, fidelity, courage and love of the chase'. The Dieppe raid was only just round the corner". Ronald Atkin in *Dieppe 1942 The Jubilee Disaster* described Lovat as "a stickler for the sort of taught discipline that saves lives in battle".

Sgt Bill Portman remembered Lovat's dictum "I don't want street corner boys – I want soldiers" the Commandos were just that, highly trained and disciplined soldiers. "Anyone in Number 4 who started a fight in a pub," recalled Portman, "was automatically out."

Now in command Lovat adopted three basic principles.

"1. I cut the dead wood in officers, NCOs and men; then looked for replacements of proven ability, at the same time accelerating promotion inside the Commando at every level of junior leaders, whose talent remained wasted while they were hanging around in Troon. 2. Individual Troops were told to get lost on commando training for not less than a week at a time, after submitting a training programme which outlined whatever form of specialised activity most appealed to their respective skills. 3. Short cadre courses began in weapon training and section leading for NCOs who were not infantrymen."

By hard, imaginative and realistic training, No 4 Commando was becoming the instrument of war that reflected the principles of its commanding officer "To sort out intentions and achieve results there are certain formulas which transcend individual merit. Pick leaders; win confidence; work hard to test initiative and adaptability. What is learnt in training is done instinctively in action – almost without thinking down to the last man. Courage looks after itself, for habit is ten times nature."

Major Derek Mills-Roberts, Second-in-Command of No 4 Commando, wrote in his autobiography *Clash by Night*, "Some of the accounts that were published after the Dieppe Raid made much of the carefree, casual, happy-go-lucky attitude which was alleged to be part and parcel of any raiding force. Nothing could be further from the truth...

The adjective "tough" was again overworked by the reporters. In fact, it means precisely nothing in the face of a hard-hitting, well-disciplined foe unless it implies mental resilience and discipline. All effective armies from the beginning of time agree on the necessity for discipline."

Encouraged to take their men away for specialist training Robert Dawson, who had climbed since his school days in Switzerland took his Troop to Bethesda in North Wales. Here assisted by David Style one of his Section officers, "They put the fear of God into the rank and file – most of whom had never abseiled – swinging down a cliff or clawing with fingertips up a rock-face... Such is the force of example, that all emerged within a fortnight as useful climbers."

Dunning remembers Dawson as a "rather shy and retiring" man who was an Emergency Commission (hostilities only) officer. He had started as a Section Officer, and would eventually command No 4 Commando with the Free French Commandos in time for D Day. His time in Switzerland had been well spent, besides climbing he had become a fluent French linguist.

While the Commando honed their military skills and waited for a mission, at the Combined Operations HQ and Home Forces Command the RUTTER/JUBILEE plans had been re-drafted with the main weight of the JUBILEE operation at Dieppe now on four beaches. The time ashore had been reduced because the planners had learned of the presence of the veteran 10th Panzer Division at Amiens. It would be a "one tide landing".

To the east of Dieppe at Puys the Royal Regiment of Canada would land at Blue Beach. Their mission was to ascend the cliffs and neutralise a small four gun battery code named ROMMEL they would then secure the eastern headland overlooking Dieppe from the rear. [The battery was one of two from the 3rd Group 302nd Artillery Regiment equipped 10.5 cm leFH 18 howitzers and supported by range finder batteries. The howitzer weighed 1985 kg in action and fired a 14.81 kg shell to a maximum range of 10,675 metres.]

At Red Beach the shingle foreshore of the town's sea front the Essex Scottish Regiment would come ashore, while at White Beach opposite the Casino and below the castle the Royal Hamilton Light Infantry were to land. In support of the troops assigned to Red and White Beaches were the 28 Churchill tanks of the Calgary Regiment and, as a floating reserve offshore, the Fusiliers Mont-Royal. These forces were to seize the town, destroy the enemy defences, radar installations, power stations, dock and rail facilities, fuel dumps, gather intelligence and assist a Royal Marine Commando "cutting out party" commanded by Lt Col Joseph Picton "Tiger" Phillips RM. The Royal Marines would remove "for our own use" 40 invasion barges that had been photographed in the harbour. To undertake these tasks a perimeter had to be seized and held against attacks by the German 110th (302nd) Division that garrisoned the area.

The ground rises to the west of Dieppe, except where the River Scie has cut through the chalk to form a shingle beach at Pourville. Here the South Saskatchewan Regiment and the Queen's Own Cameron Highlanders would land at Green Beach. One of their objectives was a Freya 125 MHz early warning radar station on high ground to the east of their beachhead. Here like the earlier BITING operation they were to capture equipment that had technical intelligence value about a sophisticated system with a detection range of 200 km (125 miles). Sgt. Jack Nissenthal, an RAF radar expert would be tasked with this technical intelligence mission. He was not to know that because of his considerable technical knowledge his bodyguard had been ordered to kill him if there was any danger of capture.

The forces that had landed at White and Green Beaches would push out of their perimeters to link up and attack the *Luftwaffe* base south of Dieppe at St Aubyn. The Cameron Highlanders were then to push south to destroy the headquarters of the 110th (302nd) Division believed to be at Argues-la-Bataille. In fact some months earlier the headquarters of the 302nd had moved forward to Envermeu, 9.6 kilometres (six miles) east of Dieppe.

The withdrawal phase of JUBILEE was based on a contracting series of timed "bomb lines" behind which the Canadian forces would pull back to the beaches, ready to be evacuated.

The whole of JUBILEE was driven by an optimism and confidence that seemed to take no cognisance of the telling quotation attributed to the 19th Century Prussian general Helmuth von Moltke 'The Elder':

"No plan survives contact with the enemy."

In late July Lovat learned of the role that No 4 Commando would play in JUBILEE, albeit in rather unusual circumstances. Brigadier Bob Laycock, now commanding the Special Service Brigade, the first parent organisation for the Commandos, arrived unannounced in the middle of a live firing exercise. Lovat was seated in the ruins of Dundonald Castle supervising selected marksmen who were firing tracer over the heads of men making an attack on the ruin.

The Brigadier and his ADC, no stranger to incoming fire, were pinned down for a time and only extracted from the exercise when, for lack of radios, an exchange of semaphore signals confirmed their presence.

"A big raid was on. He did not say where", recalled Lovat, "two Commandos were needed … to knock out coastal batteries…' Can you climb cliffs?'… Robert Dawson was summoned as we walked down to the cars. Yes, he had sixty men who could scale anything with a reasonable surface, provided there was no overhang. The word 'chalk' was not mentioned – the worst stuff to negotiate."

With Lt Col John Durnford-Slater the CO of No 3 Commando, Lovat departed for the Combined Operations HQ in Richmond Terrace, London for a full briefing on the operation. Close to the War Office in Whitehall the headquarters was an establishment for which Lovat had little love.

It "swarmed with red-tabbed gentlemen. The bee-hive illusion was enhanced by busy passages, honeycombed with rooms filled with every branch of the Services, including the powder puff variety, who looked elegant in silk stockings. There was said to be a fair proportion of drones among the inmates."

For Lovat, who in the past had been delayed by the bureaucracy of the HQ, Durnford-Slater was an excellent ally with whom to negotiate the Combined Operations beehive. The two Colonels bypassed "the smaller fry" and went straight to the top to General Charles Haydon the new Chief-of-Staff at the HQ.

Under conditions of high security – the door locked and the telephone disconnected, the General outlined the plan, described the objectives for the two Commandos, but gave no indication of the location. Haydon was well respected by both COs and Lovat recalled that he was anxious that the Commandos should do well. "Downstairs" explained the General "you will be provided with intelligence and more general information. There are good air photographs, also models of both target areas. For security reasons no maps are, at present, available." One of the briefing team was the novelist Robert Henriques, who in Lovat's words, "tried to do my thinking for me. His suggestions, as it happened, would have done us all in."

The two Commando officers left Richmond Terrace having won two valuable concessions. They would land before dawn and would be independent, free to fight in their own way, but in radio communication with the force commander to whom they would report when the task had been completed. The pre-dawn landing in nautical twilight would give the Commandos ten minutes in the cover of darkness to cross the exposed beaches or scale cliffs.

Before they departed General Haydon asked them for their opinion of the overall operation. Lovat came out strongly against a daylight assault against an objective that was presumably the port of Dieppe. "The general changed colour but stared me out. He was clearly stung. He had a hot temper but, for the moment it was under control. 'And why the devil do you settle for Dieppe, may I ask?' 'For two reasons, sir; one is hearsay based on supposition; something very similar was cancelled last month. The other is confirmatory. On the back of the picture postcards studied downstairs which show the cliffs I have to climb, there is a give-away line on the reverse side of the pictures, *Les Falaise de Vasterival près de Dieppe*. We are landing on a flank and I can understand French, sir'." Lovat recalled that the general reached for the telephone even before he had finished speaking. However even though he was clearly about to castigate the Combined Operations intelligence cell, he said civilly to Lovat and Colonel Durnford-Slater "Thank you, Shimi – I can rely on you both to say nothing to anyone."

In London Lovat was joined by Lieutenant Tony Smith, the Intelligence Officer of No 4 Commando. Smith had seen a model of the objective at Combined Operations HQ and knew that the operation would involve about 250 men. He knew that there would be a period of training on an assault ship based at Weymouth.

"The inhabitants of Weymouth greeted us with open arms", wrote Smith, "because they already knew No 4 Commando who had been there is August 1940. The people are simply charming and a good time was had by all."

At Weymouth the Commando practised their amphibious warfare and infantry assault skills. Dunning, describes the variety and intensity of the training which was divided between collective for everyone and specialised for each group according to their task on the raid.

The first priority for collective training was battle fitness. All ranks had to be capable of wading/swimming ashore, running up a pebble beach, crossing an obstacle in fighting order with weapons and equipment and moving off the beach at top speed. Dunning quotes from *Notes from Theatres of War No 11 Destruction of a German Battery by No.4 Commando during the Dieppe Raid* a training manual written by Martin Lindsay an officer of the Gordon Highlanders and produced in February 1943. "Hardening exercises, PT with weapons ["fortunately" he adds "the sea was warm and inviting, especially after a hard day's training"], [1.6 km] one mile runs every morning before breakfast. Doubling, fully loaded, over specified distances in wet clothing. Crossing beach wire with rabbit netting".

The wading and swimming training were not unwelcome to the Commandos. At the close of the month the popular British tabloid *Sunday Pictorial* explained that there had been a brief heat wave with temperatures up to 82° F. These were followed by showers as, "a quick change month from summer clothes to mackintoshes" and added coyly "P.S.- Sorry we couldn't tell you this before. Censor would not let us".

Lovat's approach to this phase of the training was, he explained like preparing athletes for a competition, each day the length of the runs increased and the tempo of training became more intense. "Every soldier would meet the events of the day like a trained athlete off his mark to the crack of the starting pistol. We were playing for high stakes. All knew it. But I held the cutting edge."

No 4 Commando had been fortunate to be allocated as their assault ship the Landing Ship Infantry (LSI) HMS *Prince Albert*[2] a converted Belgian cross Channel ferry that had escaped to Britain in May 1940. Better still the LSI was commanded by Captain Peate DSC who in Lovat's words was "a particularly nice sailor". Just as Lovat's standards and style of leadership had permeated through No 4 Commando, so too Captain Peate had made the *Prince Albert* a happy and efficient ship.

For the Commandos aboard the *Prince Albert* there were unique opportunities to buy rations and cigarettes that were now unobtainable ashore in rationed Britain. John Skerry recalled his mother's delight when returning on leave from a deployment aboard an HM ship he produced a tin of pineapple chunks – a wonderful luxury at the time.

The Commandos and ship's crew went through eight rehearsals that tested the skipper's navigation and the LCA coxwains' boat handling skills. It was vital that the troops allocated for Orange Beach 1 and 2 should board the correct LCAs in darkness with their weapons and equipment critical to the tasks they were to undertake. Loading the craft with ammunition, explosives and the scaling ladders was practised. Each man was allocated his correct position in each LCA so that when the ramp went down in France no time would be wasted reorganising – an operation that might take place under fire. Speed off the beach would be essential. Landing from the LCAs was practised first as a drill and then with full stores and equipment. Each craft carried a length of Alpine (climbing) rope that could if necessary be used to haul heavy weapons like the 3-inch Mortar or ammunition up the cliff at Orange Beach 1.

Smith noted that on August 5, two days before the dress rehearsal the troops were put ashore, "in the middle of a tank gunnery range at Lulworth. Those using the range were as surprised to see us as we were to see them… As soon as they saw us those using the range, stopped firing and an amicable discussion took place as to the rights of ourselves to continue." The tank crews and Commandos reached a compromise over the use of the area and, "Their firing made a very effective noises off for the exercise".

In an after action report prepared by Lt Commander Hugh Mulleneux RN, the special navigator attached for Operation CAULDRON, listed four practises that were conducted during training:

    i)   Boat manning (by day and night)
    ii)   Daylight landing exercises (2)
    iii) Daylight rehearsals of operation (2)
    iv)   "Dress rehearsal" of operation

In a diary note about the dress rehearsal on Friday August 7 he wrote "P.A. (HMS *Prince Albert*) got under way at 0100 and carried out a fairly full dress rehearsal for the coming operation together with the minesweepers, MGB (Motor Gun Boat)[3] and ML (Motor Launch)[4]. The sweepers laid a row of buoys to mark the channel they had swept and the P.A. steamed up to it and lowered her boats at the far end. We had a ten mile [16 km] steam in guided by the MGB. Both the PA and the MGB were out in their navigation and so we got in early and had to hang about which was a pity. Then everything proceeded to go wrong which was also a pity because Captain Hughes-Hallet (the Combined Operations Naval Adviser) and a Colonel had come down from COHQ to watch. However, we learnt a lot and succeeded in landing the soldiers at the right beach at more or less the right time. But the LCAs got out of control and started imagining signals which weren't – let's hope we do better next time as it was rather depressing after the good efforts by day although admittedly it's only by mistakes we learn".

Lovat remembered the Commando's time with HMS *Prince Albert* with affection, but on Wednesday August 5 Mulleneux noted, "Terrific fuss about changing tomorrow's programme. The Captain of the PA is away at a conference and I seem to act as buffer between Lovat and the ship's officers – the former always changing his mind, admittedly for the best, at the last moment."

The amphibious operations took place at Whorbarrow Bay an attractive sweep of the chalk coastline to the east of Lulworth Cove, an area that Lovat recalled, "had once been the property of my great-uncle, Herbie Weld Blundell". Of this phase of the training Dunning remembered that, "working relations between the RN and ourselves were cordial, whilst co-operation between soldiers and sailors at all levels was first class. Some of our enthusiasm and skills rubbed off onto the sailors, noticeably after we were asked to instruct them in the handling and firing of the Bren following the decision to equip each LCA with two Brens apiece. The sailors fired the Brens during some of the practice landings and also as they were lying offshore when they potted away at some expended floating smoke canisters, using them as makeshift targets."

Mulleneux was unaware that the Captain of Steam Gun Boat (SGB) 9 HMS *Grey Goose* was the naturalist and wild life artist Peter Scott, the son of the doomed explorer Captain Robert Scott popularised in Britain after his death as "Scott of the Antarctic". On Sunday August 16 at Fort Southwick near Portsmouth in his own words Mulleneux, "proceeded to put my foot in it" when overhearing Scott talking about the possibility of executing a painting of the St Nazaire Raid he asked;

"Do you paint?"

Evidently Scott did not take offence for a day later Mulleneux took tea with him aboard SGB9 and discussed the upcoming operation, he recalled, "the paradox of talking war in the little wardroom surrounded by his paintings of wild fowl".

Mulleneux had not been the first choice of the Combined Operations HQ staff as the navigation officer. No 4 Commando had initially been assigned a Royal Naval Volunteer Reserve (RNVR) Lieutenant known to both Lovat and Mills-Roberts from their time at Oxford where they remembered him as a cheerful extrovert. However now his "nae bother" attitude did not reassure the two officers. The Commando would be making a sixteen kilometre (ten mile) crossing over the Channel to make a landfall at a six metre (20 foot) gap in the cliffs at Varengeville. Lovat asked for "the best navigator available," and was assigned Mulleneux who, " ran us in right on time to help win the battle." In his after action report Lovat would say of Mulleneux "his cool judgement and confidence inspired all officers and ORs and in my opinion the presence of an RN Officer makes all the difference when difficult decisions and changes of plan may have to be made at short notice."

Lovat's memories of Mills-Roberts, who was two years his senior at Oxford, were entirely favourable. As undergraduates both had been members of the Oxford University Cavalry Squadron, a force that would later become the Oxford University Officers' Training Corps (OUOTC), though at this stage in their military careers Mills-Roberts held the elevated rank of Troop-Sergeant.

Nicknamed the "Mills Bomb" after the No 36 Grenade he was, "Neither short nor tall and quick on his feet, the 'Mills Bomb' of those days was jet-propelled by consuming energy and a determination". The nickname was a reflection of the character of a man who could be assertive and when he took a stand would defend his opinion forcefully. After Oxford he had qualified as a solicitor and was practising law in Liverpool before the outbreak of war put him back in uniform.

As the training on land and at sea increased in intensity and officers and men prepared for the impending operation there was a delightful Heath Robinson amphibious exercise at Portland Harbour that is recalled both by Lovat and James Dunning – it does not however feature in *Clash by Night* the autobiography of Mills-Roberts.

Assisted by Raymond Quilter a friend from the Grenadier Guards, whose firm made parachutes, Mills-Roberts had developed, "the unsinkable sea-borne container". It was intended to transport the three loads that made up the 3-inch Mortar – base plate 16.7 kg (37 lbs.), barrel 19 kg (42 lbs.) and bipod and sights 20.4 kg (45 lbs.). To Lovat the cardboard cylinder looked like a "watertight umbrella stand with a cork at one end". The payload of the container was four rifles and 300 rounds of ammunition in lieu of the 3-inch Mortar. Mills-Roberts had four large Commandos, clad only in their issue drawers stood along HMS *Prince Albert*'s rail. "Derek", wrote Lovat, "gave his final instructions in the gravely voice reserved for special occasions. 'When I say jump you go over the side; swim clear as the container is thrown in. Then try to sink the damn thing'."

Mills-Roberts explained that if the lid came off and it sank they would have to dive down and recover the rifles since he did not wish to face a court of enquiry if the contents were lost.

As ordered the Commandos jumped over the rail of the *Prince Albert* and swam clear as the container was thrown over the side. To the horror of Mills-Roberts, trailing a stream of bubbles, it plunged through the water and disappeared under the hull. Among the observers lining the rail a Royal Navy Able Seaman remarked ruefully, "She's gone to feed the fishes".

Dunning recalls the immediate reaction of the No 4 Commando Second-in-Command: "Dive down and rescue the bloody thing," he bellowed. To the relief of the swimmers, and to ribald cheers from the Commando onlookers the container broke the surface and remained afloat.

Lovat added a characteristically generous note, "I believe Derek's invention helped the Polish Resistance in the Pripet Marshes, and later the Americans made use of it in the Philippines." Dunning comments that, "the mortar team managed to get another seaworthy float with a greater carrying capacity."

It was not the only device designed to protect weapons and equipment in a wet landing. In the after action report Lt M.C. Ackernley, the No 4 Commando signals officer, noted, "The landing at both beaches was dry, so the waterproof canvas bags (issued by Col. Cole) for use with the 38-sets, were not put to the test. During trials we found them awkward to carry until we rigged up a harness, and difficult to open in a hurry when the tapes were wet. Perhaps some light container with simple opening device would be more useful."

The rehearsals with the LCAs and HMS *Prince Albert* covered both the assault and withdrawal phase. Troops withdrawing after an operation, are coming down off the adrenaline high that has propelled them into action. Some will be wounded or in shock and ammunition stocks will be low. Worse still the enemy will have had time to react and bring up fresh troops and will be keen to kill or capture the raiders.

As Lovat later observed, "On a raid it can be more unpleasant coming back than going in, especially in daylight. Final withdrawal was practised first as a drill, then with stretcher cases, then with fierce opposition, and finally under cover of smoke." Casualty evacuation at all stages was practised from the objective to the beach, from the beach to the LCAs and from the LCAs to the parent ship.

The landings might have taken place in the dark, but the withdrawal would be in daylight. Dense smoke screens produced by No 18 Smoke Generators would be essential to cover the withdrawal of the troops and LCAs as they moved inshore. Some would come from floating smoke generators but the landing craft had been fitted with two large smoke generators on their sterns to thicken up the screen. Within No 4 Commando there were designated "smoke men" tasked with producing the screen for the withdrawal. This work was so critical that there were 100 per cent reserves for the task.

Thick smoke, like fog, can be disorientating and for the officers and NCOs commanding men who might be exhausted, wounded or in shock this final phase of the operation could be extremely challenging.

Training would be the key to a safe withdrawal, but before they could consider this phase of the operation they had to attack and neutralise a well protected defended position.

The given doctrine for success is that the defenders should be outnumbered by the attackers by about three to one. Training manuals stated that the destruction of a single machine gun, dug in behind sandbags in what was quaintly called a "nest", required a platoon, about 30 men with three light machine guns.

On August 19 about an equal number of men from No 4 Commando would pit their training, skill and courage against the German battery at Varengeville-sur-Mer, men who were dug in, protected by barbed wire and minefields and ringed by supporting machine gun nests.

Notes

1   Two years later at D Day on June 6, 1944 at the Merville Battery men of 9th Battalion The Parachute Regiment would undertake a similar task albeit against a more heavily defended position. Aerial reconnaissance had identified a German coastal battery at Merville on the eastern edge of the D Day beaches. The guns, surrounded by barbed wire, mine fields and invisible in huge concrete casemates, could engage shipping as it massed off SWORD beach at Ouistreham. The commanding officer of the 9th Battalion, Lt Col Terence Otway had 35 officers and 600 men for the task. They were superbly trained and equipped with anti-tank guns, Jeeps, scaling ladders, Bangalore torpedoes and explosives. As part of the plan ten minutes before the paratroops attacked, 100 RAF Avro Lancaster bombers would pulverise the battery with 635,029 kg (140,000 lbs) of bombs.

    At dawn on June 6 the reality was different. Wind and poor navigation caused the paratroopers and gliders to be scattered over a wide area and at 02.50 a force that should have been 635 strong stood at 150 – each company was effectively 30 men. The RAF Lancaster bombers completely missed the battery but destroyed the local village. Undaunted, in a triumph of courage and improvisation, the small force commanded by Colonel Otway attacked and neutralised the position. It was then that they discovered that the concrete casemates did not house powerful 15 cm artillery, but World War I vintage captured French medium range 75 mm field guns.

    Jimmy Dunning, who after the war would serve as a Company Commander with 2nd Battalion The Parachute Regiment, pointed out that a drop at Dieppe would have to have been made just before dawn to fit in with the timings of the larger JUBILEE plan. This would have given very little time for the force to assemble on the drop zone and launch an attack. The sound of the approaching 20 converted Armstrong Whitworth A.W. 38 Whitley bombers required to drop a minimum force of two companies would have alerted the Germans and in the half light the descending parachutes would have been silhouetted against the sky.

2 HMS *Prince Albert*, Landing Ship Infantry (Small) (LSI (S)). The *Prince Albert*, a former Belgian cross Channel ferry built for the Belgian government by John Cockerill at Hoboken and launched on April 23, 1937. She was a 2,9390 tonne (2,938 ton) ship powered by 2-shaft, 22,786kW (17,000 bhp) Diesel motors that gave a top speed of 23 knots. Her dimensions were 112.7 metres length, 14 metres beam and 4.19 metres draft (370 x 46 x 13½ feet). She was converted by Harland and Wolff and commissioned for special service in September 1941. With a complement of 200 she was armed with two "very ancient" 12 pounder (pdr), two 2 pdr (40mm/1.57in) and six 20 mm (0.75in) Oerlikon AA guns. Slung from the reinforced davits were eight Landing Craft Assault (LCA) or seven LCA and one Landing Craft Support (LCS).

Copying the idea of camouflage modifications like those that had been made to HMS *Cambletown*, the *Prince Albert* was fitted with a false funnel for the Dieppe operation, however this fell off during the Channel crossing. She survived the war and was returned to Belgium in April 1946.

The Thornycroft designed Landing Craft Assault (LCA) could carry 35 troops or 362.8 kg (800 lb) of equipment. It displaced 11.17 tonnes (11 tons) and was 12.6 x 3 x 3.79 metres (41½ x 10 x 12½ feet). It was powered by a 174.2 kW (130 bhp) 2-shaft Ford petrol engine that gave a maximum speed of six to 10 knots. It had 20 mm (¾ inch) of armour along the sides and a 6 mm (½ inch) deck over the machine room; bullet proof side decks abreast the troop space, a bullet proof shelter for the coxswain and a bullet proof bulkhead forward. The complement was one officer and three ratings. The troops disembarked over a bow ramp and sufficient buoyant material was built-in to support the craft if it was swamped. The craft were "cold, uncomfortable and very wet in a running sea, but bullet-proof until the ramps went down". Dress for Operation CAULDRON included the camouflaged oilskin gas cape as a protection against sea spray stowed a quarter of an hour before landing. The LCAs had an AA mounting for the Brens or twin Lewis guns with the magazines loaded with one tracer to every three ball rounds. In current practice belted ammunition is one in five, however this higher number of tracer rounds would make it easier to direct the fire of the LMG against enemy aircraft. The orders for CAULDRON stated that the LCAs should as far as possible work in pairs to provide mutual support with their Bren guns.

The LCS – Landing Craft Support was modelled on a LCA but had an armoured boat shaped hull and was armed with either a 20 mm Oerlikon or 3-inch Mortar for firing smoke as well as twin .303 in or .50 in machine guns. It had a complement of 11. The LCS was intended to give local support for landings and its performance and proportions were similar to an LCA.

Lack of available amphibious shipping meant that No 3 Commando would cross the Channel in twenty Landing Craft Personnel (Light) (LCP9L)) also known as R Boats or Eureka Boats. These American designed craft built between 1940 and 1942 by Higgins of New Orleans had been provided under the Lend/Lease arrangements. They had a wooden construction and were powered by a 1-shaft Hall Scott petrol motor that gave a top speed of 8/10 knots. The Eureka Boat had crew of three, were armed with three machine guns and could carry 25 troops who disembarked by jumping down from the high prow.

3 Steam Gun Boat 9 HMS *Grey Goose*, with the pennant number S.309, was built by White's and launched on February 14, 1942. An elegant craft with a steeply raked bow she displaced 167.65 tonnes (165 tons) and had a complement of 27 though this increased to 34 as her armament was enhanced. Her dimensions were 44.2 metres overall, 6 metres beam and 1.6 metres draft (145½ x 20 x 5½ feet). Her 2-shaft geared Turbines produced 9,650kW (7,200 bhp) and a maximum speed of 35 knots – however extra armour and armament reduced this to about 30 knots. Her armament was formidable. It consisted of a 3 in (75 mm) gun aft, three single 2 pdr in forward, aft and amidships positions, a 20 mm Oerlikon gun in a "bowchaser" position, a single 20 mm in the bridge wings, two twin 0.50 in (12.7 mm) machine guns before the bridge and a single 21-inch (530 mm) torpedo tube abreast the funnel on either side.

4 Motor Gun Boat No 312 was a Fairmile "C" type craft, one of 23 launched in 1941. She had a complement of 16 and displaced 73.1 tonnes (72 tons). She was powered by a 3-shaft 3,619kW (2,700 bhp) Hall-Scott petrol engine that gave a top speed of between 23.5 and 26.5 knots. Her dimensions were 33.5 m overall, 5.53 m beam and 1.5/1.9 m draft (110 x 17½ x 5/6½ feet). Her armament consisted of 2 x 1 2 pdr guns, two twin .5 in (12.7 mm) heavy machine guns, and two twin mounted .303 in (7.7mm) machine guns.

During Operation CAULDRON the MGB carried four Goatley collapsible boats each stowed with a length of Alpine rope. It was proposed that the boats could be used to speed up the evacuation of the beachhead at Orange Beach 1 ferrying wounded and weapons. The Goatley boat, made from green canvas with wooden ribs and bottom, was 3.5 metres (11ft 6 in) overall, 1.3 metres (4 ft 6 in) beam, 0.5 metres (1 ft 9 in) deep and 200 mm (8 in) when collapsed. It was a light and practical craft that could carry seven men and be easily assembled by two men in about 1½ minutes.

CHAPTER 3

Training

On land, while building up their battle fitness as part of their collective training, the officers and men of No 4 Commando worked on the tactics of the impending operation as well as weapon training and marksmanship. Then, as now, the latter is known in the British Army by the slightly archaic title of "skill at arms".

Men concentrated on judging distance (JD) which would ensure that they set the sights on their rifles and Bren LMGs correctly and so increased the chance of accurate shooting. Fire control orders were practised so that riflemen and Bren gunners opened fire at the same time thus ensuring the maximum effect against the Germans. However it was essential that firing was controlled so that the limited stock of ammunition was not expended before the operation was complete.

Fortuitously in Troon in the hot summer days of July the Commando had lived off the land and shot on the ranges and each man had qualified on the rifle[1] and the Bren Light Machine Gun (LMG)[2], before they moved south to Dorset. Troop commanders noted the men who had qualified as marksmen and they received extra training as snipers. On the raid four snipers under command of Section Sergeant Hughie Lindley were deployed in France. Incidentally Lindley who had been evacuated from Dunkirk in 1940 had the good fortune to be picked up from the French coast by a Thames barge "that was full of Players (cigarettes) and rum".

A good shot is not necessarily a good sniper, he should be capable of working independently, have a high standard of field craft and ability to pick his targets to do the greatest damage. "One, L/Cpl Dickie Mann, a Reading butcher in peacetime," notes Dunning, "became very proficient. He was later awarded the Military Medal for his devastating marksmanship on his sniper rifle, with its telescopic sight, firing at individual Germans from short range in front of the battery at Varengeville." The snipers were issued with tracer ammunition in the hope that this would set fire to wooden buildings. "This arrangement was probably a mistake," comments *Notes from Theatres of War*, "since the chances of setting a house on fire with an incendiary bullet are small, and their use seldom failed to draw fire."

With the skill at arms groundwork laid on the ranges the Commandos concentrated on "field firing". This realistic and challenging form of weapons training has been described facetiously by some senior NCOs, as "shooting at bushes". In reality it is a live firing exercise that takes infantry training as close as possible to action. Troops moving across terrain, come under controlled fire from riflemen or automatic weapons firing on fixed lines and then manoeuvre to assault the enemy position – usually denoted by a trench with plywood targets. Finally with fixed bayonets they assault the position. In *Notes from the Theatres of War No 11* analysing the performance of weapons in the raid Lindsay wrote,

"*Bayonet* – There is something about a bayonet that defeats not only the armchair critic but, what is more important, the enemy. The Hun has always hated it. He may be old-fashioned but it can't be helped."

On Thursday August 13 after a conference with Lovat, Mulleneux visited the Commando while it was training and noted, "One very good practice – 100 yard sprint, 3 shots at a moving target and then 100 yards sprint back. I tried it in the afternoon."

Before the war the Small Arms Training Manual limited the use of the Bren LMG to the prone supported or tripod mounted firing positions. In the live firing training the Commandos pioneered the technique of firing the Bren from the hip. The gunner could correct his aim by observing where the bullets kicked up dust or soil near the target. *Notes from the Theatres of War No 11* noted that the Bren was more effective fired from the hip than the Thompson sub machine gun.

For the attack on the HESS battery No 4 Commando would be split into two groups each with a distinct role. The operation would be "Fire and Manoeuvre" on a grand scale. Battle school instructors summarised the principles of Fire and Manoeuvre as "one foot on the ground" or a "parrot in a cage". If both groups attempt to manoeuvre simultaneously, i.e. take their feet off the ground, like the parrot climbing up the bars of a cage failing to hang on with one claw, they would be in trouble.

For the tactics to work one group fired, while the other manoeuvred.

At first sight it looked as if the ground would restrict the tactical options available to the Commando. The coast consisted of steep chalk cliffs though to the west at Ste-Marguerite-sur-Plage/Quiberville there was a beach where the River Saâne had broken through the chalk. Close study of the shadows on the aerial photographs had shown that the cliffs were not only chalk, but worse had an overhang.

The detailed military plan for JUBILEE, described the two beaches as:

> Orange 1 Narrow stretch of shingle 600 yds wide
> gradient1/60. Exit for Inf
> (Infantry) by narrow cleft in cliffs.
> Orange 2 East of mouth of R. SAÂNE. About 300 yds
> long, 350 yds wide.
> Gradient 1/100 – 1/10. Exits for Inf and MT (Motor
> Transport).

However the two steep gullies in the cliff at Orange Beach 1 were almost opposite the battery position. In peacetime the larger of the two had been used as a route for bathers and had steps down to the sea. The shadow that showed the cliff overhang concealed barbed wire that clogged the exit from the gullies and hid the presence of anti-personnel mines laid at the top.

When Operation CAULDRON was over Captain Robert Dawson

commented in his after action report, "Much of the photographic interpretation was left to non-experts, and certain factors were not observed at all e.g., the presence of <u>LARGE</u> MASSES OF WIRE in both beach approaches."

The essence of the tactics of fire and manoeuvre are that the two elements should approach the objective on different axes – ideally at right angles.

If Group 1 composed of C Troop and a fighting patrol from A Troop was to land and use one of the gullies to ascend the cliff, they would provide the fire, engaging the battery frontally allowing Group 2 to manoeuvre.

Group 2 composed of B Troop and F Troop less the fighting patrol of A Troop were to land at Orange Beach 2 the shingle beach at Quiberville about 1.6 km (one mile) to the west, and work its way round behind the position to assault it from the rear.

This plan meant that Group 2 would need Bangalore Torpedoes[3] to breach any barbed wire obstacles and plastic explosive[4] demolition charges to destroy the guns.

German armour was not reckoned to be a threat but Group 1 would have a Boys Anti-Tank Rifle[5] to engage an anti-aircraft gun on a wooden tower in the centre of the position. This use of a large calibre rifle for long range sniping was almost fifty years ahead of its time. Today weapons like the recoil buffered American Barret 0.50 'Light Fifty' Model 82A1 and the McMillan 0.50 M-87R heavy calibre sniping rifles are in service in the US and European Armed Forces. A concept pioneered by No 4 Commando in 1942.

Within C Troop the Boys rifleman was Gunner B.K. 'Barney' Davies, however the best shot in the Commando was Gunner T. McDonough of D Troop whom Dunning remembers as "a tough, lean and dour Scotsman of average height but strong as a bull". He was "borrowed" by C Troop with Davies as the No 2 on the weapon – in this way if one man became a casualty the Troop would still have an experienced Boys rifleman. The two men worked hard together in training and would be invaluable during the operation.

Indirect firepower would come from the 2-inch[6] and 3-inch Mortars[7]. For the untrained or inexperienced, the 2-inch Mortar can be a difficult weapon to fire accurately. In essence it is a short steel tube bedded into the ground on a simple folding base plate and held upright by hand, while the other hand operates a trigger at the base. The bomb is dropped down the muzzle, the firer adjusts the angle by eye and operates the trigger – when the bomb impacts the firer judges how he should align the barrel and tries again – it can definitely be called a "hit or miss" weapon.

Dunning as TSM was in command of the C Troop 2-inch Mortar which had a two man crew, Privates J. Dale, a Glaswegian inevitably nicknamed 'Jock', who was No 1 and F.J. Horne who as No 2 carried 12 bombs, ten HE (High Explosive) and two smoke. They worked as a close and effective team and in training were able to place nine out of ten bombs in a target area 9.1 metres square (10 yards square) at 228 metres (250 yards).

The 3-inch Mortar is a more sophisticated indirect fire weapon with a base plate and adjustable bidpod with sights. It was sited to the rear of a position and fire was corrected by a forward observer who was in contact with the crew by line (field telephone) or radio. Once the first round had been fired and the mortar "bedded in" it could be very accurate. Lovat recalled that in training the mortar under command of Lieutenant Jock Ennis, with ten other ranks, fired at extreme range off the beach with the observer 548 metres (600 yards) away correcting fire over the field telephone.

On the Hardelot raid Jock Ennis had reportedly landed wearing slippers to ensure silence so earning himself the nickname "Carpet Slippers".

Rifleman and LMG gunners were now at a high standard and the mortar crews worked hard on the ranges in Dorset. The firepower of C Troop would be beefed up to three Bren LMG groups in each section. Two section Sergeants would each command three crews – six men plus riflemen. Since the Commando had recently qualified on the range, selecting the best crews was relatively easy. The training for these groups concentrated on movement off the beach, up cliffs, obstacle crossing including barbed wire and reaching a fire position unseen as two formed groups.

In the course of the training it was explained to the attached US Rangers and French Commandos that they would work as pairs, a tactical grouping known then as "Me and my Pal". Alex Szima was assigned as his "Pal" Jim Heggarty a Commando whose home was in the Irish Republic but who had enlisted in the Royal Ulster Rifles. At lunch time the men ate the packed lunches prepared by the landladies of their billets in Weymouth. With England enjoying a heat wave, they usually ate outside a pub and Szima "made it a point that Heggarty always had his pint".

Not every man in the Commando was so well catered for. Sgt G. "Honk" or "Onk" Horne, a pre-war Regular with the Beds and Herts, who had been nicknamed because his nose had been broken boxing in the Army, dismissed his landlady's cooking as muck. Collecting his ration cards, Horne shopped for his own food in Weymouth and cooked it in his mess tins over a Primus stove on the beach.

Horne may however have been prejudiced. At his lodgings in Troon his landlady was not only a generous and excellent cook, but was even prepared to return his rent if the Commando Sergeant was hard up.

Lovat recalled the intensity of the training in Dorset "When intelligence is available, only fools fail to take advantage of such information. Usually a battle is fought at short notice, with little or no plan of action. Here the data had been sorted out and sifted like a jigsaw puzzle... We knew the range and distance to be covered and learnt every fold and feature set out on the ground. The demolition squad could blow gun breeches in their sleep. Wireless communications had been tested and counter-tested. Every weapon was fired over measured marks. In camouflaged clothing, snipers zeroed telescopic sights while the Boys – anti-tank, Bren and Tommy gunners[8], and riflemen – blazed ammunition on short range practices. No 68 grenades[9] were fired on the day with telling effect."

Notes From The Theatres of War No 11 spells out in greater detail the training undertaken by No 4 Commando:

"A" Troop

Cliff climbing with scaling ladders. Fire and movement in close country. Practice fire against full scale model of the enemy battery. Fighting patrols. Street fighting.

"B" Troop

Fire and movement in close country. Use of ground. Full scale practice in lay-out against model of enemy battery. House to house fighting and assault tactics; in fighting with TMCs (Thompson Sub-Machine Carbine), grenades and bayonets. Mopping up and consolidation. Rear guard action.

"C" Troop

Forming a bridgehead. Snipers' training. J.D. Stalk and crawl. Taking up position in front of full scale perimeter. Firing 68 grenades from discharger cups. Mortar practice 3-in and 2-in. RT (radio telegraphy) in conjunction with 3-in mortar. A fighting withdrawal and final re-embarkation with (i) smoke (ii) under fire.

Training in fire and movement was carried out on terrain similar to that over which the Commandos would fight in France. "Firing practice concentrated on improvised snap and opportunity targets," writes Dunning, "simulating the conditions to be met in the assault/mopping up. No such organised targets or ranges existed for this type of training in the Lulworth area, so once again improvisation became the name of the game." Movement in close country was emphasised – the summer vegetation whilst providing excellent cover and concealment would also make control difficult since section and troop commanders would be unable see their men. Shouted words of command might also be drowned out by the noise of small arms and mortar fire.

In modern parlance there was "redundancy" in the radio communications – in other words there were different back up systems. Two men were assigned to each set, the second man ready to take over if the operator became a casualty. If the radios did not work, and this could be caused by battle damage, seawater, local atmospherics, screening by terrain or thick vegetation, line or runners would connect the 3-inch Mortar Crew to the forward observer while bugle calls or simple pyrotechnic signals would link Groups 1 and 2.

During training officers and NCOs were removed as "casualties" and their subordinates took over command. Dunning comments:

"It is a hallmark of sound and realistic planning to ensure that such measures are taken during training. For Cauldron it was an insurance policy that paid a dividend when two officers of the assaulting "F" Troop were killed prior to the assault on the battery." To cover every possibility all the men in an LCA would be written out of the exercises on the assumption that a craft might be sunk during the run in to the beaches.

The Medical Officer (MO) Capt R.J. Walker would land with Group 1 and established his Regimental Aid Post (RAP) within the bridgehead close to the cliff top. No stretchers were to be taken ashore, though they were available on the LCAs. Each man would have his first field dressing in the pocket of his denim trousers and all officers and each medical orderly would have a hypodermic and morphine.

Due to the limited time available for CAULDRON it would be impossible to evacuate the more seriously wounded outlying casualties. Lightly injured men, who were walking wounded, were told that they were to make their own way back to the RAP. Officers and men were under strict instructions that in order to maintain the momentum of the attack they were not to fall out to attend casualties. They would be the responsibility of the medical orderlies attached to the groups.

The role of No 4 Commando in Operation JUBILEE was the destruction of the battery at Varengeville. The planners addressed various contingencies. If HMS *Prince Albert* was sunk after the LCAs had been launched the Commandos were to press on with the attack. If the force suffered such heavy casualties that they could not penetrate the perimeter of the defences they were to neutralise the battery with direct and indirect fire. Finally if the force had suffered such severe casualties that it was unable to neutralise the battery, a strike by RAF fighter bombers was the final option.

For his planning Lovat was fortunate to have excellent reconnaissance photographs of the objective and the terrain along with French maps showing contours, buildings and woodland as well as a scale model of the target supplied by Maj Williams-Thompson.

Lovat's plan, drafted into a set of superbly clear orders was simple, but anticipated all possible contingencies.

For Operation CAULDRON it was essential that Group 1 be in position to engage the battery with fire before Group 2 launched its attack from the rear. The need for speed and control prompted Lovat to use only 252 men and not the whole of No 4 Commando. The essence of CAULDRON was speed and violence. In a colourful choice of words Lovat likened it to the tactics of a bank raid.

"My task was fundamental: in and out – smash and grab."

HMS *Prince Albert* would sail on the night of D-1/D and when she was approximately 16 km (10 miles) offshore the LCAs would be lowered for the run in.

Group 1 a total of 88 all ranks under command of Major Mills-Roberts would be the first to land on Orange Beach 1 and using one of the gullies would reach the cliff top and form a bridgehead to cover the advance and withdrawal. Prior to this it might be necessary to clear the holiday villas that were clustered around the top of the gully in the little hamlet of Vasterival. The Group would then move forward and engage the battery as soon as the alarm was raised or when the battery opened fire on the main JUBILEE force offshore.

The 3-inch Mortar crew would set up on the top of the cliff or sufficiently far forward "to pulverise the Battery position". After dawn ten more men would land with extra 3-inch Mortar ammunition and position the No 18 Smoke Generators that would be used to cover the withdrawal. Besides C Troop, a fighting patrol of A Troop and the 3-inch Mortar, Group 1 also had the Signal Section, IO, MO, RSM, a Beachmaster from the Royal Navy. In addition there were Canadian Army signallers, a detachment of two French Commandos, two US Rangers and the Phantom radio rear link to Lord Mountbatten at the Combined Operations HQ at Uxbridge.

RSM "Jumbo" Morris would be responsible for ammunition re-supply and prisoner handling. If any prisoners spoke English they were to be questioned about the likely location of enemy forces and headquarters. The collection of maps, documents and prisoners would be a priority once the guns had been destroyed. The orders were that, though it would be impossible to take prisoners in the hours of darkness, "After daylight, and particularly after the capture of the Battery, as many prisoners as possible will be taken... No prisoners of war cage will be established. Prisoners will be securely tied by their thumbs with fish-line in the best Japanese tradition, after which they will be handed over to the RSM and marched under escort down the cliff to ORANGE BEACH 1".[10]

In No 4 Commando, Group 2, the larger force numbering 164 all ranks would land on Orange Beach 2 in two waves. The first in one LCA consisting of a section of A Troop under command of the tall moustachioed Lt A.F.S. 'Fairy' Veasey, would land under cover of fire from the LCS at the left hand end of the beach and neutralise any opposition for the main party. It would have with it two US Ranger Sergeants, Stempson and Brady.

Aerial photographs had identified the presence of two bunkers on the eastern end of the beach and coiled barbed wire. The section would be equipped with two nine metre (30 foot) Tubular Scaling Ladders that would allow them to scale the low cliff at the eastern end of the beach. A landing before dawn was essential to complete this operation for in Lovat's words, "nobody wanted to be picked off like a fly on a wall".

After destroying the bunkers and cutting the telephone lines between Quiberville and Ste Marguerite A Troop was then to move by the shortest route to the crossroads and tracks to the west of the battery, to prevent any enemy billeted in Ste Marguerite from making their way to it to reinforce or counter attack. The standing patrols covering the road junction and patrols near the tracks in the vicinity of the lighthouse at Pointe d'Ailly would thus form what in modern terminology is called an "area ambush". Any German forces moving along the roads and tracks between Ste Marguerite and Varengeville would be certain to be "bumped" before they reached the battery.

The LCS would remain offshore to engage any enemy who moved along the coastal road from Quiberville. Once in position it was to contact Group 2 and report its position. It would then evacuate any casualties and, 90 minutes after the landing, move along the coast with the LCAs to the Orange Beach 1 ready to pick up troops. It would then be in position to engage any enemy on the edge of the cliff who might attempt to delay the final withdrawal.

Landing about three minutes after A Troop the bulk of Group 2 under Lovat would cross the wire obstacle by laying a length of chicken wire that would be flattened down by volunteers who would run forward and throw themselves down on it. This rather hazardous procedure was necessary because the Bangalore torpedoes would be required for the final assault on the battery position.

The force would then run about 915 metres (1,000 yards) along the east bank of the River Saâne and then swing east for a further 1737 metres (1,900 yards) along a shallow re-entrant to approach the battery under cover of the small wood at Blancmesnil le Bas. Lovat had allowed 90 minutes for this fast approach march. Some of the men would be carrying bulky or heavy loads like Bangalore torpedoes (four per troop) while F Troop would have Bergen rucksacks containing a total of 54.5 kg (120 lbs) of demolition charges and ancillaries.

From the start line for the final assault, radio communications[11], with a back up of three white Very[12] light signals would ensure that the whole of Group 1 was informed when Group 2 was in position for its attack. The three white Very lights fired by Lovat would be one of only two pyrotechnic signals used in the operation.

The timing at this stage of the operation was extremely tight, since 12 cannon armed Spitfire VB fighters of 129 Squadron RAF would fly in low from the Channel and attack the gun positions moments before the assault. At the same time the Group 1 3-inch Mortar would fire HE followed by smoke rounds to blind the German gunners.

If the landing at Orange Beach 2 was delayed and the dawn was breaking fast, there was a fall back option. In Plan 2 the whole of Group 2 would follow A Troop east along the top of the cliffs by the shortest route to Ste Marguerite where the Troops would be divided and allotted areas for the final assault. The signal for Plan 1 was one long call in the tone of G sounded on a bugle or hunting horn, for Plan 2 it was two long Gs.

Once the battery position had been secured by B and F Troop the guns would be destroyed by men from F Troop with "tailor made" plastic explosives charges.[13]

Of the men within the Troop designated to destroy the guns only one, John Skerry was not part of the intake of volunteers from the

Royal Engineers. Skerry as an infantry NCO who was already qualified as a marksman had completed demolitions training with the Commando at Lochailort in Scotland.

Dunning explains in *It Had To Be Tough* that the concentration of Sappers in F Troop was due to the reorganisation of the Commando in 1940-41 which resulted in the number of troops being reduced from ten to six. Among the demolition team, who were all Regular soldiers, were Lt D.B. 'Jock' McKay a Sapper Warrant Officer who had recently been commissioned, Sergeant Bill Portman who would win the Military Medal for his part in Operation CAULDRON and Sergeant Jack Lillicoe. They had all taken the opportunity to visit local coastal gun emplacements in neighbouring Portland to familiarise themselves with the most vulnerable parts of the guns. To Fusilier George Cook the plastic explosives looked "like sticks of shaving soap". As Dunning notes, "With gunners in each Troop they didn't lack any advice on the subject." The charges were made up in Weymouth and, supervised by Portman and Lillicoe, stowed in a tea chest aboard HMS *Prince Albert*.

Portman reckoned that on the operation he was carrying a rucksack containing about 38.5 kg (85 lb) of explosives "so I kept low when we landed, naturally". During the training for CAULDRON Portman had carried the rucksack even during the runs, "We used to do five mile sprint marches every day before we started training. That was with full equipment, everything, and you tried to do it in 45 minutes. The object was to do seven miles in an hour. You cursed a lot when you were doing it but it was fun, actually."

A Troop would be responsible for mopping up operations in the hamlet of le Haut de Blancmesnil to the west of the battery and for forming a roadblock.

At the close of the operation C Troop would withdraw towards the beachhead and cover it against any likely enemy attacks from Ste Marguerite to the west and Varengeville-sur-Mer to the east. The threat to the Commando as it withdrew would be from the south and west, to the east the Germans would probably be fully occupied with the larger Canadian landings.

On completion of their tasks B Troop, Group HQ and F Troop would pass through C Troop and re-embark from Orange Beach 1. A and F Troop would then follow after reporting in by radio.

Finally C Troop having shrunk their perimeter as the other Troops moved through, would pull back to the beach, leaving the Bren gunners on the cliffs as the last screen. As the Troop Sergeant Major of C Troop James Dunning was intimately involved in this phase. Training under Captain Robert Dawson began with a "chalk and talk" a verbal briefing with a sketch map, then a "walk through, talk through" as with no weapons or equipment the men practised the movement over the ground, then it was undertaken with weapons. Finally the withdrawal was practised with weapons amid swirling grey white smoke as part of the dress rehearsal.

Once on the beach troops were instructed to board the first LCA that came inshore until the Naval officer in command stated that the craft was full. A rear party had also been detailed to row Goatley boats from the MGB to assist in the evacuation of casualties and the weapons of the walking wounded.

Once Lovat had been informed by the Royal Navy Beachmaster, who with two Naval Ratings had a radio link to the LCAs, that the remainder of the Commando had been embarked, a radio message would be sent to C Troop that they were to pull back and embark. Two red Very lights would be fired as a visual signal indicating that there were 30 minutes to go before the last LCA departed. It was estimated that the whole operation would take five hours.

Under the Administration heading, the men were instructed that dress would be denims with stocking caps, and a choice of boots SV (*Soulier Vibrun* later known as Soles Vibram – boots with cleated rubber soles, later adopted by the Royal Marines as "Boots SV" and known to the public as "Commando" soles) or brown rubber and canvas PT (Physical Training) shoes. The Phantom signallers who would not have to leave the beach wore PT shoes, but took steel helmets. Most men in the Commando appear to have favoured boots and anklets, which though heavier gave better ankle support. All men would wear '37 Pattern skeleton order webbing of cross braces belt and basic pouches.

Private Clifford Leach, with F Troop was among those wore PT shoes and recalled that in the operation "in the stubble it tended to be a bit of a problem. One chap lost his PT shoe and he must have been in agony across the corn stubble". According to Austin one man with Group 2 was an Army boxing champion and wore his "black and white laced boxing pumps".

Denims were a lightweight version of the serge battle dress uniform introduced in the 1930s. They were normally worn as a "fatigues" uniform and consisted of a short blouson style jacket with two buttoned pockets on the front and an inside pocket. The trousers had two side pockets, a map pocket on the leg and a pocket for the pad and bandage known as the First Field Dressing. The trousers, that buttoned onto the blouse, were originally kept up by a belt but this was later replaced by braces. Within the Commando this combination of basic webbing and clothing was known as "Raiding Order".

Both Lovat and Derek Mills-Roberts were adamantly against the wearing of steel helmets on a raid. The latter would write that the helmet, "slows down a man like a grand piano, for it fetters him at his main point of balance. What was first-class for trench warfare in Flanders in 1915 is quite unsuitable for mobile troops engaged on an operation where speed is the very essence of the contract."[14]

The signallers who were attached to the Commando for the operation did wear steel helmets. Photographs taken on the beach in France show them as a slightly incongruous group hunched around their sets on the shingle in the morning sunshine.

It was said that the Germans regarded war as a profession, the British as a sport and the Americans as a job. Their uniforms reflected these attitudes – the Germans with insignia, badges and leather equipment, the British with baggy comfortable "grouse moor" outdoor clothes and the Americans with workmanlike boots and wool or cotton drill uniforms.

The US Rangers attached to No 4 Commando wore their olive drab herringbone twill – HBT US Army uniforms with British stocking caps and '37 Pattern haversacks, but retained their own M1923 webbing. Alex Szima who had acquired some British SV boots during the training in Dorset chose to retain his Sergeant's chevrons on his shirt. If were to be killed in action the pre-war Regular NCO intended to be recognisable as an American soldier.

On the raid Lovat would epitomise the sporting approach to war by wearing corduroy slacks, a denim battle dress blouse and beneath this his favourite sweater with his name knitted into it. William Boucher-Myers who had been commissioned into the East Lancashire Regiment in 1939, having enlisted as a Guardsman the Grenadier Guards in 1937, would to Lovat's amusement, wear a serge Battle Dress (BD) blouse and collar and tie on the raid. Presenting a "smart appearance … as befitted a former lance-jack in the Coldstream (sic) Guards." The BD blouse might be hot in August, but it would give its wearer better protection than denims to arms and elbows if he was obliged to crawl across rough terrain.

Extra ammunition was carried in the haversack, some worn on the hip and others buckled onto the webbing as a small backpack. Personal camouflage would include painting faces and hands with three colour greasepaint and the four snipers would carry camouflage nets. All the Commandos would wear a deflated Royal Navy pattern buoyancy aid a blue or brown fabric covered rubber ring with a mouthpiece and stopper, secured to the wearer with tapes.

Throughout World War II life jackets and the simpler buoyancy aids were universally known as Mae Wests after the earthy, busty, Hollywood star. The orders for operation CAULDRON read "All ranks will wear Mae Wests (of a suitable colour)".

Since speed was of the essence all troops were only to carry ammunition, no water bottles or rations were to be taken, but C Troop would carry entrenching tools. If it came under mortar fire, which happened on operation CAULDRON, the ability to dig a simple shell scrape could mean the difference between survival, injury or death.

Aboard the LCAs besides ten blankets and two stretchers there were self heating containers of soup and container of water – once offshore men would have a chance to slake their thirst. Each LCA carried 3,000 rounds of .303 ammunition as a reserve.

Officers would be armed with an SMLE, less bayonet or a Thompson SMG as well as a Colt automatic.[15]

Lovat took a Winchester sporting rifle with which he had stalked in the highlands, "It was a rifle I had done a lot of shooting with and I was dead accurate with it". Bayonets were darkened and sharpened before the operation.

Ammunition scales for the Bren Crew No 1, were five magazines in pouches and one on the gun, a Colt automatic with 50 rounds of .45 ammunition; the No 2 had six in his pouches and an SMLE with 100 rounds in two bandoleers. Within the section each man carried a Bren magazine.

Those men equipped with discharger cups on their rifles carried six 36 Grenades and one Incendiary Grenade in a haversack clipped to their webbing braces on the left side.

Men with Thompson SMGs had eight magazines in their pouches and one on the gun, with two 36 Grenades carried in trouser pockets. The SMG armed soldiers were to give assistance carrying the Bangalore torpedoes.

The No 1 on the 2-inch Mortar crew was armed with a Colt, the No 2 with a rifle and 100 rounds in bandoleers as well as 12 mortar bombs. The 3-inch Mortar crew had 60 rounds of HE and 10 of smoke which were ferried ashore.

The US Army Rangers attached to No 4 Commando for the operation would be armed with the M1 Garand self loading rifle.[16]

Signals between the two Group HQs and within Group 2 was by No 38 Set. Communications between Group 1, C Troop, the Beach Signal Station (Phantom and the Canadian Army signallers) and the LCAs was by No 18 Sets.[17]

Radio silence would be maintained until 85 minutes after the landing by Group 2. However the two Canadian signallers from the South Saskatchewan Regiment equipped with No 46 sets would be in contact with 6 Brigade HQ offshore to inform them that the beach head at Orange Beach 1 had been established. *Notes from Theatres of War No 11* records that all these communications worked excellently.

Finally that most basic form of communication, the password, for the operation was simple and memorable. The challenge or password was "Monkey" and the reply or countersign was "Nuts".

Szima recalled that training in Dorset the passwords which changed daily, seemed to be the names of English counties, or words that were either unfamiliar or unpronounceable to Americans. He wondered if this password had been selected for the benefit of the four Rangers.

On the day in darkness or heavy undergrowth a simple, memorable password could mean the difference between recognition or a burst of fire – the difference between life or death.

Notes

1 Lee-Enfield, Rifle, Short, Magazine, Mk III more commonly known as the SMLE was the standard British and Commonwealth infantry rifle for World War I and much of World War II. It was a bolt action weapon that fired a .303 in (7.7 mm) calibre round. The rifle weighed 3.96 kg (8.62 lbs.), was 1.132 metres (44½ ins) long and had a ten round magazine. Sights are set out to 1829 metres (2,000 yards). It was fitted with a bayonet with a 430 mm (17 ins) blade. At CAULDRON the cup discharger was employed for firing No 36 Grenades. Snipers used various telescopic sights including the x 2 Periscopic Prism, x 5 Winchester, x 3 Aldis and the x 3 Evans all of which had been developed in World War I.

2 The Bren light machine gun (LMG) initially built at the Royal Small Arms Factory at Enfield was based on the ZB 26 a LMG design from the Czechoslovakian small arms factory at Brno. The two names were combined to produce the Bren and LMG that soldiered from World War II to the Gulf in 1991. The Bren was an air cooled gas operated weapon that fired a .303 in (7.7 mm) round from a 30 round box magazine. It had a slow rate of fire – 500 rpm, but was very accurate with sights set out to 1829 metres (2,000 yds) and light – it weighed only 9.95 kg (22.12 lb.) and was 1155 mm (45.5 in) long. It was easy to strip and experienced gunners could change magazines or barrels in less than five seconds. Brens were also made in Australia, Canada and India during the course of the war. Like a dependable friend *Notes From Theatres of War No 11* says of the Bren in operation CAULDRON, "The Bren gun did what was expected of it".

Talking to officer cadets at the Royal Military Academy Sandhurst after Operation CAULDRON Maj Mills-Roberts emphasised that the Bren and the rifle had been the most effective weapons and the Thompson SMG of limited use.

An officer cadet queried this and asked why they were told that "tommy-guns were the answer to everything?

"Who told you that?" I asked.

He said he had read it in some newspaper.

"The real answer," I said "is that you should pay more attention to the Sandhurst Weapon Training Staff and rather less to some drivel you read".

The Commandant of RMA Sandhurst Colonel Montagu-Douglas-Scott and old friend of Mills-Roberts chuckled as they left the hall.

"I'm glad you made that point. The Weapon Training Staff will be delighted".

3 The Bangalore torpedo, named after the munitions factory in India, consisted of a cast iron tube 40 mm (1½ in) to 50 mm (2 in) in diameter and 2.4 metres (8 ft) long containing between 4.5 kg (10lb) and 5.4 kg (12 lb.) of Amanol high explosives, a primer and safety fuse. Tubes could be linked together using a "male" pin and "female" bayonet slots. At the front a pointed wooden nose plug could be fitted to prevent the Bangalore torpedo snagging on wire or vegetation as it was pushed into the wire obstacle – ideally the torpedo was not set to explode on the ground, but amongst the wire where the blast would be more effective. At the rear a safety fuze initiation set with a primer, detonator and safety fuse was fitted. When the Bangalore torpedo exploded, blast and fragments of the iron casing shredded the barbed wire and depending on the strength and proximity of the pickets created a gap between 0.76 and 3 metres (2½ and 10 feet) through the obstacle.

4 PE 808 plastic explosives, a British invention perfected at the Royal Ordnance Factory at Bridgwater just before the war, was composed of cyclotrimethylene-tritramine a powerful but sensitive explosive which the British called Research Department Explosive or RDX. Mixed as 91% RDX and 9% plasticising agent it was a stable, water-proof and shock proof, putty like material which could be moulded into containers or directly onto a target.

It was a yellowy brown colour and came in 75 mm (3 in) x 30 mm (1¼ in) 100 gram (4 oz) waxed paper cartridges. PE 808 had a characteristic marzipan smell and if handled and inhaled would give the user a splitting headache, known as a "gely (gelignite) headache".

As a demolition charge it was set off using a Composition Explosive (CE) TNT primer and No 27 Mk 1 detonator. The detonator was a 45 mm (1¾ in) long thin aluminium tube containing fulminate of mercury at the closed end. Safety fuse was inserted into the open end and crimped in place with special pliers called "crimpers". Safety fuse No 11 consisted of a black powder core surrounded by a waterproof fabric cover. It burned at 0.6 metre (2 ft) a minute.

5 Rifle, Anti-tank, 0.55 inch Boys Mk 1 was developed in 1934 with the code name "Stanchion" but following the death of Captain Boys the leader of the design team, just before the rifle entered service, the name was changed. At the beginning of World War II it was the British Infantry platoon anti-tank weapon. It was a bolt action rifle with a five round magazine that fired a 13.97 mm (0.44 in) 930-grain steel cored bullet that despite the flash eliminator on the rifle produced a pronounced muzzle flash. It could penetrate 21 mm (1 in) of armour at 300 metres (328 yards). On early marks the sights were set out to 274 metres (300 yards) and 457 metres (500 yards) later marks had fixed sights. It was not a popular weapon because its formidable muzzle velocity of 990 metres/second (3250 feet/second) produced a pronounced kick and its weight of 16.56 kg (36 lb.)

6 Developed from a Spanish Ecia design following trials in the mid 1930s the Ordnance, M.L. 2-inch (51.2 mm) Mortar was the standard British Infantry Platoon support weapon. It weighed 3.32 kg (4.1 lb) had a maximum range of 456 metres (500 yards) and fired a 1.02 kg (2.25 lb) HE bomb which on hard ground could cause casualties up to 150 metres (164 yards) from the point of impact. Other ammunition included smoke, illumination and signal flares. No 4 Commando were equipped with the early Mark II mortar that had a hinged base plate and "twist turn firing device" trigger. On the move the base plate and barrel could be folded at 90° and the weapon carried balanced across one of the crew's shoulders. The mortar remained in service into the early 1980s and though after the war the HE round was phased out, it was reintroduced during the Confrontation in the mid 1960s in Borneo.

7 Ordnance M.L. Mortar 3-inch (76.2 mm) Mk 2 was the standard British Infantry Company support weapon that weighed 57.2 kg (126 lb) in action. It had a minimum range of 114 metres (125 yards) and maximum of 2,516 metres (2,750 yards) with an elevation from 45° to 80° and a traverse of 11°. The HE and smoke bombs weighed 4.54 kg (10 lbs), and an experienced crew could fire 15 bombs a minute. The mortar could be broken down into three loads – base plate 16.7 kg (37 lbs.), barrel 19 kg (42 lbs.) and bipod and sights 20.4 kg (45 lbs.) and carried by men or mules to remote locations.

8 The .45 inch Thompson sub-machine gun Model 1928A1, Thompson Machine Carbine (TMC) or "Tommy Gun", was designed by J.T. Thompson in the United States in 1918. It was intended for trench fighting in World War I and was known as the "Trench Broom", but was delivered too late to see service. In the inter-war years the sub machine-gun was widely associated with the gangland turf battles of the Prohibition years in the United States. Senior staff officers in the British Army referred to sub machine-guns disparagingly as "gangster weapons".

Following the Fall of France in 1940, any reservations that the British War Office may have had were forgotten in the face of the threat of German invasion and orders were placed for the Model 1928. This gun saw service in North Africa and Italy. It weighed 4.88 kg (10.75 lbs.), was 857 mm (33.75 inches) long, had sights set out to 549 metres (600 yards) and had a cyclic rate of 600 to 725 rounds per minute with 20, 30 round box or 50 round drum magazines. Most Commando sub-machine gunners favoured the 20 round magazine that fitted into a 37 Pattern ammunition pouch and made for easier movement in close country.

9 The Grenade No 36 M was an improvement on the First World War Mills Bomb or Grenade Hand No 5, designed by Mr Mills of Birmingham and adopted by the British Army in 1915. It weighed 0.6 kg (1½lbs) and consisted of a cast-iron

segmented body, with two tubes, the central containing a spring-driven striker, an ignition cap and a short length of safety fuse, the smaller outer tube housed the detonator. The striker was held back under pressure by a fly off lever which pivoted on "shoulders" on the top of the grenade. A safety pin with a ring held the lever down. Grenades were packed 12 in a box with 12 igniter sets – cap, fuze and detonator. Priming consisted of unscrewing the base plate at the bottom, checking the two tubes were clean and that the pin and lever worked smoothly. The igniter set was inserted and the base plate screwed back.

When the grenade was thrown there was a four second delay before it exploded, it could kill or injure up to 18 metres (60 feet), but on hard ground fragments could go as far as 152.4 metres (500 feet). For ambushes, with the base plate removed, grenades could be linked together with explosive detonating cord fed through the central well to form a chain. The No 36 remained in service with the British Army into the 1970s when it was replaced by the L2A2.

The Discharger No 1 and No 2 Mk 1 fitted to the muzzle of an SMLE loaded with a ballistite cartridge, enabled soldiers to fire a 36 Grenade up to 182.8 metres (200 yds).

The No 77 Smoke Grenade weighed ½lb and was filled with white phosphorus. It had a tinned metal plate body with a screw on tin plate cap at the top. Removing the cap exposed a weighted tape attached to the safety bolt. When the grenade was thrown the tape unwound and withdrew the bolt. A creep spring held the striker back, until the grenade hit the ground when the impact overcame the creep spring and the grenade exploded producing dense white smoke for about 30 seconds. It would be used in action for the first time by No 4 Commando.

10 One of the 104 copies of the detailed orders for JUBILEE with similar instructions about securing prisoners was taken ashore by Brigadier William Southam of the 6th Brigade of the 2nd Canadian Division and found after the operation. It read "Wherever possible, prisoners' hands will be tied to prevent the destruction of their documents". The capture of these orders would lead to 1,376 Allied PoWs of all ranks being held in manacles in Germany, while in PoW Camps in Canada and Britain German PoWs were then chained in retaliation. On December 12 the practice was stopped after the International Red Cross had intervened, but the Germans refused to unshackle their prisoners until the British Government had given an assurance forbidding the binding and shackling of prisoners under any circumstances.

11 The Wireless Set No 38 Mk II or Mk II* was the platoon radio set at the outset of World War II. Prior to Operation CAULDRON all officers, NCOs and runners from No 4 Commando received refresher instruction in its use. The radio consisted of the set, signals satchel and canvas aerial (antenna) case with the telescopic radio antennae. It was a high frequency (HF) radio with a frequency range of between

7.3 to 8.8 MHz and weighed 12.4 kg (27½ lbs) complete. The output was 0.5 watts that gave an expected range of 1.2 km (¾ mile) with a 1.2 m (4 foot) rod antenna and two miles with the 3.65 m (12 foot) antenna. The two sockets for the long and short antennae were automatically tuned. However screening by woods or terrain could reduce the range of the radio. The signals satchel held ancillaries including the throat microphone, headphones with a canvas headband, two H.T./L.T. dry batteries, four aerial rods, a junction box, adapter plugs for ground aerials and spare valves. In the after action report the No 4 Commando signals officer Lt M.C. Ackernley wrote of the No 38 Set that it was a "great success, being lighter and less bulky, also requiring only one operator, it has obvious advantages for some Commando tasks in preference to the No.18 set, even though its range is not so great."

12 Very Pistol, a single shot 1 inch (26 mm) signal pistol broken for loading like a shotgun. It fired flares of different colours that could be used for signalling or short range illumination at night. The name came from Lt Very of the US Navy who designed the pistol and ammunition in the 1880s.

13 The 10.7 kg (20 lb) PE808 charge was a cylinder, large enough to fit into the breach of the 155mm guns, fitted with two percussion igniters or pullswitches. An igniter consisted of a brass tube about 100mm (4 inches) long weighing 100grams (2¾ oz) containing a spring-loaded firing pin held under tension by a safety pin and split pin to which was attached a short length of waxed string. Once the safety pin had been removed a sharp tug on the string removed the split pin and released the striker to fire a .22 cap. This ignited safety fuse inserted into jaws at the opposite open end of the device. A rubber sleeve could be fitted over the fuse and jaws to ensure that the igniter was water proof. John Skerry recalls that the igniters were either Pullswitch Type III WS 5-40 or Type A.N. or MD.1/13.

14 The knit cap rather quaintly known as a Cap Comforter, because it could also be worn as a scarf, lives on with the Royal Marine Commandos as part of Dress Regulations BR81 and is a slightly modified headgear called a Headover. The Headover, folded like the old Cap Comforter, is worn by recruits during the Commando phase of their training at the Commando Training Centre Royal Marines (CTCRM) at Lympstone in Devon.

15 The .45-inch Colt 1911 was the automatic pistol with which the US Army had fought World War I. It was modified in 1921 with a longer horn on the grip safety, a slightly shorter hammer horn and cutaway portions below the trigger to accommodate the trigger finger and so became the M1911A1. US servicemen carried the Colt 45" through World War II, Korea and Vietnam and it was also widely issued to Allied forces. It was 216mm (8½ ins) long, weighed 1.1kg (39 oz)

had a seven round magazine and a muzzle velocity of 262 metres a second (m/s) 860 feet per second (f/s). Ammunition from the Colt 1911A1 would have been compatible with the Thompson sub-machine gun Model 1928A1 carried by some officers and soldiers in No 4 Commando.

16 The Rifle, Caliber .30, M1 "Garand" was designed by John Garand of the Springfield Arsenal in the late 1920s and adopted by the US Army in 1936. It was a robust semi-automatic gas operated rifle that weighed 4.313 kg (9½ lb.) was 1107 mm (43½ ins) long and had an eight round box magazine. Sights were set out to 1097 metres (1200 yards). Though it had the minor tactical drawback that the clip was ejected with a distinctive ping when the last round had been fired, General George S. Patton described the M1 Garand as "the best battle implement ever devised".

For Szima training with No 4 Commando had been his first chance to familiarise himself with the M1 Garand rifle. In the US Army his personal weapon as an NCO in the headquarters was a Thompson SMG, but over the ranges he would be engaging the enemy a rifle would be a more effective weapon.

In the first practice he would be firing an un-zeroed rifle on the ranges in Portland. His American accent and GI uniform and the right side of his face scarred from a pre-war cycling accident had already lent him the reputation of a mystery man to British soldiers whose knowledge of the United States in the 1930s and 40s was derived largely from Hollywood films. His "beginners luck" on the ranges would add to it.

To any British soldier who has fired on the old pre-electric target ranges, the orders issued at the end of a firing practice:

Cease firing.

Unload.

Show clear.

Stand up.

Dress down the range and check targets; are as familiar as a temple mantra to priests and worshippers.

On the words "…check targets" firing point instructors and students run the distance that separates the firing point from the targets or butts to check the hits and so accuracy of the sight settings on the rifle and the marksmanship of the shooters.

To Szima and his fellow US Army Rangers British Army this range procedure was novel, almost exotic

"Surprising and not so surprising: at the cease fire, everyone on the line ran like a herd of buffalo with Maj. Mills-Roberts leading the pack."

Walking back from the targets Mills-Roberts met the US Ranger Sergeant. The British officer was shaking his head and Szima was convinced that his shooting was in British range parlance a "wash out" and that every round had missed the target.

In fact his five rounds were in a tight 200 mm (8 inch) group.

"Sergeant are you a member of the American Army rifle team?" asked the Commando officer.

"No Sir" came the reply; "I'm just a bartender from Dayton, Ohio"

17 Wireless Set No 18 was a manpack radio set for short range communication between Battalion and Company HQs. It consisted of a transmitter, receiver and dry battery in a canvas carrying frame. When not in use the front of the set was covered by hinged metal flaps and a canvas hood that protected it in poor weather as well as concealing light from controls. The 0.30 metre (1 ft) antenna rods were clipped to the side of the set. The Wireless Set No 18, with ancillaries, weighed 14.5 kg (32 lb), it was 44 .45 cm (17½ in) high, 26.67 cm (10½ ins) long and 27.9 cm (11 ins) wide. The 3V LT, 150V HT and 12V GB dry batteries produced a power output of 0.25 watts. It had a frequency range of from 6 to 9MHz. Using a3.35 metre (11 ft) rod antenna and transmitting on Carrier Wave (Morse) it had a range of over 16 km (10 miles), with the same antenna voice signals would work over 8 km (5 miles). The 1.8 metre (6 ft) rod antenna was more practical and gave a range of between 3.2 and 8 km (2 and 5 miles). On CAULDRON the No 18 had a two man crew an operator and assistant who carried a spare battery and valves.

Kenneth Kennett who was an assistant radio operator with A Troop recalled, "The radio sets were the old No 18 and they were quite heavy things to carry. I always thought they were very vulnerable but they did their work very well. They got their messages back and forward". Kennett was a skilled and experienced signaller, who after CAULDRON was promoted to Lord Lovat's Brigade Signals Sergeant by D Day and was later awarded the *Croix de Guerre* for his services in Normandy.

CHAPTER 4

Departure

Though the men from No 4 Commando who had been selected for CAULDRON had a clear idea that were to attack a gun battery and what their roles were within the operation, they did not know the location of the target. The training in Dorset had been described as a build up for an exercise. Security remained a priority – the raiding party would have no identifying insignia, and it was axiomatic in this type of operation that no marked maps or orders would be carried. They were however tasked that following a successful attack they should gather as much intelligence as possible about the German position and the formation manning the battery.

Lovat recalled one security alarm during the training; "the arrival of six (sic) Free Frenchmen sent by Dudley Lister, who swaggered into Weymouth all covered with weapons and insignia. They had uses as interpreters, but first they were told to change into something less conspicuous." The French Commandos were wearing the distinctive naval cap with its red pompon and beneath the Commando flash on their battle dress blouses the national insignia France. The three men from No 10 Commando attached to No 4 all returned safely from the raid, however those with No 3 who were taken prisoner, were reportedly shot when the Germans saw the words Commando and France on their uniforms. The French Commandos with No 4 were to gather intelligence from the local population a role that would be invaluable.

Concern about security even prompted Smith, the Intelligence Officer to request that two Norwegian soldiers, normally based in

London, should be temporarily posted to Weymouth and make sure they were seen with uniforms showing the Norway title on their shoulders. It was hoped this would spread the rumour that the Commando was destined for another Norwegian raid.

With the assistance of Inspector Martin of the Dorset Constabulary in Weymouth the French Commandos were moved by police car to billets inland in Dorchester.

Despite the efforts at concealing the location of the objective Private George Cook recalled, "One or two blokes looked at the map and worked out that we were going to Dieppe because of the sort of places we were practising our landings at."

Both Lovat and Mills-Roberts recall attending a security film about the Second Front that was presented to No 4 Commando. It had as its major protagonists a "clean-cut youth with curly hair, who knew more than was good for him ... walking out 'all innocent-like' with the wrong kind of girl". She it turned out was a Nazi agent whose family were under pressure by the Gestapo who had arrested them trafficking in Berlin's black market. "Unless the daughter's treachery pays dividends", comments Lovat in *March Past*, "all have been earmarked for a Concentration Camp. And a good thing too!" She charms the secrets from the youth.

To compound the youth's crimes an Air Ministry official mislays his briefcase in a restaurant (today it would be a laptop computer). The final scene sees the battalion, including its Brigadier being mown down in terrain familiar to generations of British soldiers, the Long Valley training area in Aldershot.

"The Brigadier looked like some antediluvian relic", commented Mills-Roberts, "and tactically one felt his demise was perhaps well merited. He bore little resemblance to our own Brigadier, Bob Laycock of the Blues, whose youthful appearance and red tabs were the cynosure of all eyes in London."

Security was however a serious priority for all ranks within the Commando. While the propaganda value of some of the dramatic press coverage of Commando operations was indisputable, it might also be a potential source of intelligence. "Those who talked to the press," recalled Lovat, "got the sack".

The Commanding officer of No 4 Commando felt that, "The press did not help the Commando image with a presentation of reckless, devil-may-care fellows who acted in a slap-happy and generally irresponsible manner. The public lapped it up. Nothing could have been further from the actual truth. Unorthodox, yes; but there were no short cuts to eventual proficiency."

Donald Gilchrist commenting on the press coverage said, "There is a lot of nonsense talked about Commandos, as though they were six foot between the eyes or something, but in actual fact all they were was a bunch of highly-trained blokes dedicated to the idea of getting fit and doing the job. They were not supermen. They were ordinary men who had been super-*trained*."

However the Commando was not averse to keeping a record of events and had its own unit photographer, the bespectacled Sgt Geoffrey Langland who was equipped with a German Leica camera captured on the Lofoten raid. It even had its own artist. After operation CAULDRON, Corporal Brian Mullen of the Intelligence Section would work up some of the grainy photographs taken by Langland into atmospheric charcoal and pastel sketches. Mullen who would be killed at D Day, was not only an accomplished self taught artist but also a shrewd businessman who had copies made of the sketches and sold them to the men of No 4 Commando following the operation.

As with all rules there was one exception. It was the war correspondent A.B. Austin of the *Daily Herald* who would accompany the Commando and land on Orange Beach 1. Lovat would say of Austin that he, "was a friend and physically up to the task (he) was given a rifle at Dieppe: later he was to get himself killed, poor fellow."[1]

Mills-Roberts remembered him as, "a fair thickset fellow I had noticed earlier dressed as a subaltern officer ... (he) asked questions and wanted factual information about our battle plan. He did not appear to be the type of reporter who would, at the end of an operation, feed the reading public with, 'What the curly-headed sergeant had for breakfast' supplemented by a photograph of some half-wit with a parrot perched on his shoulder." The excesses of tabloid journalism covering operations by the British Army, who would now be dubbed "our boys", are clearly not new.

Austin would not carry a rifle as a non-combatant correspondent, however when the landing took place he worked as a runner carrying messages between the cliff top and the beach to the Phantom Signals section and moving ammunition from the beach to the 3-inch Mortar crew. "Even if you are not allowed to carry arms there is always plenty to do in a modern battle," he would later explain to his readers.

For the larger JUBILEE operation the media coverage would be extensive with journalists aboard the warships offshore and at the ports to conduct interviews when the troops returned. The Canadian Army public relations staff had requested that five US correspondents in the UK be invited to cover the operation. Among them was Quentin Reynolds of *Collier's* magazine, Drew Middleton of Associated Press, while the Canadian angle would be covered by Ross Munro of Canadian Press, Fred Griffin of the *Toronto Daily Star* and Wallace Reyburn of the weekly *Montreal Standard*. Only Austin would file for the British Press, then known collectively as Fleet Street, as a pool contributor for ten national newspapers.

On Sunday August 16 a despatch rider delivered the top secret maps of the target area to Lovat. He also received instructions to ring a London extension by a secure scrambler telephone at 12.00 am on Monday. He rang and was answered by Colonel Anthony Head, a staff officer, who explained to Lovat the elaborate security measures that were to be taken to move the Commando to Southampton docks, ready to board HMS *Prince Albert* that had already sailed from Weymouth.

The plan was for a very early departure on Tuesday morning with No 4 Commando travelling by truck from Weymouth to Ringwood. Here Lovat would make a call over an open line to Head to confirm the arrival of the troops. For security they would be referred to as "stores". If the sea conditions in the Channel were favourable he would be told "Well, just as well get them loaded".

"Anyone who thought it possible to find and rouse up to two hundred men, in widely scattered billets during darkness, ought to have his head examined," asserted Lovat. "Apart from waking every citizen or suspect agent in Weymouth, it showed small consideration for personnel unlikely to sleep for the next thirty-six hours."

The two men worked out a compromise. Troop leaders would be told the afternoon before that there would be an early start for a two day exercise. The men were to parade on the waterfront in marching order with small packs at 05.00 hours.

Lovat on edge and angry told Head that a despatch rider should be at Ringwood Post Office as a back up in case enemy air attacks severed telephone links "Or, if your place gets a direct hit, which is the best thing that could happen to it".

In Weymouth Gilchrist knew that the operation was On, and that it was not to be another exercise when, "quite suddenly, as I was hurrying towards the hotel where the officers were staying, I saw something that stopped me in my tracks. Three Commandos moved across my line of vision carrying something that glittered in the sunshine. Armfuls of British bayonets. Sheffield steel, guaranteed. This was it."

In Portsmouth Peter Scott had received orders for the operation on August 14. It was 60 to 70 typewritten pages with photographs and charts. "I sat far into the night trying to form a picture of our particular jobs in the Combined Plan."

Trooper George Cook interviewed by the IWM recalled that on August 17 at Weymouth, "We were told one night when we finished (training) "Settle up with your landladies, pay your bills and be on parade", I think, "at 6 o'clock in the morning."

Despite having had a hard day's weapon training every man paraded on time in the early morning. "One good soldier – who appeared with a bursting bladder, as the clock struck the hour – relieved himself (and had his name taken) before the roll call ended. There were no defaulters," remembered Lovat with satisfaction.

The trucks had arrived, but no officer from Transport Command to command the convoy. "Here he comes sir," Lovat recalled the drivers saying, "as an individual emerged from the shadows with a greatcoat collar turned up and a Woodbine dangling from his lip."

"My nerves were frayed by this time," admits Lovat, "It was too dark to identify the offender, but I took the cigarette away with a swipe that put the gentleman on the floor. 'You step to the rear, my lad, and go into report for being late for parade.'"

At the Warnford transit camp Mills-Roberts recalled that they ate an enormous lunch and he enjoyed a pint of beer. They departed at 14.30 with the canvas side curtains of the trucks in place to conceal the soldiers on board. The IO Smith noted, "There were several other convoys entering Southampton about the same time as we did and none of these had their sidelines down." The streets were full of interested spectators as the convoys arrived.

Sergeant Szima had been given a note by the Ranger's Sergeant Major from Major Darby that read, "I am Sgt Szima 1st American Commandos, reporting to Lt Col The Lord Lovat." The Sgt Major had added a post script "and don't forget <u>The Lord</u>". Szima recalled that the new US Army special forces formation had not yet received the title Ranger. Searching for Lovat on HMS *Prince Albert*, Szima encountered the Second-in-Command Major Mills-Roberts, however because all ranks had removed insignia prior to the operation, he initially mistook the stocky Guards officer for a deck hand.

Szima was shown into Lovat's quarters, but before he could complete his formal report Lovat, burdened with the responsibility of CAULDRON, interrupted him, shook his hand and to the surprise of Szima, the Regular Army NCO, greeted him with, "Glad to have you with us". Thirty six years would elapse before Szima would meet Lovat again at a reunion at Varengeville and this time he would have the satisfaction of completing his report.

The Rangers, like the Frenchmen from No 10 Commando were not strangers to the men of No 4 Commando having joined them for 18 days in the work up training and exercises in Dorset.

The training was now behind them and on board HMS *Prince Albert* watches were synchronised by Lt Commander Hugh Mulleneux. The orders for the operation had stated that all troops and support parties should have more than one watch in their group – Derek Mills-Roberts had a watch on each wrist.

Once they were on board, at 17.30 the men were visited by the CCO Lord Louis Mountbatten who gave them a morale boosting speech that began with " a couple of saucy jokes".

Koons recalled, "He struck me as a grand guy and very full of fight; he made us all laugh and we were cheerful." For Dunning the presence of Mountbatten on the ship was confirmation that this was not another exercise, but the raid was on. "The die had been cast. Lord Louis left us in no doubt that we had a vital role and we must destroy the Battery. He was confident that we would – and so were we… For every five men going ashore, there would be a fighter aircraft."

Sergeant Hughie Lindley remembered the Admiral assuring them that the operation "was not the Second Front but a reconnaissance in depth". Bill Portman recalled that Mountbatten said, "I don't give a damn what Germans you kill or what you don't … but don't forget you have to get the guns".

Austin who had heard Mountbatten addressing Canadian troops earlier in the day recalled that the speech was similar in some respects, but that the CCO had prefixed this one with,

"Four Commando's task is most vital. If you don't knock out that German howitzer battery near Varengeville, the whole Dieppe raid will go wrong. You have to do it even at the greatest possible risk."

George Cook of F Troop had a rather jaundiced view of the speech, "Mountbatten gave us a lecture. He said he wished he was coming with us. Once we realised where we were going I think 200 blokes thought "I wish he was going instead of us". But, yes, a very nice talk and off he went, we cheered him and then we started priming grenades and drawing ammunition."

As men found space to sleep on the ship Dunning like many others went up on deck for a final view of the English shore. For Dunning however it was even more significant. Looking out over Southampton docks the 22 year old Troop Sergeant Major reflected that the home of his widowed mother was only one and half miles away. "I took a long look in the direction of our house and home, took a deep breath and rushed off to join the rest of C Troop on the mess deck."

Mills-Roberts regretted his lunch and pint when in the wardroom, "Tea and small brittle cakes were now placed before us" he noted that "the elderly steward had a cold eye which discouraged constructive criticism." Austin remembered the evening meal as, "lukewarm clear soup, pork chop, potatoes, peas, jam tart, sardine on toast", for which he was later charged 1s 6d – (7½p).

At 19.00 HMS *Prince Albert* cast off its mooring lines from Berth 103 in Southampton Docks and got under way. The ships leaving Southampton were departing before the onset of the short but lovely summer night and so were elaborately disguised as a coastal convoy as a cover against detection by Luftwaffe reconnaissance aircraft.

To Mulleneux the atmosphere onboard the assault ship was "enthusiastic and electric". Like a perfect host Lovat passing A.B. Austin smiled and apologised:

"Sorry we're in such a state of flux, but you see how it is. No doubt there'll be lots to talk about on the way home."

Austin later observed Lovat as he, "sat in the wardroom, rested for a minute or so, and then began to talk in his high-pitched, rather lazy voice. He seemed very casual, lolling back in the wardroom settee, but he was really drawing together all the loose threads he could find, tidying up the eleventh-hour odds and ends. He spoke to every officer in sight, flung sudden, searching questions at them in an airy, almost bantering way."

Now the ships were under way. "We slipped at 2037," recalled Peter Scott, "There was a great feeling of elation to be started at last. "We're off, we're off, we're off." No. 9 slid so neatly and quickly into the adventure – followed so docilely behind the assault ships – past Fort Blockhouse and down the narrow channel to Spithead. We turned west there, along the Solent, to meet our group which was coming from Southampton, and found the *Prince Albert* in the dusk. "Are you P.A.?" we flashed and were told to take up our appointed station."

HMS *Prince Albert* still had cabins from her days as a ferry and it was to one of these that Mills-Roberts retired for the overnight crossing. "I took off my jacket, boots and socks and climbed into my bunk – the ordinary top bunk of a cross-Channel steamer. Then I remembered that I had forgotten to wind my watch, and after I had done this I went to sleep."

Below deck the Commandos, Free French and the four US Rangers were priming grenades, during training they had each carried five un-primed in their haversacks. As they sat in the late summer evening unscrewing the baseplate of each grenade and carefully inserting the igniter assembly, the four Americans were silent, lost in their own thoughts.

"It was obvious that some of the gloss was missing," recalled Szima, "one of us shouted some abuse at his Company Commander's decision to order him on the raid as a way to trim the overage on the roster of Rangers trained at Achnacarry. Achnacarry allowed for a 10% overage for casualties while training."

Watching the sun sink over the Channel Alex Szima wondered if it would be his last. George Cook remembered it as "a beautiful evening sailing down the Solent and past the Isle of Wight".

The Rangers, Frenchmen and Phantom Signallers who in Austin's phrase were the "semi-detached members of the Commando force" had an opportunity to study the model of the battery and adjoining terrain. The model was about the size of a tea tray, but unlike maps or aerial photographs was easier to assimilate being three dimensional and in colour. Hunched over it Austin heard one signaller say to his mate,

" 'If we don't pull off this job, it's finish Four Commando' and he turned his thumbs down.

In that gladiatorial mood they landed on the enemy beach nine hours later."

On board HMS *Grey Goose* Peter Scott tried to sleep in a deck chair on the bridge. "It was a clear starry night that moved gently round the foremast rigging. I lay wondering upon the outcome and thinking of many things past. The sea was calm but for the washes of the great convoy ahead."

In his bunk Mills-Roberts awoke during the night and hearing the reassuring thud of HMS *Prince Albert*'s engines as she made steady progress across the Channel, rolled over and fell asleep again. Szima resolved the problem of sleep by using one of the six £1 notes (each the equivalent of about £24 today) he had with him to buy an illegal pint bottle of Service Rum Dilute (SRD) or Pusser's Rum from a sailor on the ship. The seaman had saved the treacly spirits from his traditional Royal Navy daily rum tot. The powerful spirits were duly watered down and shared out between the Rangers.

The passage towards Dieppe by the 13 naval groups was made in darkness and only the sailors saw the moon in its first quarter disappear below the horizon at 23.16.

At 01.15 Mills-Roberts was awakened by his batman Lance-Corporal E.A. Smith, dressed and went down to the wardroom for breakfast. "There I met the usual depressed breakfast crowd that one finds before the start of a day's work. On the eve of a big race, or before any event of even minor magnitude, there is rarely a gladiatorial spirit at the breakfast table ... most of those present were suffering from that uncertain feeling which is experienced by very nearly everyone about to come under starter's orders, or on the point of proceeding to the wicket".

The meal was mutton stew, which Mills-Roberts felt needed more salt "but no one reached for it and most people ate in preoccupied silence". As he left the table a steward presented him with his mess bill for 13s 4d (about £16 today).

Austin remembered the morning meal clearly – was it breakfast or supper at 01.45? The steward told the officers he thought it was supper, besides the stew the officers had bread, butter, marmalade and coffee.

"We sat round, eating the stew and swallowing unusually large spoonfuls of marmalade, in a kind of moody silence that had more to do with the hour than the coming fight. If Hitler could have looked in upon us then, he would probably have been greatly cheered by the seemingly low morale of British Commando officers."

Lt Donald Gilchrist, who would also land at Orange Beach 2, awoke, washed and dressed and "told myself I would make a well-groomed corpse". While Mills-Roberts remembered the preparation for battle on the mess decks of HMS *Prince Albert* as having "a general air of quiet concentration" to Gilchrist it "gave the impression of a Hallowe'en party, not a major operation. Everywhere men were applying grease-paint to their faces. It varied in colour. Some achieved the desired nigger minstrel effect. Others resembled Red Indians.

A Sioux brave in khaki approached me, 'You haven't got your face blackened, sir. I'll fix it for you.'

He smeared me with a greasy substance, the smell of which made me sick.

'Where the hell did you get that?' I demanded.

'Right from the cook's pan, sir,' he grinned."

Austin fared rather better. He "shared a burnt cork with the doctor, because he had a tube of Vaseline for a foundation, perhaps as a faint memory of some university amateur theatricals. This," he recalled, "made it almost impossible for me to recognise men I had hardly begun to know by sight with their faces clean."

Not everyone endured these improvised camouflage paints. Dunning recalls that for the first time in the war No 4 Commando had been issued grease paint camouflage in tubes of brown, ochre and green.

Seven miles off the French coast the ship's engines slowed to a stop and Lovat addressed the Commando.

"This is not the hour for a speech. None of us feel very strong at this hour of the morning. But I'd like to say this is the toughest job we've had, and I expect every man to contribute something special.

Those of you who are going into action for the first time, remember that noise always sounds worse than it is, and that if you're hit in the dark it's just bad luck.

I know you'll come back in a blaze of glory. Remember that you represent the flower of the British Army."

George Cook, who had celebrated his 21st birthday only two weeks before, remembered, "We were warned that casualties were expected to be heavy and that if a man got wounded he would be left behind". It was a warning he would have cause to remember.

Lovat drew to a close by telling the Commandos that the German soldier was not at his best at night, and that therefore the Commando had an advantage since the first part of the operation, the landing, would take place just before dawn at 04.30 hours, Before Morning Nautical Twilight or BMNT.

He ended by saying that he wanted a little extra from each man on this occasion. The Commando dispersed and in a brief moment of quiet Lovat took his Second-in-Command aside and asked.

"D'you think you'll find your crack in the cliffs all right, Derek?"

"Yes, there's no need to worry," replied Mills-Roberts with a confidence that he later confessed did not reflect his real feelings.

Now the captain of the *Prince Albert* took over and his voice carried through the ship's Tannoy public address system.

"Hear ye. Hear ye.

This is your Captain speaking.

The crew to action stations and commanders to their assault craft."

RSM Jumbo Morris followed with an equally typical Army command.

"All right you lot, get cracking."

At the signal to embark the men began a well rehearsed procedure. However as they filed through the ship to their boat stations, Mills-Roberts noted that, "even disciplined paragons of the barrack square – are incapable of moving at a controlled and consistent speed along constricted corridors".

To Dunning the Commandos, "went, almost automatically, in single file along those familiar gangways and up the stairs as we had done so many times during the past couple of weeks, out into the darkness and along the deck to our boat stations, there to clamber and struggle aboard the landing craft in complete and disciplined silence to our allotted seats."

Austin holding the belt of a Commando officer as he shuffled his way through the corridors of the now darkened HMS *Prince Albert* heard

"The full hoarse voice of a Commando trooper behind us (tell) his mate:

'An' don't forgit the other bastards is twice as scared as you'.

By now I had heard quite a few eve-of-battle speeches, but I think that this was the most compact and most comforting".

The Channel was a flat calm as with a low whine from the electric winches, the LCAs, some of which were heavily loaded, were lowered into the sea.

As at 03.00 hours the craft moved away from HMS *Prince Albert* the assault ship appeared as a vast dark silhouette. Before dawn she would move back across the Channel to be under Allied air cover. Once the LCAs were under way the Commandos inflated their Mae Wests. After the early start Mills-Roberts found himself dozing as the craft moved through the water.[2]

Austin had fallen into a doze, but awoke with one arm, side and leg dead with cramp. Looking around, "There was just enough light to show the dozing huddles of men all down the boat, with faint sounds, shiftings and mutterings coming from them like a dark fowlhouse clucking itself awake in the early morning."

Mulleneux in MGB 312 now had the responsibility of navigating the small convoy to Orange Beach 1 and 2. The LCAs were formed into two lines with MGB 312 on the starboard beam and SGB 9 HMS *Grey Goose* astern of the flotilla. At a steady 7 knots they begun to approach the French coast. Twenty minutes into the journey they passed the darkened shapes of the landing ships HMS *Beatrix* and *Invicta* carrying the South Saskatchewan Regiment. The ships were close together and to Mulleneux "appeared to be in trouble which was confirmed when three blasts were sounded on a siren, sparks were seen to fly and an ominous scrunching sound heard."

At 03.40 hours the Commandos and sailors saw star shell and tracer fire on their port bow. It woke Mills-Roberts and one Commando muttered, "Some poor so-and-sos are copping it out there". It was No 3 Commando whose fragile Eureka boats had encountered a German convoy moving along the coast. The firing lasted about half and hour and to Mulleneux "indicated that our landing was not opposed". To Alex Szima also dozing in the LCA, it seemed as if "the whole ocean lit up … so much that you could have read a newspaper". Peter Scott recalled "The starshell died and a tracer battle broke out, fierce white tinsel-like tracer being fired from the south and purposeful red tracer, much of it aimed too high from the north."

At 03.50 hours Mulleneux sighted three darkened vessels on port bow passing from west to east. He guessed that they were probably part of a German convoy or its escort, because he could see the flashing signal of the lighthouse on the Pointe D'Ailly and concluded it was to allow the enemy ships to navigate safely along the coast. He "considered it prudent to evade rather than investigate more closely. The course of the flotilla was therefore altered fairly drastically to starboard in order to pass well clear and astern of the suspicious vessels."

The heavy responsibility made him feel, "rather naked whilst contemplating the extreme vulnerability of the flotilla of landing craft in spite of the presence of MGB312, SGB9 and the knowledge that our destroyers were operating to the Westward."

The lighthouse at Pointe D'Ailly flashed for about five minutes every quarter of an hour, the harbour lights of Dieppe were visible to port of the flotilla and two miles off the coast Mulleneux was confident that he had navigated them to the point where they could divide for the final approach to the beaches. He transferred to the LCS and at 04.30 the groups split.

In the darkness Lovat shouted, "Good luck", across to Mills-Roberts.

LCAs 2, 4 and 6 escorted by MGB312 skippered by Lieutenant A. R. H. Nye RNVR, a veteran of an earlier No 4 Commando raid, started their approach to Orange Beach 1, while LCAs 3,5,7 and 8 under Mulleneux, escorted by SGB9 proceeded towards Orange Beach 2.

On board SGB9 HMS *Grey Goose* Peter Scott sniffed the air and detected "a warm wind blowing from the south, laden with the smell of hayfields". Like Mulleneux he had seen the lighthouse earlier and thought, "The Germans had left their lighthouse burning to guide us. Then we *were* achieving surprise!"

To Mills-Roberts as the beam from the lighthouse, "swept across and over us ... we felt like thieves in an alley when the policeman's torch shines. It is extremely hard to pick out low-lying craft from the shore at night, and we reassured ourselves with this consoling thought."

Aboard one of the landing craft approaching Orange Beach 2 George Cook was less sanguine, "The naval officer, a 'one ringer' (Sub-Lieutenant or in Naval slang "Snotty") said "Oh, they've got all the harbour lights lit". I looked over the prow of the boat and you could see lights on in the harbour because this I suppose was where the (German) convoy was going. The lighthouse at Varengeville (sic) was flashing so I thought, "Cor Blimey, all the lights on, everybody's awake, we're going to have a pretty bad welcome here".

Destined for the same beach the young Gilchrist looked across at a veteran Commando hunched in the LCA. "He wore spectacles with metal rims. A Tommy gun was cradled lovingly in his arms. Across the muzzle was a strip of adhesive tape to prevent water getting in when he splashed ashore."

The LCA had slowed to half speed and was moving silently towards the shore. "Was it going to be a dry landing?" wondered Gilchrist, "Was it going to be unopposed?

It wasn't."

Notes

1   With the rank of Wing Commander A.B. Austin, a Scotsman, had been head of the Press Section at Fighter Command Headquarters during the Battle of Britain. After the battle he had published *Fighter Command* a book that was favourably reviewed by Ritchie Calder in the *Daily Herald* but more significantly also by the recently retired Air Chief Marshal Sir Hugh Dowding in the *Sunday Chronicle*. *We Landed at Dawn* the book that described amphibious training and the No 4 Commando action at Vasterival was published in January 1943 and by March that year was into its fourth impression. Austin aged 39 at the time of the operation and almost 20 years older than some of the Commandos, emerges as an acute observer, a modest man, who is at pains to remind the reader that he is a non-combatant. His work as an ammunition carrier and messenger during CAULDRON put him at considerable risk from sniper fire and possible injury from the anti-personnel mines laid in the area.

2   For many men in Operation CAULDRON sleep seems to have come easily. They slept on HMS *Prince Albert*, in the LCAs on the run in to their respective beaches, and understandably on the return journey to England. Part of this was fatigue – they had been training hard in August and on the day had risen early. However it is also the human body's subconscious reaction to stress or a serious impending challenge. It closes down and builds up all available reserves through sleep. Private Richard Whitaker a US Marine with the USMC 6th Division observed this behaviour in himself and his comrades as they hunched in the Amtracs running in to the beaches of the Japanese held island of Okinawa on April 1, 1945. Years later on a psychology course at college in the USA he discovered the reason for this reaction.

CHAPTER 5

Hostile Shores

The defences on the darkened shore of German occupied France that the Commandos were fast approaching were not yet known as the *Atlantikwall*. These coastal defences, that would feature in propaganda films and photographs, would eventually stretch from the Spanish border to the North Cape in Norway some 2,685 kilometres (1,668 miles). They would combine coastal artillery to engage shipping offshore plus infantry and artillery positions, protected by minefields and barbed wire, to delay and destroy any troops and vehicles that managed to make a landing. Huge tonnages of concrete and steel reinforcing bars would go into the *Atlantikwall* and vast armies of slave labourers would live and work in appalling conditions to construct them.

The responsibility for engaging targets onshore or offshore would by 1944 be divided so that the *Kriegsmarine* – German Navy, gunners would man the guns that fired on shipping, and would have their own spotting and fire control system. *Das Heer* – the Army would defend the beaches and harbours. In 1942 this division had not been established so though the men of No 813 Battery at Varengeville were from the Army, their observers and fire controllers were Naval personnel. It might seem rather complex, but clearly the logic was that the men of the *Kriegsmarine* could accurately identify Allied and German warships, whereas Army gunners might, in modern parlance, cause casualties by "blue on blue" or "friendly fire".

Immediately after the Fall of France in 1940 the German forces had occupied French naval installations and with them the local defences. Later, after Britain had failed to sue for peace, field defences had been dug along the coast and barbed wire entanglements and minefields positioned to block beaches that might be used by amphibious raiders. They were not the concrete bunkers that were constructed in 1943 – 44, but many were timber reinforced zigzag slit trenches.

In 1941 the *Organisation Todt* (OT), the German government civil and military engineering construction organisation that took its name from its head the civil engineer Dr Fritz Todt, had concentrated on reinforced concrete U-boat pens, *Luftwaffe* airfields and bases and coastal gun positions in the Pas de Calais. The guns at Calais would cover the narrows of the Channel and subject Dover and a corner of Kent to periodic shell fire. "Hellfire Corner" would remain under threat until the late summer of 1944. Between June and September 1942 no major construction work had been undertaken on coastal defences, late in the year the situation had begun to change.

Nazi Germany was committed to the war in the East against the USSR and units that had been engaged in heavy fighting in Russia were rotated back to Germany or France to recover and integrate new conscripts that had been posted to bring them up to strength. The rotation of units through France meant that sometimes a sector could be defended by an exhausted formation that was under strength and ill equipped, or one, soon to be posted back to Russia, that was rested and well equipped. British and Canadian intelligence officers believed that the 110th Infantry Division held the Dieppe area though in fact it had returned to the Eastern Front over twelve months earlier and been replaced by the 302nd Division. The 110th was, not unsurprisingly, described by Allied intelligence as battle weary. Even while Infantry and Armoured Divisions were resting and re-equipping in France they could lose infantry regiments, and supporting battalions to reinforce those that had suffered battle casualties in the East. A survivor of the HESS battery contacted after the war by the researcher and historian Emyr Jones recalled that, "in Spring '42 I was one of the oldest and already in August '42 I was one of the youngest. Because of the war in Russia, Africa etc whole troops of young soldiers were withdrawn and replaced by older men."

Breaking up a military formation like No 813 Battery, either by posting away individuals or sub units would have been damaging to efficiency and morale. Military formations, even a section or squad, are a team. Men build up confidence and knowledge training together and this solidarity is reinforced by active service.

Life in France however was far from unpleasant for German soldiers, the value of the German currency the *Reichsmark* had been pegged by the occupying authorities in Paris. At the favourable exchange rates even lowly private soldiers could afford to buy luxury items like perfume, sweets and lingerie to send home to families and girl friends. If the soldiers were not based close to a city, they could still live well on the fresh farm produce bought in local markets. Since their victory in 1940 the Germans had behaved very correctly in Occupied France and the French population had developed a reasonable working relationship with their conquerors.

Following the Armistice of June 1940 between France, Germany and Italy the two Axis partners had carved up the defeated country and annexed or taken under direct control large areas of eastern France. This included Alsace Lorraine on the Rivers Saar and Rhine where Gauleiter Buerckel administered the territory. The Germans planned to extend westwards to include an area with a north south line from Mezières, through St-Dizier to Chaumont, and change its ethnic character by settling it with Germans.

From March 1942 *Oberbefehlshaber West* (Commander in Chief West), a post that included France, was held by the veteran Field Marshal Gerd von Rundstedt.

The Occupied Zone in France or *Militärbefehlshaber in Frankreich* resembled an inverted letter L included Paris, the Atlantic coastline and the English Channel and was administered from Paris by General Karl von Stuelpnagel. From former French naval and air bases the Germans were well placed to wage sea and air attacks against Great Britain

The *Zone Libre* to the south, more commonly known as Vichy France, was administered from the spa town of Vichy by Pierre Laval with the World War I hero Marshal Philippe Pétain as Chief of State. It included the cities of Limoges, Toulouse and Lyons. Following the

Allied landings in North Africa this area was occupied by the Germans in November 1942.

Recalling his time in the Dieppe sector earlier that year Joachim Lindner, who would rise to the rank of General but was then a Captain and Adjutant of the 571st Regiment, part of the 302nd Division, recalled nostalgically, "It was a paradise compared with Russia".

For *Unteroffizier* – Sergeant, Friedrich Waltenheimer, food was no problem, "We were well provided with enough food, but were able to buy more on the open market if we needed to. We used to barter with fishing boats. The fishermen were not officially permitted to sell their catch to us but they used to exchange fish for cigarettes. If you could speak French, as I did, the connections were very good."

The garrison in Dieppe had their own cinema with a programme that changed twice weekly and a military brothel that ensured that relations with the local population remained correct. Even these facilities appear to have been insufficient for some; among the papers gathered up from No 813 Battery was a report drafted on August 18 by the *Wachefuhrer* (Guard Commander), *Feldwebel* Sergeant Major Holzer. After sunset he had been informed that a woman's screams could be heard coming from the tented camp of Pioneer troops in Varengeville. When he arrived with a patrol he found a French girl cowering in a tent and a young German soldier who asserted that she had tried to knife him. Holzer resolved the situation by admonishing the soldier for fraternising with a French civilian within barracks and by arresting the girl as a spy.

For the purposes of defence, the coast of this "paradise" was divided into Army Sectors. The Dieppe front was part of the German 15th Army sector commanded by Colonel General Curt Haase.

Of the three Corps that made up the 15th Army, the LXXXI commanded by General Adolf Kuntzen, with its headquarters in Rouen, covered the coastal area that included Dieppe. The vicinity of Dieppe was the responsibility of the 302nd Infantry Division commanded by Major General Conrad Haase. The CO of the 302nd was unrelated to the commander of the 15th Army but amongst the officers the Army commander was known as "*Der Grosse Haase*" – Big Haase and the Divisional commander as "*Der Kleine Haase*" – Little Haase.

General Curt Haase, a 60 year old veteran of the First World War who had been recalled to the Army was described rather patronisingly by British Intelligence as having "all the characteristics of an old and worried German general". In September 1939 commanding III Corps, 4th Army, part of Army Group North under the difficult General Fedor von Bock, General Haase had advanced into Poland along the river Vistula. These glory days now seemed remote to the elderly general in the relative backwater of France.

However both "*Der Grosse Haase*" and "*Der Kleine Haase*" appear to have taken their responsibilities for coastal defence in France very seriously. Aware perhaps that the troops under his command were not of the highest calibre and that the "real war" was being fought in Russia and North Africa, Major General Haase took heed of the warnings about raids and landings. These had been issued from the HQ of the Commander-in-Chief West the veteran Field Marshal Gerd von Rundstedt. In the summer of 1942 Haase summoned the officers under his command to his HQ and ordered them to take an oath to defend their positions to the death. He himself swore to die rather than retreat or surrender.

General Curt Haase may have been a worrier, but he was well served by his staff. They identified three periods in the summer of 1942 when the Channel tides and moon state favoured enemy amphibious operations – July 27 to August 3, August 10 to 19, and August 25 to September 1. On these dates he urged the men of the 15th Army to be, "at the highest degree of watchfulness and readiness for action. Be on guard! Eyes and ears alert! Kick the Anglo-American and his helpers in the snout!" On August 10 using the language of Nazi rhetoric rather than military logic the General issued an order warning about the risk of enemy landings. Though the German Army had suffered a set-back outside Moscow in 1941–42, the style of this order is more reminiscent of the desperate exhortations issued by senior officers in grim years of 1944–45.

Order of the Day

G.O.C. XV Army   Army H.Q. 10-8-42

The information in our hands makes it clear that the Anglo-Americans will be forced, in spite of themselves, by the wretched predicament of the Russians, to undertake some operation in the West in the near future. They must do something

(a)   in order to keep their Russian allies fighting;

(b)   for home front reasons

I have repeatedly brought this to the attention of the troops and I ask that my orders on this matter be kept constantly before them so that this idea sinks in thoroughly and they expect henceforward nothing else. The troops **must** realise that it will be a **very sticky** business!

Bombs and naval guns, sea weapons and Commandos, assault boats and parachutists, airborne troops and hostile citizens, sabotage and murder will have to be coped with. Steady nerves will be required if we do not want to **go under**.

Fear does not exist! When the hail of fire pours down upon the troops, they must wipe their eyes and ears, clutch their weapons harder and **defend themselves as never before**!

THEM or **US**!

That must be the slogan of all!

The German Army has in the past received all kinds of tasks from the Führer and has always carried them out. The Army will carry out this task too. **My soldiers won't be the worst!** I have looked into your eyes! You are German men! You will willingly and bravely **do your duty! And thus remain victorious!**

Long live our people, our Fatherland
Long live our Führer ADOLF HITLER!

Your Commander, HAASE,
Colonel-General

The slightly hysterical tone adopted by General Haase and his determination that his soldiers would not be the worst may have reflected his underlying fear that in fact that this rather mixed and unmotivated force might not perform well in action.

The full strength of the No 813 Battery at Varengeville under command of the comparatively elderly 48-year-old *Hauptmann* – Captain Schöler was 130 men, but when Operation JUBLIEE was launched on the morning of Wednesday August 19, only 97 men were on duty. Though some were veterans of the Eastern Front, the battery that was No 4 Commando's objective, also included men who had been recently conscripted from the areas of western Poland. This zone had been deemed German and absorbed into the *Grossdeutsches Reich* – the Greater German Reich and these men were thus classified as *Volksdeutsch* – or ethnic Germans and liable for military service.

Of the prisoners taken by No 4 Commando, only one the *Unteroffizier* Leo Marsiniak was German born.

Bronislav Wesierski and Max Kussowski were told that if they refused to serve in the Wehrmacht they would be sent to a concentration camp. They accepted the lesser of the two evils and along with 1,200 other Poles were mustered at the port of Rostock on the Baltic. After a six day journey 200 men were posted to the Dieppe sector on August 10. Their military training had lasted three weeks. The poor level of training meant that, unlike young Germans who had been immersed in a military culture since 1933, these new recruits required as part of their daily training programme such basic lessons as Recognition of Badges of Rank.

As a PoW in England Kussowski explained to his interrogators that he had been rejected for service in the Polish Army because he suffered from chronic bronchitis. According to the intelligence officers who interrogated them, all the men were in poor physical condition and would have been rejected on medical grounds for service in the British Army. Kussowski stated that when he explained about his health problems to the German Medical Officer (MO) who examined him he received the disconcerting reply,

"For cannon-fodder all are good."

Wesierski, who had flat feet and a heart condition had collapsed when he arrived at Rostock but was told by the examining MO that if Germans were fighting and dying in Russia, Poles could do the same.

Even the earnest bespectacled *Gefreiter* – Lance Corporal Leo Marsiniak was not in good physical condition. He told his captors that following frostbite injuries to his feet on the Eastern Front in the winter of 1941-42 he was now excused marching.

One ten man infantry section in Dieppe was made up of a German *Gefreiter* in command, one Sudeten German, a German who was believed to have been a priest, five Poles, one Belgian and a Czech. These were men, who being over 18 the German recruiting system had classified as members of the *Ersatzreserve I* – untrained men under 35 who had not yet been drafted. Only invalids were exempt from classification, which makes it particularly hard on men like Kussowski who found themselves reluctant soldiers of the Third Reich.

At Pourville about three miles along the coast to the east of the battery in a hotel commandeered as an HQ a local Frenchman Maurice Mallet observed his occupiers.

"One young soldier was a shoemaker and a Communist. He used to sit all evening with his fist raised, all alone. Another lad of the same age had worked on a pig farm. He was not at all a Nazi, not at all a Hitler supporter. There was another one, a very nice lad, a stage manager from an Essen theatre. I asked him once if all Germans supported Hitler and he said there was no choice. One night the pig farmer was sitting in a chair in the hotel kitchen and getting in a mood. He said he was not going to stand up ever again for an officer and if the war wasn't over in six months he would kill himself. In our area the Germans weren't too bad. There were very few Fascists, just the odd one. We weren't occupied by really nasty elements."

However as history had already shown even poorly trained troops armed with functioning weapons, sufficient ammunition, under good or firm leadership and in well sited and built positions could be a formidable opponent. The drawback for the Germans was however that many of the men were still receiving "on the job training" – this might work with the relatively simple skills of an infantrymen. For more technical arms like the artillery the proper drills and skills had to be instilled from the outset or the results of poor training could be fatal as would soon be demonstrated at the battery at Varengeville.

The garrison in the Dieppe area had had time to dig its positions, wire and lay mine fields, site weapons, calculate ranges and ready themselves for an attack.

The construction of the battery, originally code named PIGEON, that would be the objective of No 4 Commando's attack, began in November 1941. The position straddled the road between Ste Marguerite-sur-Mer and Varengeville-sur-Mer at the fork of the minor road running down to Vasterival. It was an area of woodland, fields and holiday villas.

Living close to the Hotel de la Terrasse at Vasterival Gerard Cadot a 14 year old French boy studied the German soldiers with the intense interest that many young boys have for military equipment and operations. Though some houses were abandoned and some had been commandeered in the hamlet of le Mesnil around which the battery position had been constructed, some houses were still occupied. Mme Lefevre lived next to the villa that had been taken over as the Officers' Mess. At the western end of the hamlet was the home and workshop of Lucien Benoit a carpenter and cabinet maker and across the road was the house of the Raymond Boullier. Other residents included the Operes, Bertins, Maillets and in the outlying farms the Varins, Lefeveres and Boies.

Gerard Cadot watched as 90 gunners from the 72 Battery deployed six 15.5 Kanone 418 (f)[1]. The guns were initially sited at Petit Ailly but later moved. The soldiers were billeted in the villas in Vasterival and at the lighthouse on the coast. At low tide the gunners used the funnels of a ferry that had sunk off l'Ailly in 1940 for target practice.

A rail-mounted 2 metre searchlight was positioned close to the lighthouse.

In the autumn of 1941 the men of the 72 Battery departed reluctantly for the Eastern Front and were replaced by No 813 Battery. In the early months of 1942 construction work began on the position and guns were dug in a line of open emplacements that were revetted with concrete topped with a sand bag parapet and concealed under camouflage nets. A command post (CP) bunker was constructed at the road junction and the officers' mess was set up in a small villa to the south across the road. The CP was linked by two telephone lines to the observation post (OP) by the lighthouse. One line was on telephone posts and the other was dug into a trench below 80 cm of earth and marked by a red rubberised strip. Though some of the work would have been undertaken by men of the Artillery Regiment, they might have been assisted by the Pioneer Battalion from their parent the Infantry Division. It must have been dusty work, photographs of the site taken by RAF reconnaissance aircraft show the area from the gun pits back to the road immediately behind them white with exposed earth and chalk. Even when grass had grown back, the subsoil thrown up in front of the gun positions remained as a neat row of obvious "U" shapes.

The crews were billeted in houses in the village immediately behind the gun line. Across the road from the guns were a line of fifteen *Munibunker* – ammunition bunkers. There were also three *Mannschaftsbunker* – shelter positions for the battery personnel. The site had an Artificers Store, Medical Orderly's Office and Clothing Store in requisitioned houses. The battery had its own chemical warfare protective equipment store. A house near the south east perimeter of the position had been taken over as the *Schreibstube* – Battery Office and the canteen.

There were conflicting reports about the number and type of anti-aircraft (AA) defences. Some Allied intelligence reports stated that there were two AA guns one at grid reference 149673 and the other at 151671. They were code named respectively PINCER and PIEFACE. The latter was described as a "2 cm Pz Kw K.38 (mounted for flak purposes)". However PINCER sited behind the main road on a 10 metre high timber Flak tower was according to Cadot a 37 mm gun[2] however Allied intelligence asserts that both were 2 cm guns.

Tony Smith the Intelligence Officer of No 4 Commando identified three light Flak positions. PIEFACE which he put at grid 151673, one on the ground approximately 150 metres north west of the centre of the battery and a third on the ground 175 metres north east of the battery just outside the wire. The two ground mounted positions also had machine guns for local defence. A three gun configuration would fit with the standard German Flak *Zug* – AA Section.

Nine machine gun posts[3] or *Kampfstände* were dug covering the two roads running from east to west through the battery position and the open ground to the rear. Within a German Artillery regiment there were 24 machine guns allocated for local defence. Since the field guns nearer Dieppe were within the main defences, the outlying batteries received most of these weapons. Of those positions identified by Cadot four covered the east side of the position and only one the south west corner. There were two depth positions within the perimeter and the AA gun on the Flak tower used in the ground role would have helped cover this flank.

Machine guns are most effective if their fire overlaps or interlocks, so when they open fire they catch an attacker in two arcs of fire. Most of the positions were sited effectively at the battery, but not all.

The numbered *Kampfstände* were also named after their locality within the battery and were 1) Pfordestall 2) Hunihaus 3) Varengeville 4) Ginsterstand 5) im Grunde 6) Sportplatz 7) Ste Marguerite.

Allied intelligence identified two *Kampfstände* numbers 6 and 7 near the southwest corner. Positions in this locality were to cause casualties in Group 2. When in the assault on the battery the men of Group 2 started to neutralise these positions they discovered that they were sited to give supporting fire to the other if it was under attack.

A single coil barbed wire fence[4] covered the south of the battery position enclosing the villas, CP, huts and *Munibunker*. The coiled wire had a sloping fence on either side, known by the British as an apron, to give the obstacle greater depth. In itself barbed wire would not stop a determined attack by adequately equipped soldiers, however it would delay them long enough for the defenders to bring their fire to bear on the attacking force. Though barbed wire was often sited to run along exiting features like hedges or ditches to help camouflage its presence, where it ran across fields the grass or crops grew long where it could not be cut and thus stood out clearly in photographs. Once the defensive perimeter of the battery had been established the buildings and defences could be located within it. To the front of the battery the fence was a double coil that followed the line of the wood that had a salient facing south towards the battery. The total area enclosed by the barbed wire was about fifty acres.

Concertina wire five metres high was used to block the gullies at Vasterival, anti-personnel mines were also buried in these defiles.[5]

A barbed wire fence three coils deep blocked the beach from the Quiberville cliffs to those at Ste Marguerite. Two bunkers were built and equipped with captured French 75 mm guns[6] and nearer the beach three field positions with machine guns were dug. The fields behind the beach were flooded by closing the sluice gate that stopped the slow flowing River Saâne running out to the sea. The coastal road between the two villages was forbidden to French civilians and the garrison of fifty German soldiers were housed in commandeered villas in Ste Marguerite. Though some of the houses within the battery area at le Mesnil had been commandeered by the German artillerymen, some were still occupied by their French owners, with troops billeted in them. In August 1942 these positions were manned by men of the 571st Infantry Regiment, with a platoon of the 3rd Company in Quiberville and possibly the 1st Company in the Ste Marguerite area.

By January 1942 the construction work was complete and the garrison was reduced. The searchlight was removed from the Phare d'Ailly but 25 sailors from the *Kriegsmarine* remained in the OP at the lighthouse. In addition to the sailors the OP had five soldiers from the battery. Two 36 mm AA guns crewed by ten men from the *Luftwaffe* were sited at the lighthouse.

During the fighting on August 19 somewhere to the south and east of the battery an 8.1cm mortar line[7] was established. The crews may have pre-registered targets and one of these was the tree line immediately to the front of the battery.

Allied intelligence actually over-estimated the strength of the defences of the battery. They were given as two AA guns, at least seven machine gun posts, two in bunkers and an anti-tank gun.

Besides manning their "Stand To" positions in trenches and machine gun positions at dawn and dusk, the men of the battery mounted regular standing patrols of the area by night and day. The young Gerard Cadot watched two soldiers leave the lighthouse walk down to Vasterival along the road, stand guard at top of the gully leading to sea for one hour and then return through the woodland and scrub. A second patrol of two men would leave the battery, pass the

Hotel de la Terrasse, patrol the plateau – the open ground to the east of the hotel and then return through the woods to the battery. Though the main threat would come from the shore to the north, standing patrols also probably covered the flanks and rear, walking out to 1000 to 1,500 metres along the roads and tracks.

German war artists like Müller-Gera and Franz Martin Luenstroth attempted to portray this boring sentry duty in a romantic light with works like *Sentry on Duty on a Starry Night (Mont-Saint-Michel, France, 1943)* and *Sentry Post on the Beach Near Ostende, 1940*. In these pictures the lone soldier, with rifle slung, stands facing north towards the hostile shores of Britain.[8]

For the men of the coastal garrisons there were three states of alert. The Continuous State of Alert, which was the normal routine; Threatened Danger when troops should be ready for action; and Highest Degree of Alert or Action Stations.

On the evening of August 18 the troops were on Threatened Danger Alert since the reported weather conditions and tide states were favourable for an enemy operation. The Luftwaffe meteorologists reported the weather for the coming night and following day as, "Light winds chiefly from the South, increasing later to a minimum of two to four. Few clouds, visibility about 4 to 10 kilometres, morning mist on the coast with decreasing visibility. Later on an increasing haze may be expected from the West with a ceiling of low cloud… High water at Dieppe 04.30 hours on 19 August."

At Puys to the east of Dieppe *Hauptmann* Richard Schnösenberg commanding the 3rd Battalion of Infantry Regiment 571 of the 302 Infantry Division recalled that because he had put his soldiers through a training exercise they were on full alert. However, "my neighbouring battalions at Dieppe and Pourville had only night crew operating – the rest were asleep." Recalling the positions that the 3rd Battalion were manning he said, "We had enough ammo stockpiled to keep us going for days on end if it had been necessary.

All we needed to do was take the machine guns in our hands and fire. We'd had so many practices with live ammo, we knew what to do."

In Spring and into the hot August weather of 1942 the gun crews of the battery at Varengeville had run to their "Stand To" positions and fired practise shoots out to sea. To keep cool and to save their uniforms from wear and damage they wore their *Heeres Drillichanzug* an off-white denim fatigue uniform of a plain drill jacket with no pockets and trousers with two pockets.

In North Africa and the Eastern Front soldiers were issued with special reed green or sand coloured hot weather uniforms, but in France they made do with this uniform that traced its origins back to a previous century. The *Heeres Drillichanzug* was easy to wash and dry, but what little colour there was in the unbleached fabric soon disappeared. Since they were not front line troops the need for camouflage clothing in the field, they reasoned would not be essential. It would be a fatal mistake for many.

Clearly some of the men wore this uniform regularly for any heavy or dirty work at the battery since among the prisoners taken by No 4 Commando one man had repaired his uniform with sacking. The white colour of the uniform led many of the men of No 4 Commando to assume that the Germans were wearing shirts or initially that one man who was seen was in "cook's whites" – the white cotton drill uniform of an army cook. However during the fighting at the battery several men reported seeing a German wearing a cook's cap, rather than a steel helmet, fighting with surprising determination.

The NCO's commanding the MG 34 machine gun positions around the battery perimeter would have been armed with the MP 38 sub machine gun[9]. The 30 round magazines for the weapon were carried in six leather and canvas ammunition pouches with a special pouch for the loading tool on the left. The NCOs and Officers would also have been equipped with the 6 x 30 *Dienstglas* the standard Army issue prismatic binoculars.

Rank for NCOs was displayed by chevrons or aluminium thread ribbon edging to their collars. Both NCOs and soldiers would have carried the distinctive German *Stielgranate 24* stick grenade[10]. These were often carried with the wooden handle stuffed into the tops of marching boots or behind the soldier's belt.

The officers living in the comfort of the villa close to the gun line would have been easily distinguishable by their dress and weapons. Though many infantry officers used the MP38/40 SMG in action, those in No 813 Battery would probably have been armed with either the P 08 Luger or Walther P 38 automatic pistol[11]. Firing his pistol *Hauptmann* Schöler the battery commander would fight a running battle with the men of B Troop No 4 Commando when they assaulted the position.

The cut and quality of officers' tunics with britches tucked into superior quality leather boots would have distinguished them as well as the *Schirmmütze* peaked cap with its silver chin strap cords and the red *Waffenfarbe* trim of the Artillery around the crown. The officers' pistols in leather holsters would have been worn on brown leather belts with open double claw buckles.

It would have been hard to distinguish the sailors who worked alongside the army gunners. Both wore very similar uniforms and this led the young Cadot to believe that the battery had Marines as well as sailors among its personnel. The men of the *Kriegsmarine* Coastal Artillery had gold coloured naval buckles on their belts, green backing to the *Reichsadler* eagle and swastika badge on the right breast of their tunics and green backing to collar and epaulets. The ordinary *Matrosen* – ratings had an insignia on their epaulets that showed an anchor surmounted by a flaming shell with a numeral above it.

However in early spring of 1942 a *Kriegsmarine* film and stills camera crew visited the battery and the *Matrosen* – sailors, were clearly distinguishable in their double breasted dark blue jackets, side hats and trousers. A member of the film crew, one of the 8,577 veterans of the fighting in Narvik in 1940, proudly displayed his gilt metal *Narvikschild* – Narvik Shield on the upper left sleeve of his jacket.

So though No 813 Battery might be crewed and commanded by officers of *das Heer* it was tactically the responsibility of the Coastal Artillery branch of the *Kriegsmarine*. In the after action reports that were a mixture of sound analysis and self-congratulation Field Marshal Gerd von Rundstedt put his signature to Fundamental Remarks of Army HQ No 8 issued on August 22, 1942. Paragraph four stated:

"There are still many coastal batteries in absolutely wrong positions which could not oppose a close infantry attack well led.

The reason lies in the fact that these were established in 1940-41 when conditions were quite different to the present (then more of an offensive nature firing against distant naval targets. Now it is coastal defence against landing operations and supporting the principal fighting forces)".

In the months before operation JUBILEE the Naval staff pressed the Army to have the battery sited closer to Dieppe so that it could be included within the defensive perimeter. Three 10.5 cm field artillery batteries, two to the west and one to the east were within this perimeter. Writing about the Varengeville battery in an after action report Admiral von Fischel the Admiral Channel Coast stated:

"It was tactically and absolutely wrongly sited ... for three long months the 302nd Division had declined each of three suggestions without even making one positive proposal."

The Army finally agreed to a new more defensible site, but no work had begun by August 19, 1942. In his report Colonel General Curt Haase, CO 302nd Infantry Division would write:

"The two coastal batteries were outside the main sector of Dieppe and through lack of personnel were not able to be defended sufficiently by infantry. The critical position of No 813 was known, and its inclusion in the Dieppe defences proper should have been made earlier".

Fundamental Remarks of Army HQ No 8 stated; "The winter programme for work of fortification must eliminate this trouble. We shall have to find and will find a solution so that these batteries will be able to protect themselves."

Part of the problem had probably been lack of mobility. The big 15 cm guns would have required tracked prime movers like the 12 or 18 tonne SdKfz 8 or 9 half tracks to move them from their current positions. A standard artillery regiment had a nominal strength of 2,700 officers and men with 38 motorcycles, 35 motor vehicles, 226 horse drawn vehicles and 2,211 horses. As part of a low priority coastal defence division the regiment was under strength in both manpower and vehicles. Many of the vehicles were captured and were already worn out and unreliable when they were allocated to the division. Spare tyres were in such short supply that units attempted to buy them on the civilian market. According to Joachim Lindner transport for most of the units in the Dieppe area was horse drawn, "We were not mobile. Horses and bicycles were the only means of transport."

For the commander of these ill equipped, poorly motivated men one of the greatest problems was keeping them at the proper level of readiness. "It was very quiet, day after day nothing," recalled Lindner. "We had a problem with the men guarding the coast, the poor man walking with his rifle along the cliffs. Nothing happened but the waves coming and going, coming and going. Sometimes he slept. Yes, we had a problem to keep them awake."

At the battery office at Le Mesnil a conscientious clerk had drafted the training programme for the day the *Dientsplan für miitwoch den 19 August 1942* and pinned it up on the notice board on the evening of the 18th. After rouse at 06.00 the gunners would have *Frühsport* – fitness training and after breakfast and an administration period between 10.45 and 11.45 they would conduct *Geschütz-exerzieren* – firing practice.

In the minutes before dawn on August 19, 1942 the men of the No 813 Battery at Varengeville would receive a violent wake up call and this time it would not be a training exercise.

Notes

1 The *15.5 cm Kanone 418(f)* was a captured French 155 mm piece, the *canon de 155 GPF (Grand Puissance Filloux)* known as "Fillian". The gun was first used in World War I in 1917 and adopted by the US Army as the 155 mm Gun M1918 M1. In World War II many of the 449 that were deployed by the French were captured and subsequently used for coastal defence. Those at Varengeville had previously been used by the French on the Somme in 1940 and appear to have been mounted on German carriages. The *15.5 cm Kanone 418(f)* weighed 10,750 kg (23,699.6 lb) in action, had a traverse of 60° an elevation of 0° to 35° and a muzzle velocity of 735 metres (2,411 ft) a second. This could propel a 43 kg (94.7 lb) shell out to 19,500 metres (21,325 yds) and though the given rate of fire was one round a minute, this could be doubled over short periods. For coastal artillery work the split trails were opened and fitted into a circular track. At the centre the wheels of the carriage were bolted onto a turntable. Though now static, the gun could be aligned quickly to engage targets over a 180° arc.

2   During the war the Germans fielded four 3.7 cm (1.45 in) AA guns the Flak 18, 36, 37 and the Flak 43, though this last gun would not have been located at the battery.

The Flak 18/36/37 operated by barrel recoil and residual gas pressure and had a practical/cyclic rate of 80/160 rpm (Flak 18) and 120/160 rpm (Flak 36/37). The guns were clip fed from the side and fired HE-tracer, HE-incendiary-tracer, Armour Piercing HE, HE-incendiary and HE projectiles.

The weight in action for the Flak 18 was 1,757 kg (3,873 lb), and the Flak 36/37 1,544 kg (3,403.9 lb). The elevation was -5° to + 85° and 360° traverse with a muzzle velocity of 820 m/sec (2,690 ft) (HE) and 770 m/sec (2,470 ft) (AP) at ground targets. The guns had a maximum vertical range of 4,785 metres (15,698 ft) and horizontal of 6,490 metres (2,129 ft).

The sights for the guns were the *Flakvisier 33*, the *Flakvisier 37* for the Flak 37 and the *Schwebedornvisier*.

The 2 cm Flak 30 weighed 483 kg (1,064.8 lb) in action, had an elevation of -12° to + 90°, a 360° traverse on its tripod base. Its muzzle velocity was 899 metres (2,949 ft) a second with HE ammunition or 830 metres (2,723 ft) a second firing with armour piercing (AP) in a ground role. The maximum vertical range was 2,134 metres (7001.3 ft) and horizontal 2,697 metres (8,848.4 ft). Practical rates of fire were 120 rounds per minute (rpm), though the gun had a cyclic rate of 280 rpm.

The Flak 38 was an almost identical weapon except that it weighed 406 kg (895 lbs) in action and its practical rate of fire was 220 rpm and cyclic rate 480 rpm. It elevation was from -20° to + 90°. Both weapons were fitted with a single seat for the gunner.

All were recoil operated and could fire single shots or bursts using a twenty round box magazine. A light armoured shield could be fitted where there was a threat from small arms fire, but with those guns used in the Defence of the Reich it was normally discarded. The guns were equipped with one of three types of magnifying optical sight, the *Linealvisier 21*, *Flakvisier 38* or the *Schwebekreisvisier 30/38*.

3   The MG 34 machine gun, loosely known the Spandau, was the section automatic weapon with which the German forces entered World War II. Designed by Louis Stange of Rheinmetall it was the world's first General Purpose Machine Gun (GPMG) a weapon that could be used in the light role firing off its bipod, or in the sustained fire role on a folding tripod with an optical sight. Its design drew on German experience in World War I, where water cooled Maxim machine guns were too cumbersome to be used effectively in the trenches.

The tripod on the MG 34 gave greater stability and consequently a longer effective range – however if the crew were attacked from another axis it was difficult to dismount the gun and re-deploy it quickly. The MG 34 could also be used as a light AA gun with a ring sight on a special mount. Tanks and other AFVs were equipped with the MG 34. Infantry crews carried two spare barrels in a metal tubular container these were changed after they had fired 250 rounds. The air cooled machine gun was 1,219 mm (48 in) long with a 627 mm (24.75 in) barrel, weighed 11.9 kg (26.7 lb.) in the light role and 31.07 kg (68.5 lbs) on the sustained fire mount. With a muzzle velocity of 755 metres (2,480 ft) a second it had a maximum range of 2,000 metres (2,187 yds) and a cyclic rate of 8 – 900 rounds per minute. It fired from a 75 round saddle drum magazine or 50 round non-disintegrating belts that could be reloaded for subsequent use and carried in two or more ammunition boxes.

4   Barbed wire obstacles. German military barbed wire – *koppelzäne* differed from that used for agricultural fencing, the barbs were about 20 mm (.75 in) long and were spaced at about 40 mm (1.5 in) intervals. The wire might be deployed as a simple fence – *einfacher koppelzäne* with pickets driven in at 3 to 4 metre (9 to 13 ft) intervals to support it, or as a double fence with a coil between it – *doppelter koppelzäne verstärk*. The two fences were about 1.10 metres (3.6 ft) high and 1 metre (3.2 ft) apart and the gap was filled by coiled barbed wire. The coiled wire *S-Rolle* known as concertina or Dannert wire by the Allies, was easy to deploy since it could be folded flat for transport and then pulled out like an extended spring. Roads could be blocked quickly with portable barbed wire barriers consisting of a two metre (6.5 ft) length of timber or metal angle irons with "X" shaped supports at either end these obstacles were known to the Allies as "knife rests" or *chevaux de frise* and to the Germans as "Spanish Riders".

5   Anti-personnel (AP) mines fall into two classes – blast or fragmentation. In German use the former were designated *Schü-Minen* and the latter *S-Minen*. Mines were usually buried 50 to 100 mm (two to four inches) below the ground spaced at two metre (6.5 ft) intervals. Minefields were marked with boards showing a skull, crossed bones, the letter "M" or the warning *Achtung Minen* – Attention Mines. Barbed wire might be wrapped around fence posts in a distinctive pattern to indicate the edge of the minefield. Live minefields were marked with upright lettering and dummy with slanting. Throughout the war the markings were changed to confuse Allied intelligence. Though anti-tank (AT) mines would have been laid on ground that was accessible to vehicles, the gullies near Vasterival would have been blocked with AP mines.

The two types of AP mine most likely to have been used were:

The *S-Mine* that was a cylinder 5 in (130 mm) high, 4 in (100 mm) diameter and weighed 4 kg (9 lbs), it had a 395 gram (14 oz) TNT filling with a propelling charge of 226 gram (8 oz) of powdered TNT. It operated either by pressure of about 6.8 kg (15 lb) on the three prongs of an S.Mi.Z 34 igniter or pull on one of the two trip wires on the Z.Z.35 igniter that had been screwed into the top of the mine. This would release a spring loaded striker that would fire a percussion cap, a delay of about 3.9 seconds would follow before the powdered TNT blasted an inner cylinder about 0.9 to 1.5 metres (3 to 5 ft) into the air. At this height it exploded and 360 ball bearings or chunks of mild steel rod were blasted in all directions causing death up to 20 metres (22 yds) or injury up to 100.5 metres (110 yds).

The *Schü-Mine* literally "Shoe Mine" that might have been laid in the Dieppe area would have used the Z.Z.42 igniter with a No 8 Detonator screwed into a 1928 Pattern 200 grm (7 oz) TNT Slab Demolition Charge. The igniter and charge were fitted into a black compressed fibre container – the low metallic content would have made it harder to detect with electronic mine detectors. Under pressure the Z.Z. 42 igniter fired the detonator and when the main charge exploded it had a blast area of 10 m (10.9 yds).

The *S-Minen* were buried at four metre (13 ft) intervals in lines while the *Schü-Minen* were buried at one metre (3.2 ft) intervals. The angle of the sides of the gullies at Vasterival may have made it harder for the German soldiers to follow these mine laying criteria.

6   The French Model 1897 *Canon de 75 mm* (2.95 in) field gun saw extensive service in World War I and by 1918 more than 17,000 had been produced so it was therefore still in widespread use in World War II. It was the first field gun to have an effective recoil buffering system and consequently a trained crew could achieve a rate of fire of between15 to 30 rounds per minute. The Seventy Five fired a 7.25 kg (16 lb) shrapnel shell or a 5.32 kg (11.75 lb) HE shell to a maximum range of 8,230 metres (9,000 yds).

7   The 8 cm *schwere Granatwerfer 34* the medium mortar deployed by the German army entered service in 1934 and was still in use in 1945 it was carried into action as a three man load, base plate, barrel and bipod.

A wide range of ammunition was developed including the 8 cm *Wurfgranate 39* "bouncing bomb", other rounds including conventional HE, smoke, target illumination and target marking. The exact calibre of the mortar was 81.4 mm, it weighed 56.7 kg (125 lb) in action, had a barrel 1,143 mm (45 in) long, elevated from 40° to 90° and traversed from 9° to 15°. The minimum range for the 3.5 kg (7.72 lb) bomb on Charge 1 was 60 metres (65.6 yds) and maximum on Charge 5 was 2,400 metres (2,625 yds). An experienced crew could fire 12 round a minute that at maximum range had a 50% chance of landing in a target area 65 x 14 metres (71 x 15 yds).

8   On patrol the gunners of the No 813 Battery wore the field grey *Heeres Dienstanzug Modell 1936* – Model 1936 Service Uniform that consisted of a four pocket jacket with a total of nine grey metal buttons and matching trousers made from a wool/rayon mix. The trousers were tucked into studded black leather *Marschstiefel* – marching boots. As artillerymen they would have been distinguished by the red Arm Colour – *waffenfarbe* piping on the edges of the

epaulets of their tunics and on the front of their *Feldmütze* – side hats. In action they wore the distinctive "coal scuttle" Model 1935 *Stahlhelm* – steel helmet. Pouches for ammunition varied according to the weapon issued to the soldier. Most men who were issued with the *Kar 98k* rifle had the six 1909 Pattern leather pouches that held a total of 60 rounds.

One of the Commandos photographed at Newhaven has a captured *Kar 98k* bayonet with the distinctive NCO's coloured knot or *Troddel* looped through the scabbard.

The *Karabiner 98 kurz* – *Kar 98k* or Short '98 Carbine, was developed from the Mauser commercial rifle called the Standard model first produced in 1924 in Belgium. The *Kar 98k* first produced in 1935 weighed 3.9 kg (8.6 lb), was 1107.5 mm (43.6 in) long, and in its ten year production life it was manufactured in thousands in Germany, by FN in Belgium and Brno in Czechoslovakia.

A trained soldier armed with a *Kar 98k* could fire at 15 rounds a minute, however like the *Gewehr 98* the new rifle had only a five round magazine, which could be a liability in a fire fight. Like all the 7.92 mm calibre rifles the maximum effective range of the *Kar 98k* was 800 metres (2,624.6 ft).

In addition on their belt, with its distinctive aluminium buckle with the motto *"Gott Mit Uns"* – "God With Us" and supporting harness, the soldiers would have had a gas mask in its ribbed metal container, a 1931 Pattern water bottle and sometimes a *Brotbeutel* – bread bag, a light haversack. The *Brotbeutel* held the soldier's *Feldmütze*, washing and shaving kit, knife, fork and spoon and rations.

In the driving autumn and winter rains that blew up the Channel the soldiers wrapped themselves in their camouflaged triangular *Zeltbahn* – groundsheet/tent quarter shelters and plodded around their patrol routes.

9 The *Maschinenpistole* MP 38 and MP 40 sub-machine guns originally manufactured at the Erma-Werke at Erfurt had several revolutionary features. No wood was used in their construction, only steel and plastic, and the sub-machine guns had a folding metal butts, which made them ideal for paratroopers and armoured vehicle crews. The weapon was universally known as the *Schmeisser* by the Allies, however despite this accolade the German small arms engineer Hugo Schmeisser had no part in its design.

The 9 mm calibre MP38 and MP40 both fired from a 32 round box magazine with a distinctive cyclic rate of 500 rounds a minute. They were 833 mm (32.6 in) long with the butt extended and 630 mm (24.8 in) with it folded. Manufacturing changes to increase production, reduced machining and replaced it with welding and steel pressings. This reduced the weight of the MP 40 to 4.027 kg (8.87 lb), compared to 4.086 kg (9 lb) in the MP 38.

10 *Stielgranate 24* the Stick Grenade was 356 mm (14 in) long, 70 mm (2.75 in) in diameter, weighed 0.596 kg (1.31 lb) of which 0.17 kg (0.37 lb) was explosive fill.

Once the metal cap at the base on the handle had been unscrewed the porcelain ball on the end of the friction igniter cord fell clear. When it was given a sharp tug, there was a 4.5 second delay before the grenade exploded producing a blast radius of 13 m (43 ft). The practical distance that the *Stielgranate 24* could be thrown varied according to the tactical situation but it was about 35 metres (115 ft) – which the men of No 4 Commando were to note was further than the range of a British No 36 Grenade. The relatively thin casing of the *Stielgranate 24* meant that in modern terminology the grenade was both "offensive" and "defensive" so the thrower did not need to take cover to avoid injury from fragments.

11 The 9 mm Walther *Pistole 38* or P 38 was designed as a substitute for the P 08 Luger, which was complicated and difficult to manufacture. The weapon has the distinctive design feature of a positive safety catch that prevents accidental firing even when it is cocked with a round in the breech. A pin indicator, which could be felt in the dark, showed if a round was loaded. The P 38 was safe, easy and cheap to manufacture. It was 219 mm (8.6 in) long, had a barrel length of 125 mm (4.9 in) weighed 0.96 kg (2.1lb) loaded and had a muzzle velocity of 350 metres (1148 ft) a second. The magazine held eight rounds that could be fired in 20 seconds with an effective range of 50 metres (164 ft).

Production was undertaken not only in Germany but also by FN in Belgium and Czechoslovakia. Eventually the unit cost to the German Treasury was reduced to 32 *Reichsmarks*.

The older Luger self loading pistol, known in German Army service as the *Pistole 08* from its year of adoption, was named after Georg Luger a designer at the Ludwig Löwe small-arms factory in Berlin. The first military Lugers were made in 1900 to a Swiss order and the type was adopted for the German Navy in 1904. The standard pistol had an eight shot box magazine and fired a 9 mm (0.354 in) Parabellum round with a maximum effective range of 70 metres (230 ft). The toggle-joint mechanism was complex, but made the weapon comfortable to fire and therefore more accurate.

In the 1920s the British firm of Vickers manufactured Lugers for export to the Netherlands. The standard pistol had a 103 mm (4.06 in) barrel an overall length of 223 mm (8.75 in) and weighed 0.876 kg (1.93 lb). The Naval Luger weighed 1.060 kg (2.3 kg) had a 200 mm (7.8 in) barrel, a tangent sight and could be fitted with a 32 round "snail" magazine making it effectively a light sub machine-gun.

ove: Battery 813 before Operation CAULDRON. The 15cm guns have their carriages bolted ...to simple turntables to give them a 180° traverse. Camouflage nets have not been ...sitioned, but ammunition magazines with doors open and charges visible can be seen in the ...ncrete wall of the revetments. (EJ)

low: Orange Beach 1 a few minutes after H Hour on August 19, 1942. In this picture, one ...several taken on the raid by Sgt Geoffrey Langland, an LCA has nosed up to the beach, ...obably landing ammunition and stores. (IWM)

The elegant Edwardian holiday villa at Le Mesnil that was commandeered by the German army as the officers' mess. It was from a flag pole in the garden that the Union Jack continu to fly hours after No 4 Commando had departed from the battery. (WF)

974 VARENGEVILLE
Descente à la Mer
Gorge de Vasterival

A late 19th Century post card of the Port de Vasterival the gully leading to the sea and Orange Beach 1. By 1942 the sides were less steep, however the figure of a woman just visible on the steps gives an idea of the height of the cliffs. (EJ)

above: A postcard of La Volière the holiday home for children from Rouen. It was this building that dominated the battery and was the position from which Maj. D. Mills-Roberts gave the order to fire. The barn was to the right of La Volière and it was in the trees between them that TSM Dunning and the 2-inch Mortar crew took up position. (EJ)

below: "Varangeville Battery - 0607 hrs" Brian Mullen's charcoal and pastel sketch of the moment the cordite at the battery exploded following the hit by a 2-inch Mortar bomb. The Flak tower is visible on the skyline, while in the right foreground the Mortar Officer Lt J.F. Ennis hunches over his field telephone. (BM/JD)

ove: The abandoned gun pits of 813 Battery photographed in 1944. The barn is visible by
e trees on the horizon, but La Volière wrecked by flak shells and mortar fire has been
molished. (EJ)

low: The smoke screen drifts across the water at Orange Beach 1 partially concealing the
As circling offshore. The picture taken by Sgt Langland shows the sides of the gully in the
reground and the beach below. (JD)

above: "Dieppe - Withdrawal from Beach" Mullen's sketch shows the gully, Commandos wading out to the LCAs and a Goatley boat at the stern of the craft in the centre. The lighthouse at Pointe d'Ailly is visible on the horizon on the right. Above German Messerschmitt Bf 109 fighters attempt to hinder the operation. (BM/EJ)

below: A press photographer aboard HMS *Calpe* captured the moment when Lt Col Lord Lovat LCA approached the destroyer and he requested orders from General Roberts the JUBILEE force commander. The censor has erased the smoke generate on the stern of the near LCA. (AP)

above: An RAF fighter sweeps low across the Commando LCA flotilla as it makes its way home across the English Channel. Some of the dogfights were so low that Capt. Boucher-Myers recalled that empty cases from the fighters' machineguns and cannon rattled onto the decks of the craft. (JD)

below: "Rescue of US airman in Channel" Mullen's sketch shows a moment recalled by many of the Commandos. An LCA put about and the crew and Commandos had the pilot on board within moments of his parachuting out of his blazing fighter. "How's that for service Bud?" said the soldiers. (JD)

above: Gunner Len Ruskin gives the Army photographer a shy grin as he lands at Newhaven. A medical orderly has ripped the leg of his denim trousers to position a first field dressing. Below him on the right Pte E.L. Fraser of F Troop sports a captured German field cap and Kar 98K rifle. (IWM)

right: Surrounded by Bren gunners, possibly from C Troop, *Unteroffizier* Leo Marsiniak one of three Germans captured at the HESS battery approaches the ladder leading to the quayside at Newhaven. Ironically Marsiniak as a spectacle wearer was not blindfolded. (IWM)

left: Guiding a blindfolded PoW and holding a captured rifle L Cpl Joe Walsh moves briskly across Newhaven quay. The German wears a now grubby *Heeres Drillichanzug* an off-white denim fatigue uniform. On the left a C Troop Commando can be distinguished by the entrenching tool strapped below his small pack. (IWM)

ht: With Marsiniak lowing in the ckground the rman PoW is nded over to the nadian Provost at whaven. An lication of the lack preparedness of the ttery is the footwear the German gunner - ock and a carpet oper. (IWM)

left: US Ranger Sgt Ale
Szima accepts a light fo
his cigarette from Sgt A
"Bunny" Austin in one
the classic photographs
of the war in Europe.
Towering over the grou
is Cpl Bill Brady with
face of Sgt Kenneth
Stempson partially
concealed. (IWM)

right: The American
journalist Walter
Knickerbocker, dressed in
a US Army khaki tan
summer uniform,
interviews the four US
Rangers at Newhaven.
Cpl Franklin Koons is
out of the picture to the
right, Stempson faces the
camera, while Szima has
positioned his face so
that Brady's rifle conceals
the scar. (IWM)

left: A group of Commando signallers skirt a collapsed Goatley boat that holds some rudimentary flotation equipment and a single boot. The signallers appear to have favoured the brown gym shoes in preference to boots. On the right in the background Cpl John Skerry can be seen, bareheaded and with a German rifle slung over his shoulder. (IWM)

right: From the look of concentration on the faces of Captain Boucher-Myers and Lord Lovat may be checking preliminary casualty returns for No 4 Commando, the bare headed Captain Gordon Webb can be seen looking over their shoulders. On the right the fair hared Len Ruskin and Lou Chattaway await news of friends and comrades. (IWM)

...ptain Pat Porteous VC who led the final assault on the guns. The terrier, which is often ...pped out of this photograph, was probably his mother's dog. (IWM)

FRANÇAIS!

Ceci est un coup de main et non pas l'invasion.

Nous vous prions instamment de n'y prendre part en aucune façon et de ne faire quoi que ce soit qui puisse entraîner des représailles de la part de l'ennemi.

Nous faisons appel à votre sang-froid et à votre bon sens.

Lorsque l'heure sonnera, nous vous avertirons. C'est alors que nous agirons côte-à-côte pour notre victoire commune et pour votre liberté!

The leaflet dropped by the RAF that explained that JUBILEE was a raid and not an invasion. In Dieppe many Frenchmen heeded its instructions not to take any action that might lead to reprisals by the Germans. The population around Varengeville who assisted the Commando were punished by the Germans. (WF)

above: No 4 Commando Square in Ste Marguerite. Jimmy Dunning commissioned the upper plaque from a craftsman in Romsey, Hampshire. (WF)

left: Surmounted by the Free French Cross of Lorraine a plaque at Ste Marguerite commemorates the three French Marines from No 10 Commando who took part in the attack. (WF)

REMEMBER THE BRITISH SOLDIERS
WHO DIED IN THIS ACTION AND
GIVE A SPECIAL THOUGHT TO THE
SIX WHO HAVE NO KNOWN GRAVE

SOUVENONS NOUS DES SOLDATS
BRITANNIQUES MORTS AU COURS
DE CE COMBAT ET ACCORDONS
UNE PENSEE SPECIALE AUX SIX
D'ENTRE EUX DONT LE LIEU
DE REPOS EST INCONNU

† L.CPL. L.BISHOP	THE SOMERSET LIGHT INFANTRY
PTE. W.O.GARTHWAITE	THE LOYAL REGT.(N.LANCS)
L.CPL. F.M.GOOCH	THE EAST SURREY REGT.
L.CPL. E.P.H.HECKMAN	THE ROYAL BERKSHIRE REGT.
L.CPL. J.KEENAN	THE ROYAL ULSTER RIFLES
† LT. J.A.MacDONALD	1ST.ROYAL DRAGOONS, R.A.C.
PTE. S.McGANN	THE SOUTH LANCASHIRE REGT.
† L.CPL. D.T.MERCER	THE KING'S REGT.(LIVERPOOL)
L.CPL. A.MILLS	THE SOUTH LANCASHIRE REGT.
L.CPL. J.MOSS (SERVED AS TAYLOR)	THE LOYAL REGT.(N.LANCS)
† CAPT. R.G.PETTIWARD	THE BEDS. AND HERTS.REGT.
PTE. G.H.SUTTON	THE EAST YORKSHIRE REGT.
SIGMN. G.A.TUCKER	ROYAL CORPS OF SIGNALS
† RFN. J.WATTERS	THE ROYAL ULSTER RIFLES
L.CPL. J.WHATLEY	THE OXFORD.AND BUCKS. LT. INF.
† GDSMN. J.WHITTAKER	GRENADIER GUARDS

† HAVE NO KNOWN GRAVE

The No 4 Commando role of honour at Ste Marguerite. (WF)

CHAPTER 6

Landing

Off the French coast the predawn silence was shattered by the distinctive growl of the Rolls Royce Merlin engine of a fast approaching fighter, an RAF Supermarine Spitfire Vb[1]. It flew in low from the west along the coast and with cannons roaring strafed the area close to the HESS battery and the ochre and green camouflaged lighthouse on the headland at the Pointe d'Ailly.

In the dust and smoke of exploding 20 mm cannon shells and .303 inch machine gun fire the light in the tower was extinguished and tracer fire from German 2 cm Flak positions arced up into the darkness.

"Streams of ... white tinselly tracer went up from the battery round the lighthouse, which," Peter Scott recalled, "seemed to consist of about five guns. To the eastward along the coast was more tracer, but all going upwards – still the landing craft were undetected."

The operational log for August 19, 1942 of the Thorney Island based No 129 Squadron RAF records:

> "0447 – 0600
> Two Spitfire VB of 129 Squadron attacked a lighthouse on the coast.
> Sgt Reeves attacked lighthouse 'causing gun flashes in the lantern'."[2]

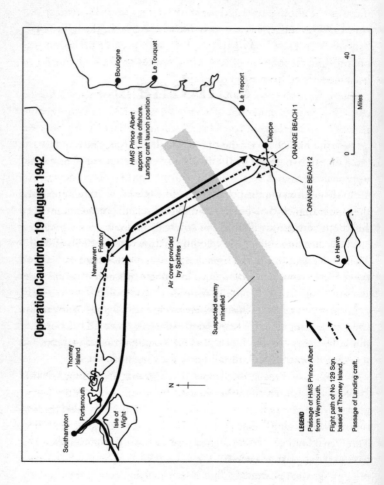

Operation Cauldron, 19 August 1942

Boulogne
Le Touquet
Le Treport
Dieppe
ORANGE BEACH 1
ORANGE BEACH 2
Le Havre

HMS Prince Albert
approx 1 mile offshore.
Landing craft launch position

Air cover provided
by Spitfires

Suspected enemy
minefield

Southampton
Portsmouth
Thorney
Island
Isle of
Wight
Newhaven
Friston

N

40

0

Miles

LEGEND

Passage of HMS Prince Albert
from Weymouth.

Flight path of No 129 Sqn.
based at Thorney Island.

Passage of Landing craft.

The LCAs 2, 4 and 6 escorted by MGB 312 were now beginning their stealthy approach to the looming cliffs at Vasterival. Mulleneux remembered a nagging doubt that they would not make the exact planned landfall. In the darkness the cliffs appeared more vertical than those on the photographs and the model. *Notes from Theatres of War* says that though it was not easy to see the beach, the lighthouse, "served as a useful navigation guide, and greater precision was obtained by recognition of two white houses on the cliff which had been memorised from air photographs."

These were the moments, which aboard HMS *Prince Albert* a cheerful young Commando officer had assured A. B. Austin would probably be their last, and the journalist confessed with frank honesty, that in that old R.A.F. saying "I had kittens". "But," he reported, "I hung, in my rising funk, onto the thought that "the other bastards" were twice as scared as me.

"One question worried all of us in those last silent 20 minutes after the long cramped voyage in the starlight. Would the Germans be ready for us? A sergeant crouching in front of me kept up a whispered running commentary: "About 500 yards now ... see the cliffs?... There's the crack we want... Look at the Jerry tracer bullets... Don't think they're firing at us though ... hundred yards now ... fifty."

The young Ranger Cpl Franklin "Zip" Koons dozing in the LCA was awoken when seawater splashed on his face. Watching the tracer fire and hearing the low flying aircraft he remembered, "I began to think 'Hey this is really World War II'. I had been reading about the war since I was in 6th Grade and now I was really in it".

In LCA 6 a Free French soldier was unable to suppress his excitement as the craft approached his homeland – a country he had not seen for more than two years. Operation JUBILEE would the first time in World War II that Free French Forces would land in France. The Frenchman kept wriggling to his feet through the heavily laden Commandos and was cursed "in various English accents which he did not understand" and pulled back down into the craft.

In these final critical moments the Phantom Signals officer, the stocky Capt A.R.M. Sedgwick, hunched in the landing craft close to Austin gave a jerk, screwed up his face, and said,

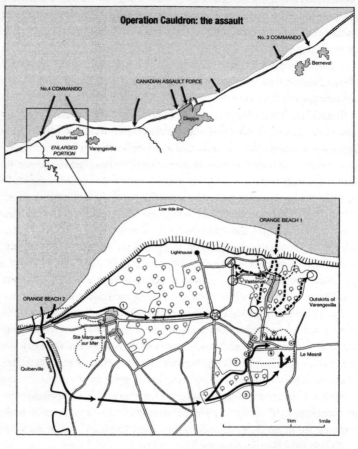

Operation Cauldron: the assault

No. 3 COMMANDO

Berneval

No.4 COMMANDO

CANADIAN ASSAULT FORCE

Dieppe

Vasterival

ENLARGED PORTION

Varengeville

Low tide line

ORANGE BEACH 1

Lighthouse

Vasterival

ORANGE BEACH 2

Outskirts of Varengeville

Ste Marguerite sur Mer

Le Mesnil

R.Saane

Quiberville

1km   1mile

LEGEND

Marine Battery	▲▲
A.A. Battery	⊕
Machine gun	⊙
Barbed wire	
Defensive perimiter	
Standing patrols	○

N

Route taken by Fire Group under the command of Major Mills-Roberts

Arrows showing the Assault Group under the command of Lt Colonel the Lord Lovant M.C.

① A Troop. Veasey

② F Troop. Pettiward

③ B Troop. Webb

"Blast! I've got cramp. Hell, damn and blast! I've got cramp."

The coxswains of the LCAs closed with the coast and began to move eastwards along it trying to find the two gullies. Smith recalled an earnest whispered discussion between Dawson and Mulleneux about where the correct location was for Orange Beach 1. The Army opinion prevailed.

At 04.52 in the strange half light of Before Morning Nautical Twilight, known to French sailors as *'entre chien et loup'*,[3] the passengers and crews of LCAs 2 and 4 felt the hulls grate on the shingle. The ramps clattered down and with less than a metre to jump the Commandos landed dry shod and stooping ran quickly ashore, braced for action. They had landed at Zero + 2 minutes.

Speed off the beach had been emphasised in training since this was the area most likely to be covered by enemy fire.

"As usual we went split arse across the beach," recalled Dunning. "It was the old rule, once the ramps were down it was get out and get off the beach as quick as you can".

The burst of activity quickly loosened up Sedgwick's cramped muscles.

It was high tide and on the narrow shingle beach the men were met by complete silence.

To Mills-Roberts the landing "seemed rather like stealing round to the back door of a house where a noisy party is in progress, and finding nothing but silence". They were followed by LCA 6, which with an excellent eye for history was recorded by the unofficial unit photographer Sgt Langlands.

One of the Free French Commandos stepped off LCA 6 and after the excitement of the run in, celebrated his return to his homeland with almost Anglo Saxon understatement, muttering under his breath,

"*C'est drole*" – This is funny.

Smith confessed that he was very surprised by the dry landing "we had been given to understand that it was likely to be very wet. We had been told by the Navy that we should probably have to swim ashore and that we should certainly have to swim back after the show to the LCA."

As Lt David Style's section moved quickly along the foot of the cliff to examine the two gullies, LCAs 2 and 4 moved back to begin ferrying additional men including the beach parties and mortar ammunition and stores from MGB 312 lying a mile offshore. Later in daylight Orange Beach 1 appeared to Mulleneux "a delightful little cove more suited to a bathing picnic than to a battle".

In the half light the coastline appeared to Austin as, "the cold-looking, unscaleable, chalk-white cliffs of Orange Beach 1". Style, an experienced climber, initially examined the eastern gully, but found that after 35 metres it was clogged with three coiled barbed wire obstacles as well as lumps of fallen chalk. This gully had been the one that Mills-Roberts had favoured as an access, so a worried Style moved on quickly to examine the larger western gully. To Mills-Roberts the speedy reconnaissance seemed to be taking an age.

Suddenly an urgent whispered message.

"There's someone on top of the cliff".

Lindley remembered the figure on the cliffs in an interview with Emyr Jones;

"As we were approaching this chap was on top of the cliff. Why he didn't see us I don't know. He could have stopped us by throwing a couple of grenades over."

This figure may have been a man from lighthouse garrison, a force that would thankfully be conspicuously passive during the operation. It may equally have been shadows and tension playing tricks on men already on edge. Looking down into the shadow of the cliff it would have been hard for any German soldiers who might have been on the coast to see the Commandos in the half light.

Style returned to report that the other gully was also blocked by wire and so it would be necessary to clear it with a Bangalore torpedo. "This was the time when one's highest hopes began to be tempered with feelings of tense frustration," recalled Mills-Roberts, "For us surprise was essential".

A Bangalore torpedo was brought up, pushed into the wire and the fuse lit, Dunning reassured the nervous Austin as, pressed against the cliff, they waited in the tense silence for the charge to explode.

"The fuse was a normal one," recalled Mills-Roberts, "but I looked over at Robert Dawson and could see that he too felt the delay interminable. Was the fuse a dud? With a loud report, magnified by the narrow gully, it blew." Though some of the wire had been cleared it was necessary to use a second Bangalore torpedo to make a viable gap. Style, his head ringing from the explosions for having lit the fuse he had been obliged to take cover only a few metres away, led the way up the gully. Incredibly the sound of the two explosions was masked by the gully and the cliff face and the sound of low flying fighters strafing targets close to the battery and the Flak engaging them.

The explosion prompted the same thought with Smith and Austin.

"Had the Germans prepared their defences properly we would not have had a chance. One platoon with a machine-gun could have held the beach against a fair-sized army."

Smith remarked :

"I could not help thinking that had there been anyone at the top of the cliff with a supply of grenades he could have done us all in".

At 05.20 with dawn rising the Commandos moved off quickly and chose a route along the left side of the gully to avoid the AP minefields that they suspected might have been laid at the top.

Speed was essential, the explosions might have alerted the Germans and if they reacted quickly Group 1 would be trapped in the gully and on the beach.

"Get a bloody move on! Get up the bloody cliff!" yelled TSM Dunning as he urged the men to climb up through the churned mud, chalk and smashed concrete and through the gap in the wire. For Szima the climb was "two foot forward sliding back one" as he struggled up the slope that still smoked and reeked of high explosives. Dunning recalling the ascent commented, "our climbing skills came in useful as did our special footwear we were wearing, the newly available rubber soled climbing boots."

At the top the men saw that their precautions had been justified for they were German minefield markers with their grim skull and cross bones, facing inland and the warning *Achtung Minen!* it was also written in French for the benefit of the local population – *Danger Mines*. This prompted one Commando in C Troop to remark within earshot of Dunning, "Cor, they're an obliging lot, they've even written it in English for us."

On the spur formed by the two gullies the Commandos would later discover that the Germans had in fact dug a machine gun position with supporting trenches. Fortunately that night it was unmanned. Cpl George Jones, a Bren gunner with C Troop recalled that they had been warned there might be a position covering the gullies. "But," he recalled "the Jerries had done a bunk."

The air attacks and response by the German Flak emplacements at the lighthouse and golf course had awakened the Cadot family. As shrapnel and 20 mm cannon cases rattled down on the houses the family decided to take cover in the shelter at a villa named "La Maisonette". They dressing quickly and with the kitchen clock showing 5 o'clock and his mother clutching a blanket they crossed the road to the adjoining house.

As the Cadots were making their way to shelter Mills-Roberts' force had reached the top of the gully and the sections had split off to their allotted tasks. A section of C Troop under Dawson moved to search the houses on the right of the road leading to the battery, among his group was Szima and his Commando battle partner Heggarty. Once the buildings had been cleared a group of Dawson's C Troop under Sgt Langlands established a defensive perimeter around the gully.

Smith glanced back towards the sea. "The sun was now rising over Dieppe and the scene I could only describe as Wagnerian. To seaward the sky was struck yellow by the rising sun, the Mustangs which were flying down the coast seemed to me to be silhouetted against the sky, I could see their black shapes clearly in the morning light. The cliffs stood up white but I could not see the assault party go up the cleft because it was cut obliquely in the face of the cliffs."

To the left of the axis of advance a section under Style began clearing the houses. "The grass had grown long and the gardens looked wild and unkempt. The early morning sun shone down on forbidding-looking rows of shutters which were fast shedding their paint. To our left lay the Hotel de la Terrace, once, no doubt, an attractive summer hotel." (sic)

Two of Style's leading scouts returned from one of the weather-beaten villas escorting a barefoot old man wearing a nightshirt. He was enraged that the Commandos had pushed through the hedge surrounding his vegetable garden and trampled through its contents. Undeterred by the fact that he was surrounded by armed men, shaking his fist at them he growled,

"*Bande de salopards!*"

"I felt sorry for the poor old chap," recalled Mills-Roberts, "How could he preserve his dignity in such garments?" When, with the assistance of the Free French Commandos Corporal R. Rabouhans and Private R. Taverne, Mills-Roberts was able to explain that they were British soldiers and not Germans, he seemed surprised. "It is a curious thing," mused Mills-Roberts, "but many of the canvas uniforms worn by the armies of separate nationalities don't vary much in shape or colour".

The old man had thought they were a German patrol and was going to remonstrate with them for the damage to his hedge and vegetables, which by August would have been ripe and ready to pick.

As he was being escorted back to his house an attractive girl appeared on the veranda and asked without emotion, "Are you going to shoot Papa?" She was assured that they were not, but warned that everyone should remain inside. Mills-Roberts noted the house had no telephone wires to be cut, but would take no chances "even with those who appeared to be loyal Frenchmen". It was not yet 05.40, and despite the delay at the gully Mills-Roberts was pleased that his group was on time.

Close to the Hotel de la Terrasse Austin spotted a cow grazing, "She gave an occasional worried moo, but, in spite of all the bullet whine and mortar crash, never budged from the corner of the field...

"Beyond her, over the fields at the edge of the cliffs, a small gibbet stood up against the sky. A shapeless figure was hanging from it, presumably a dummy." Austin wondered if this bizarre object was an elaborate scarecrow or some German artilleryman's black joke about the possible fate of would be attackers.

Dunning too had spotted cows grazing peacefully in the dawn sunlight. By the end of the morning he would remember them dead, innocent victims of the small arms fire and mortar fragments that had turned the pastures into a killing ground.

The Free French Commandos had a strange but not unfriendly

encounter when a local man appeared out of the woods carrying a basket of eggs and offered them to the Commandos. Evidently Nazi propaganda had been effective for, proffering the basket, the man said earnestly to Rabouhans and Taverne.

"*Tenez. Vous devez mourir de faim en Angleterre*" – Take them. You're dying of hunger in England.

The Commandos thanked their compatriot and explained that at the moment they did not need them.

This was the first of the reported "egg encounters" that would punctuate the day during Operation CAULDRON.[4]

Szima passed the Hotel de la Terrasse. "There in the road was a fresh killed German. He was on his back with an undetonated potato masher (stick grenade) and apparently his other grenade went off because his insides were steaming in the cool dawn. Considering that we had lamb or mutton for a hot breakfast, the rum with it probably saved the meal."

In the summer dawn there were other encounters with the local population. A patrol commanded by the young and slightly built Lt Knyvet "Muscles" Carr, tasked with cutting the telephone link between the battery and the lighthouse OP encountered a young French woman. To Tony Smith and his Intelligence Section NCO Corporal Ken Phillot she asserted that she was a gardener at the lighthouse. Smith was not convinced, "It was possible that she was the local prostitute and that her duties at the lighthouse extended beyond the garden. She appeared very frightened, both of our troops and lest the Germans should take reprisals if she helped us. She did not volunteer any information, but was not altogether unwilling to talk when questioned. She stated that there were 80 German sailors at the lighthouse area."

Carr's patrol cut the telephone line in two places to ensure that it could not be repaired by a simple splice. Soon after Carr's patrol had moved off the main body of the Troop commanded by Boucher-Myers came under sniper fire. Fearing that this lone enemy soldier might pose a threat to the telephone line cutting patrol, Boucher-Myers ordered his men to kill the sniper before they moved forward to the battery. "This we did without much difficulty, killing him as he broke cover.

We then split into sub-sections formation, got into the village and swung left-handed towards the battery."

The first house Szima and Heggarty checked was empty, but the second had a locked bedroom door. "I psyched myself to do a two step run and stomp my rubber soled Commando boots near the empty keyhole – the door sash gave. Before me was a table, bottle and a candle and jacket over the chair and I turned right and there was a cot and a large pile under sheet or blanket. I fired one round intentionally and by reflex action another. Then stepped thru the door and Heggarty said, 'Did you get him?' I said, 'Nothing there'. He 'What did you shoot for'. No answer. I didn't want to go back in there." It would later emerge that it was merely crumpled bedding that had been shot twice.

As the Commandos moved up through the scrub, woodland and buildings they heard a sound that they dreaded – an explosion that Austin described as a "dull, hollow sound like an explosion in a quarry".

The guns of No 813 Battery had opened fire.

As the first shells fired from the battery whistled overhead Mills-Roberts received a message from Smith now back at the beach, who besides being the IO, was acting as the Adjutant to Mills-Roberts. They were the words he least wanted to hear.

"Convoy in sight, apparently within range of enemy battery." The timing for JUBILEE was now running fifty potentially fatal minutes ahead of schedule.

Austin looked out to see, "splashes and felt a little cheered. They were just spouts of water, not the smoke and steam of hits. Perhaps we'd be in time yet."

Not far away the Cadots were in their nearest air raid shelter when they heard the battery open fire. The first shells appeared to be aimed at targets near Dieppe and then fire was switched towards Quiberville. The family assumed that the target was a British convoy that was sailing too far to the south. As they emerged from the shelter they saw a German sailor running towards the lighthouse – he may have been a runner sent by the battery commander after the line had been cut by Carr's patrol.

Moments later four Commandos, three armed with Thompson SMGs and one with an SMLE, all in raiding order with their faces camouflaged appeared in the road. They may have been Carr's patrol because the after a conversation in English that was incomprehensible to the Cadots, three men left in the direction of the lighthouse. The remaining soldier appeared surprised that the Cadots did not follow him as they had decided to return to their home. The AA fire had increased and the family could see the shipping massing off Dieppe. When they reached home he made some gestures, presumably indicating they should remain indoors, and at about 06.00 moved off back to the gully.

"It was no good cursing some erratic staff work on the part of someone outside our orbit," thought Mills-Roberts as the Commandos heard the fire of the155 mm guns, "the only thing to do was to improvise as fast as possible".

The OC of Group 1 realised that the exact timings of operation CAULDRON would place Lovat's Group 2 in their final assault position in 50 minutes time. The aim of their operation was to neutralise guns at 06.30 but the guns were now already in action and had fired at the shipping off Dieppe. It would later emerge that all the shells fell short – but the shipping was approaching Dieppe and so closing the range.

Accompanied by Lt Ennis the Mortar Forward Observation Officer (FOO) and their two signallers Mills-Roberts with his runner LCpl E.A. Smith, pushed inland as fast as possible through the woods on the left hand side of the road. The Bois de Vasterival was thick with waist high saplings and summer vegetation and it was hard work as the small party went "crashing ahead like a herd of elephants". The hardening exercises and fitness training in Dorset was paying off.

Mills-Roberts had sent a runner back with a message for Style to bring his section forward. By now the Free French Commandos and others had been able to establish from the locals that there were no Germans in the villas by the beach and Group 1 could concentrate on its main effort in the operation.

"Suddenly the wood ended," recalled Mills-Roberts, "We topped a little rise and came face to face with the battery itself." The group dropped to the ground and crawled forward to a patch of scrub about fifty metres in front of the wood and just over 100 metres from the perimeter of the battery. They were so close they could distinctly hear the words of command as the battery fired another salvo.

To his right on the edge of the wood he spotted the barn like structure of La Volière and decided that it would give them a better view of the target. Accompanied by Smith he worked his way back to the wood and ran the 90 metres to the building. Here he met Style on the track by the barn and taking two snipers forced open the door to La Volière. They raced upstairs to the apartment on the first floor. Approaching the windows carefully they looked out and realised that they were about 140 metres from the perimeter wire and 170 from the battery. As they watched they saw the three guns on the left fire a salvo.

Meanwhile the men of A and C Troop were making their way rapidly forward through brambles and ferns in the woods to positions covering the roads to the west of the battery. With the battery in view Szima could see the AA gun and hear the German shouted orders. He found himself a fire position in the barn and Heggarty by a tree.

The signal for opening fire was given by Mills-Roberts who had selected the sniper's target, a tall German who was shouting orders in the battery position, and then watched as, "He settled himself on a table, taking careful aim. These Bisley chaps are not to be hurried; we waited whilst he took first pressure… At last the rifle cracked, it was a bull's-eye and one of the Master Race took a toss into the gun pit. His comrades looked shocked and surprised – I could see it all through my glasses."

The noise of the shot would have been masked by the sound of the artillery fire and the German gunners initially had no idea what had happened or where the shot had come from. To Mills-Roberts, "It seemed rather like shooting one of the members of a church congregation from the organ loft".

Now at 05.50 hours Group 1 went into action. No 1 Section of C Troop had approached closest to the enemy, entering a small salient strip of scrub facing the forward wire of the battery about 250 metres in front of them. The three Bren gunners, under L/Sgt F. McCarthy firing short aimed bursts, one from a range of only 150 metres engaged the battery with "well controlled and aimed fire". On the right the gun commanded by Gdsm H. Humphries killed a sniper who had taken a position on the roof of a building and engaged a forward position. In the centre LCpl G. Hampton had taken a position in a building and from here he destroyed a machine gun position as well as directing effective fire on the battery. On the left Cpl Wallis also engaged the gun positions.

The enemy were sometimes difficult to see, "It was a case of keeping their heads down" recalled George Jones who had taken a position on the left flank with his Bren gun. Between firing bursts the Bren gunners shifted their positions to ensure that they were not located. "We were on the move all the time. You can't stop in one position for too long."

Riflemen picked their targets and one of the snipers L/Cpl Dickie Mann, with his face painted green and with the camouflaged netting of his face veil breaking up his outline, worked his way forward to a position 120 metres from the battery. Mann, who before the war had been a butcher in Reading, would win the Military Medal for his courage and marksmanship as he "conducted his own little war with the battery with his sniper's rifle".

From his position Sergeant "Hughie" Lindley could see only the gun pits and two machine gun posts, but the snipers he had trained were ruthlessly efficient. Interviewed by the IWM in 1989 he described how he indicated targets to the snipers. Spotting a Germans soldier dressed in white drill fatigues he whispered to Mann, "'There's a sitting target for you' so he ups with the telescopic sights and we saw him go down."

The snipers had been equipped with incendiary ammunition in the hope that hits on wooden huts might start fires – it did not, but "their use seldom failed to draw fire" records *Notes from Theatres of War*.

However the training manual notes that, "It was necessary to weigh the conflicting claims of making the maximum display possible from this direction at the same time conserving ammunition." In the original plan the Troop would have opened fire at 06.15 hours. Would their ammunition be sufficient, or would they have to call on the reserve stocks held on the beach and offshore LCAs?

The men of A Troop under Boucher-Myers had moved up to positions in buildings on the right of the perimeter wire.

Koons with A Troop had taken up a position in a barn and "found a splendid spot for sniping, just over the manger, and I fired through a slit in the brick wall. I fired quite a number of rounds on stray Jerries and I am pretty sure I got one of them".

Despite Koons' modesty and lack of certainty he is now credited with being the first American soldier in World War II to kill a German in fighting on land. Not far from Koons his fellow Ranger Alex Szima was also in action. Rifle fire was dangerously close and concrete splinters from a near miss hit the left side of his face and eye. Besides enemy fire he had other problems, the hot ejected .45 inch cases from a Commando sub-machine gunner began to cascade over him. As the Commando changed magazines Szima took a running dive and landed in a manure heap. It might be an unsavoury fire position, but it was one that gave him some excellent targets. Spotting a German helmet he shouted to the big Lt Len Coulson;

"'Mr Coulson, I see him' and his shout back to me while laying prone at the hedge line, 'Well get him Yank'. Although he only said it once, my subconscious kept repeating the message and did so until I cleared most of the crap off the sights, eased the barrel forward and all the while the helmet didn't move … the sun was up by now and there was no mistaking what your eyes saw. I put all six on him and when I looked the helmet was gone."

Close to the beach the Cadots could hear the sound of small arms fire coming from the battery. The shelling stopped but later they heard further explosions that were the 2-inch, 3-inch and the German 8.1-cm Mortars coming into action.

The French family returned to their home and moments later heard footsteps. Rabouhans and Taverne, appeared at the door. The former was armed with a .45 Colt and the latter with an SMLE and unlike the men of No 4 Commando had uncamouflaged faces. The tall Rabouhans holstered his pistol and to the surprise of the Cadot's addressed them in French.

" Do you want to leave for England?

"You're French?" replied my father, very surprised.

"Yes, I'm French"

"We cannot leave, our family would wonder where we are. But what's going on exactly?"

"Well, it's a raid and in two hours we'll be gone again".

They said goodbye and at 06.30 hours moved back towards the gully where they joined the perimeter defence of the beachhead and gully.

It may have been the Cadots who later appeared in Smith's report as "a man and his wife about 30 and a small child. They were probably "petit rentiers" and seemed well nourished. They were quite friendly and gave information quite willingly when questioned, although they did not volunteer any information... They were obviously very frightened, not only of the battle but lest they should be implicated in any way. They definitely did not want to be dragged in, and did not want to come away with us."

Back at the edge of the wood the fire fight between C Troop and the battery was beginning to grow in intensity. Mills-Roberts was aware that one detachment of three guns had been reloaded and were ready to fire. He was determined that this should not happen. The pressure must be maintained. "When engaged by a rifle or light automatic, it is not easy to pinpoint the exact spot from where the fire is coming. This was the Germans' difficulty; we made it no easier for them." The gun crews had stopped firing and taken cover behind the parapet.

A German survivor who was in a gun pit on the western edge of the battery, described the experience of being on the receiving end of the Commandos' fire to Emyr Jones. "The man next to me was in a sitting position after being shot through the neck. I myself came out of it with a shrapnel wound in the shoulder. We saw nothing and had no idea of where we were being shot from." He tried the old trick of putting his steel helmet on his rifle and raising it above the parapet. "It was hit instantly. After that I could do nothing but remain perfectly still until the nightmare was over."

The gunners on the Flak tower in the centre of the battery depressed the barrel and opened fire at the tree line. "We could see the streams of phosphorescent shells as they raked the edge of the wood and exploded amongst the tree trunks," recalled Mills-Roberts. "Fortunately this fire tended to be high."

OC Group 1 made his way to Ennis the FOO to request the supporting fire that was part of the plan. Ennis cranked the handle on the field telephone and hunched over the handset waited for the reply from the 3-inch Mortar position. It was silent, he tried again and realised to his horror the line was dead. Somewhere in the woods it had been cut. To further add to the confusion the Corporal in command of the mortar crew had brought them too far forward. The 3-inch Mortar was a critical weapon for Group 1, it could reach parts of the battery that were either out of direct sight behind buildings or trees or beyond the effective range of the infantry weapons.

On the beach Smith had co-opted every man in the HQ including Signallers, Medical Orderlies and Austin to carry two four-round ammunition cases up to the mortar position. "We thus kept the mortar supplied with ammunition at the risk of giving no local protection to Headquarters, but I judged that risk worth taking because I felt that to get the mortar into action was the most vital part of the show".

From over the buildings to the left of the battery, the Commandos heard the frightening and distinctive hollow cough of medium mortars opening fire. The crews seem to have known the exact range of the woods and moments later the trees were filled with the crash of exploding bombs, splintering wood and the stink of high explosive. Tree bursts are the most lethal effect with mortar bombs, none of the explosive energy is lost in the ground and the shrapnel hits the soldiers below.

One Commando initially thought that their own 3-inch mortar had opened fire and misjudging the range dropped bombs short of the intended target. The 8.1-cm crew may not have been part of the German battery but could have come from the Support Company of the 1st Bn 571st Rgt that was beginning to move northwards towards Dieppe and Varengeville from the direction of Offranville.

"The infantry soldier dislikes a mortar intensely, particularly when he is not dug in," commented Mills-Roberts. "With it you can lob explosive bombs into otherwise inaccessible places. A man can use his wits in finding cover from rifle and machine-gun fire, but once a mortar gets his range and locality things become difficult".

Two support weapons had come forward and one would be critical in the action. The Boys Anti-Tank Rifle crew of Gunners T. McDonough and B.K. 'Barney' Davies opened fire against the Flak position.

"It ceased to revolve and gave the appearance of a roundabout checked in full flight," recalled Mills-Roberts. Having neutralised the AA gun the crew switched targets to the machine gun posts. Assisted by the Bren gunners they proceeded to win the fire fight with the three forward MG 34 *Kampfstände* on the north of the battery.

With the 3-inch Mortar still not in action the 2-inch Mortar crew of Ptes Dale and Horne under command of TSM Dunning would be the only indirect fire weapon available. They had not received the message they were to stop searching and move forward as fast as possible and Dunning recalled that they were surprised that the firing had begun early. They quickly took up a position in the wood between the barn and the now increasingly battered La Volière.

The 2-inch Mortar is a simple weapon, it has no sights and no tripod, the firer judges by eye the angle at which he should hold the barrel and how it should be aligned. As Dunning recalled setting up the mortar was simple, "Just plonk it on the ground and point it in the right direction". To the untrained this may seem almost as accurate as lobbing a ball underhand. After the No 2 has dropped the bomb down the barrel, the No 1 operates the trigger by the baseplate. The single propellant charge increment explodes and the bomb is on its way. The recoil from the explosion of the first bomb sometimes helps the base plate to bed in to soft ground.

The first round fired that morning may have been at too high a trajectory but could have bedded in the mortar. Aware of the relative inaccuracy of the weapon Dunning had told the crew to take the centre of the battery as their point of aim. With a crump and cloud of black smoke it exploded according to some witnesses to the left, halfway between the buildings and the battery.

The crew corrected their aim, the next bomb rattled down the barrel, the No 1 fired and it landed in the middle of the battery but appeared to have no appreciable effect.

No one could have anticipated the effect of the third bomb they fired.

Back at the beachhead Austin, busy carrying 3-inch Mortar ammunition up the gully to the cliff top and messages back down to the Phantom Signal team on the beach, had time to notice swallows twittering around their nests on the chalk cliffs. His brief reverie was broken when, "An explosion ... louder and longer than anything we heard that morning, made us crouch suddenly. It seemed to be the father and mother of all explosions".

It was heard by the men of Group 2 moving inland, and seen by the A Troop fighting patrol who, after cutting the telephone link to the lighthouse, had worked their way round to the right of the battery.

The explosion they all heard was the result of the third mortar bomb fired by the C Troop crew. It had exploded amongst the bagged cordite charges by the No 1 gun in the battery. The battery did not fire again.

It was 06.07 hours and the battle had swung dramatically in favour of the Commandos.

Recalling the event many years later Dunning modestly confessed, "It was luck, nothing more than luck... Probably the luckiest mortar shot of World War II."

Why the German gun crews had adopted such sloppy ammunition handling procedures is hard to explain. It would prove a fatal mistake.

The bagged charges may have been brought forward from the ammunition bunker, taken out of their containers ready to be stuffed into the breach and fired in the next salvo. They may simply have been stacked in their containers close to the gun pits for some of the guns were later discovered to be loaded and ready to fire. The pits appear to have had secure ammunition stowage positions in the concrete revetment that would have been proof against indirect fire. The heavy volume of small arms fire from Group 1 had forced the crew to take cover and thus unable to load the charges had left these highly inflammable explosives lying exposed.

Another explanation may have been the poor level of training of the German artillerymen. This coupled with the fact that the battery was not at full strength, meant that they cut corners to ensure a steady rate of fire. They were bringing the bagged charges forward faster than the crews could load and fire them. The soldiers were certainly not very disciplined, many had ignored the Threatened Danger alert and undressed and gone to bed on the night of August 18. Many were now in action only partially dressed, including one man wearing carpet slippers.

The Commandos watched as the charges "ignited with a

stupendous crash, followed by shouts and yells of pain. We could see the Germans as they rushed forward with buckets and fire extinguishers, and everything we had was directed on to this area." To add to the mayhem the fire appeared to cause secondary fires and explosions in other cordite dumps behind the guns.[5]

Above the village of le Mesnil, identified as "the town" RAF fighter pilots had also seen the explosion and the intelligence report of the Hornchurch Wing (81,122,154 and 340 (FF) Squadrons notes.

"Much gunfire was seen near Orange 2 from the wood towards the beach. A thin spiral of smoke was seen ascending from the town. A long sheet of flame (approximately 500 feet) came from the front of the town and was suddenly extinguished. The pilot who observed this thought that flame-throwers were being used."

At the beach Austin recalled, "Mills-Roberts came back through the trees grinning. 'We've got their ammunition dump. Mortar shell, bang on top of it. Bloody fools, they'd got their ammunition all in one lot'". The journalist was sent to scramble down the gully to the beach with a message for Sedgwick and his Phantom radio operators who were in contact with General Roberts, the JUBILEE Military Commander aboard the destroyer HMS *Calpe*.

"Tell them 'Battery demolished'".

The signal logged between 06.30 and 07.00 at the Phantom Rear H.Q. at R.A.F. Uxbridge in the UK was less dramatic, it read.

> "4 Commando demolished enemy ammunition dump and engaged six-gun battery.
>
>   The R.A.F. were engaged over target. The Commando which was intact, put in a further attack at 0630 hrs. There was no contact between the Commando and the troops on their left though the Camerons had landed. Our troops were pinned down on White and Red Beaches and unable to land at Blue."

Co-located on the shingle with the Phantom signals group of Capt Sedgwick RTR, Tpr B Randell The Royal Scots and Fus C King The Royal Fusiliers, was a one from The South Saskatchewan Regiment,

Privates Michael Faille and Paul J Karesa. They were tasked with establishing a radio link with their regiment and the Cameron Highlanders of Canada who were landing at Green Beach. Theirs would be the tragic task of monitoring the increasingly garbled and erratic transmissions that indicated the Canadian landing at Pourville had failed.

Closer to the beach Tony Smith recalled, "After the ammunition went up I had a very anxious moment because I did not know that the Germans were not in a position to open fire again and on looking out to sea I saw a whole fleet of TLCs moving in fairly close towards Dieppe. I remember thinking 'If we don't silence the German battery at once, it will play havoc among those ships'".

The battery was now silent, and in effect No 4 Commando had fulfilled its mission, the enemy however were still resisting. With a shattering explosion a mortar bomb detonated in a tree behind Mills-Roberts and a severed branch crashed down close to his position.

The men of C Troop with the attached men of A Troop were spread out in two distinct localities half in the scrub with the 3-inch Mortar FOO party and the rest of Group 1 in the area of La Volière. The men in the scrub were harder to spot, and mortar fire was over-shooting their position and landing in the trees. The obvious target of La Volière attracted more fire and Style moved his Bren gun teams away and further to the left. The LMG crews fired in short bursts on a pre-arranged plan so that they conserved ammunition but kept up a steady rate of fire.

Mills-Roberts was pleased that the fire from Group 1 had neutralised the battery, but now the German reaction was building. Mortar and machine gun fire became more accurate. Several men were wounded and when Pte M. Knowles fell on the track at the edge of the wood LCpl W.O.Garthwaite raced from cover to dress his wounds. As he knelt over the wounded Commando there was a flash and the thump of an exploding mortar bomb and he was mortally wounded. Knowles was subsequently dragged into cover.

Blast from another mortar bomb ripped off most of the right trouser leg of LCpl A.Fletcher's denims, but miraculously he was only lightly wounded. At about 06.15 however the slightly groggy Fletcher had no idea if he would survive the fire fight at the battery, let alone make it back to the United Kingdom. Amidst the crash of exploding mortar bombs, the stink of cordite and dust Mills-Roberts however was remarkably sanguine. "On the whole we were getting away with it far better than we expected," he recalled. As he considered the situation Corporal E.A.Smith panted up from the beachhead and reported, "Your message has reached Uxbridge, sir".

A new German crew had made their way to the PINCER Flak position and directed accurate fire at the scrub. Eventually three crews would have manned the gun and been cut down by rifle and Bren gun fire. From the upper window of La Volière the redoubtable Boys Anti-Tank Rifle crew of McDonough and Davies took on the Flak position. By the close of the operation they had fired 60 rounds, mostly rapid shots, which given the formidable recoil of the weapon was a feat of considerable endurance. The tungsten slugs punched through the armoured shield and the Flak gun eventually fell silent.

For Mills-Roberts and Group 1 time was running out. If by 06.30 hours Group 2 had not attacked the battery, following the strafing run by Spitfires, he would have to commit his now depleted force to the assault.

His radio operators had been unable to contact Group 2 and indeed Mills-Roberts did not even know if the force had landed safely at Orange Beach 2. The enemy mortar fire was becoming heavier and more accurate, the southern face of La Volière was now scarred and smashed by German light Flak and small arms fire.

Urgently Mills-Roberts' radio operator signalled to him, leaning close to the officer he shouted that Group 2 was in contact. They were ready in their forming up point (FUP) to the south west of the battery. Two factors had prevented earlier communication, the screening of the woods and the hilly terrain, but most importantly LCpl P. Flynn of the Royal Signals, a critical signaller in Group 2 had been stunned by an exploding mortar bomb at Orange Beach 2. Realising that he was a key link in the operation he caught his breath, swung his radio onto his shoulders and set off at a run alone along the right bank of the river Saâne. He linked up with Lovat and his HQ party just as the two sections of Group 2 were about to attack.

The volume of fire from riflemen and Bren Gunners in Group 1 increased. By the close of the action they would have fired 12 out of the 16 twenty-five round Bren magazines they had brought with them. It was manifestly clear that Ennis had established radio communications with Cpl Nankivell and the 3-inch Mortar crew as it "came into action with a heartening crash". Ennis was now using the No 18 set of Mills-Roberts' radio operator to communicate with the HQ Troop back at the beachhead. It was a problem that had been anticipated in training and a procedure that had been rehearsed.

At 06.25 hours after firing HE, both mortars switched to smoke and "deluged the whole battery area". The 2-inch crew had fired all ten of their HE bombs and now expended the two smoke they had with them. The smoke bombs may have obscured the visibility for some of the men in the battery, however for the 8.1-cm Mortar crew in a depth position the vertical smoke trails of the 2-inch bombs gave an accurate aiming point. Because the 3-inch crew had been late coming into action they had not fired all of the 60 HE rounds but now fired some of the ten smoke rounds that had been brought forward. The remaining unfired ammunition would prove valuable later in the operation.

At 06.28 hours as clouds of white smoke curled above the buildings and gun positions the air strike went in. The Spitfires came in at tree top height and the area disappeared in boiling dust and smoke in a roar of exploding cannon shells. Dunning recalled that the men in the building and lying in the woods and scrub, "had the distinct feeling, lying there, of being a bit too near for any error. It was quite an experience."

The twelve aircraft from 129 Squadron led by Squadron Leader Rhys Thomas DFC had seen the smoke rising from the burning cordite on the battery site.

Lovat in his after action report said that the attack "was only partially successful as the Squadron came in mixed up with enemy Focke-Wulfes (sic)[6] and their cannon fire raked some of the houses from which 'A' Troop were sniping the enemy on the west flank. No damage was fortunately caused although I understand that two Ranger Sergeants attached for the operation were covered with bricks and mortar and shot out of the roof under which they were sheltering."

Undeterred Stempson returned to his roof top position and continued to fire at the battery.

Though it was reported that enemy fire had wounded TSM Williams of A Troop there are indications that his injuries may in fact have been caused by the RAF air strike . Under heavy enemy fire Sgt L. Heaynes and L/Bdr H. Larment dashed out to pull the wounded TSM into cover. After he had received some basic first aid the TSM, realising that his severe injuries would slow down the later withdrawal in company with another wounded Commando, L Cpl J. Jackson began to make his way back through the woods to the beach head.

The *Luftwaffe* Focke-Wulf Fw 190A-3 fighters that attacked the Spitfires were from *Jagdgeschwader(JG)* – Fighter Wing 26 "Schlageter" which along with JG 2 made up the *Kanalgeschwader* the Channel Wing, a force that during the day would conduct the air battle over Dieppe. The aircraft in this action were probably those operating from the St. Omer-Arques airfield. In the brief air battle Pilot Officer J.B. Shillitoe put a burst into an FW 190 and claimed to have damaged it.

The intelligence log of the RAF squadron records the ground attack mission with business like economy.

0540 – 0710
12 Spitfire VB of 129 Squadron attacked gun positions which were already burning on their arrival.

12 Spitfire Mark VB of No 129 (Mysore) Squadron took off at 05.40 hours to attack gun post "Hess" to W, of Dieppe. Perfect landfall made at lighthouse and target located by burning buildings. One attack made and position thoroughly raked all return fire being silenced. 12 Fw 190s arrived from the South as the squadron came over the Target and several dog-fights took place. 2 machines were hit by flak but none seriously damaged. All aircraft landing safely at base by 07.10 hours."

The squadron was identified to the men of No 4 Commando by the code name THRUSTER. The pilots acknowledged the target by repeating the code word HESS over the radio and giving their expected time of attack.

In the detailed plans for JUBILEE the possibility of the loss of HMS *Prince Albert* and with it No 4 Commando had been considered. In this situation the fighters would have been tasked with the destruction of the battery.

At 06.30 hours, exactly on time, the men of Group 1 saw three white Very lights soar up in succession in a steep arc above the smoke and dust hanging over the battery.

Lovat and Group 2 were about to attack.

Notes

1 Supermarine Spitfire Mk VB
   Type: Single-seat interceptor fighter
   Power plant: one 1,074 kW (1,470 hp) Rolls-Royce Merlin 45M V-12 piston
   Performance: maximum speed at sea level 534 km/hr (332 mph)
   maximum speed 574 km/h (3576 mph)
   maximum range 756 km (470 miles)
   service ceiling 10,820 metres (35,500 ft)
   Weights: empty 2,291 kg (5,050 lb)
   loaded 3,016 kg (6,650 lb)
   Dimensions: wing span (clipped) 9.80m (32ft 2 in)
   length 9.11m (29ft 11 in)
   height 3.02 m (9ft 11 in)
   Armament: two 20 mm Hispano cannon; four .303 in Browning guns; some modified to carry two 227 kg (500 lb) bombs.

2 The attack on the lighthouse marked the first Spitfire loss during JUBILEE. Two Spitfire Vbs flown by Flying Officer H.G. Jones with Sgt R.L. Reeves as his wingman had taken off from Thorney Island at 04.47 hours. They made their landfall about 8 km (4 miles) west of the target, alert German Flak crews opened fire hitting the aircraft flown by Jones. It caught fire and crashed into the sea. This AA fire may have been the "tinselly" tracer observed by Peter Scott. Reeves flew on to complete the mission. He subsequently tangled with two FW 190s on his return journey and though injured put a head on burst into one enemy fighter and saw it go down streaming thick black smoke. The FW 190s had just shot down an RAF Boston bomber and Reeves seeing the crew in

their life rafts was able to report their position. They were rescued by a Walrus flying boat.

3 Nautical twilight with the sun 12° below the horizon commenced at 04.31; twilight with the sun 2° below the horizon was at 05.15 and sunrise was at 05.50.

4 According to the account by Raymond la Sierra a similar generous gesture was made by an elderly Frenchwoman dressed in traditional widow's black costume. Like an urban myth the "egg story" has improved with the telling. In an obituary for William (Bill) Boucher-Myers one writer in a British newspaper asserted that at the close of Operation CAULDRON every man in No 4 Commando returned to England with a freshly laid egg.

5 The Germans were unable to establish how the battery had been destroyed and initially put it down to hits by cannon fire from the RAF Spitfires. Later this was changed in the report drafted by the Chief of Staff of Army Group D General Major Zeitzler who wrote "Fighter planes attacked it, swooping down and igniting the cartridges of nearly all the guns with small incendiary bombs".

   Field Marshal von Rundstedt put his signature to the report Fundamental Remarks of Army HQ No 8 that stated:

   "(6) Conservation of Ammunition
   British fighter planes ignited the cartridges of one battery with tracer bullets, obliging the personnel to employ themselves in extinguishing the fire, after which the enemy attacked the battery with infantry.

   Lessons deduced – Re-examine all the arrangements of ammunition, especially of cartridges, to see that they stored safely."

   Part of the reason for the German confusion was that in the days immediately after CAULDRON they did not appreciate that there had been two landings and the role of Group 1 supporting the attack by Group 2.

6 Focke-Wulf Fw 190A-3
   Type: Single-seat interceptor fighter/ fighter bomber
   Power plant: One 1,268 kW (1,700hp) BMW 801D-2 14-cylinder two-way radial
   Performance: maximum speed at sea level 509 km/h (312 mph)
   maximum speed 615 km/h (382 mph)
   maximum range 800 km (497 miles)
   service ceiling 10,600 m (34,775 ft)
   Weights: empty 2,900 kg (6,393 lb)
   loaded 3,980 kg (8,770 lb)

Dimensions: wing span 10.5 m (34 ft 5½ in)

length 8.8 m (28 ft 10½ in)

height 3.95 m (12ft 11½ in)

Armament: two 7.9 mm MG17 machine guns in upper cowling; two 20 mm MG 151 and two 20 mm MG FF cannon in wings.

CHAPTER 7

Attack

A white signal flare[1] had arced up close to the lighthouse as the four LCAs with the LCS and MGB approached Orange Beach 2 at 04.30 hours. It was followed by a green one fired from the eastern end of the beach. The Commandos of Group 2 hunched in their landing craft wondered if this was a German signal for opening fire or sentries firing flares for illumination on the vague suspicion that something was out at sea.

A few seconds before LCA 3 touched down on the eastern end of the beach, RAF fighters flew in low and Mulleneux noted they, "proceeded to occupy the attention of the enemy light flak guns. This happy synchronisation almost certainly enabled the second flight consisting of the LCS, LCAs 5,7 and 8 to disembark troops without opposition."

Writing afterwards Lovat said that once the white flares had been fired he ordered the Senior Naval Officer (SNO) to increase speed. "Almost simultaneously with the challenging star shell, the first air sortie was made by our fighter bombers up the valley of the River Saane. This timely diversion had the effect of drawing a concentration of flak and L.M.G. tracer bullets on the aircraft, three in number, which passed almost over our heads heading inland. This tracer served to unmask almost all the enemy positions."

Peter Scott recalled the landing. "The pillbox at the eastern end of Orange II opened fire along the beach, and the fire was returned by the L.C.S. The Huns behind the beach fired a six-star green firework – no doubt an invasion signal – and the party was on."

The sub-section of A Troop under Lt Veasey who were the first ashore doubled up the shingle and positioned light weight tubular ladders against the low cliff at the eastern end of Orange Beach 2. Among the men who raced ashore in the half-light in were the US Rangers Sgt Stempson and Cpl Brady. Brady from Grand Forks, North Dakota towered over the Commandos.

The section suffered four casualties but destroyed the two machine gun positions that covered the beach. One position was unoccupied but the Commandos spotted a German laden with ammunition boxes running to the second. Stempson opened fire. He later recalled, "When you hit them they rolled over like jackrabbits". They raced towards the position and a red headed Commando pitched grenades into it killing the crew.

Only eighteen minutes after landing and under intense small arms fire the slightly built Trooper William Finney, later awarded the Military Medal, climbed up a telephone pole and cut the lines linking Quiberville and Ste Marguerite.

Using the techniques for crossing obstacles on the assault course the agile Finney had placed a foot in the cupped hands of the 1.85 metre Brady who, braced against the pole heaved the Commando onto his shoulders. In training in Dorset Brady had confessed that "his big concern was Finney's boots would not rip off his ear". Miraculously both men survived the heavy fire that cracked past them and thudded into the telephone pole.

Further along the beach the main landing by the LCAs went in. "Our boats landed on a front fairly close together, each one about a cricket pitch apart on a beach about 150 yards wide," recalled Lovat. "It was a nasty beach, quite a steep affair, and the wire on top of it in the half-light looked almost as high as a ceiling."

As the LCAs withdrew to seaward after landing the troops, they came under heavy fire. "The fire was wild, however, no serious damage was done and a useful purpose was probably served by thus drawing the enemy's fire whilst the troops evacuated the beach."

Seen from the sea a mortar or howitzer shell appeared to explode on the beach, but Mulleneux knew that by now the troops were off it and on their way along the River Saâne. Two craft remained a few hundred metres off the beach ready to evacuate casualties if requested. Unable to see any, and receiving no summons they withdrew about one kilometre out to sea.

"I have subsequently discovered," wrote Mulleneux a few days after the operation, "that one or two casualties had actually been left on the dead ground on the landward side of the beach and the fact that they appear to have been abandoned both by the army and the navy is much regretted".

Peter Scott 's boat about 1,000 metres offshore opened fire on a bunker with its 3-inch gun. "One or two bursts seemed fairly near in spite of the fact that we had only open cartwheel sights. But, although we did not hit it, the pillbox ceased fire after we had fired about six rounds. Ten minutes later, however, it recommenced, so at 0515 we opened fire for a further three minutes' bombardment. The L.C.S. was firing most accurately with Oerlikon, and after that the pillbox was silenced for good."

On shore the landing by Group 2 had not been unopposed. Streams of red tracer fire and the thump and concussion of exploding mortar bombs greeted Lt Donald Gilchrist who was in action for the first time. He saw Captain Gordon Webb grab his shoulder, hit by a mortar fragment, but as they ran up the beach, "Webb (was) still with us".

Lovat had emphasised the importance of clearing the beach rapidly. No one was to lie down, unless they were wounded. The crews of enemy mortars, artillery and direct fire weapons like machine guns would know the exact range of the beach and it would be a potential "killing ground".

"If we had hesitated on that beach, as some do when they get windy and flop down, we would have been in trouble. When that happens. with bad troops you've had it, you can't get them up again."[2]

Lovat had told his section commanders to take the name of any man who lay down on the shingle and if they survived the raid they would be returned to their parent unit.[3]

On the beach the mortar fire that had wounded Webb also wounded or killed the men of B Troop who, wearing leather jerkins and carrying the rabbit wire matting that would flatten the coiled barbed wire, had doubled forward. They were quickly replaced by more Commandos and afterwards Lovat paid tribute to their bravery. "These men really tore the wire apart in a way which I can't believe was possible, looking back on it. They really rolled about in it and they went through like loose forwards following a rugger ball."

George Cook was in one of the two man teams with wire netting and recalling Lovat saying of the tracer fire, " 'They're firing too high', quite casual. Lord Lovat was about six foot, I'm five foot four so I thought, if they're firing over his head there's no danger they're going to touch me."

In a classic of understatement Skerry remembered that, " the landing was obviously a bit scary, but at least it was fairly dry."

The German mortar crews had by now decided the landing craft and HMS *Grey Goose* offshore were more lucrative targets and lengthened their range. It would give the men of Group 2 the critical seconds that would allow them through the wire and off the beach. As on the Orange Beach 1 the minefields, helpfully marked in French and German, were avoided.

"We were in occupied France," recalled Gilchrist, a Scotsman with a keen sense of humour, "This was the Dieppe raid. I was in action for the first time. A keen young junior officer. Proud to be a section leader on No 4 Commando. Determined to be a credit to my country and an inspiration to my men. And then my trousers started to come down. I still shudder to think of it."

Working his way forward through the wire he confessed that he "did everything a rogue elephant would have done except trumpet. In protest against these unnatural strains, British buttons sawed themselves free. And down slid my trousers... Clutching my trousers in one hand, Tommy gun in the other, I raced inland... If any of my comrades had noticed my predicament, and said the wrong word – I'd have shot him dead and burst into tears."

At about this point three Douglas Havoc II night fighter/intruder aircraft[4] roared in low across the coast distracting the German fire. The first German Gilchrist ever saw killed fell victim to one of these aircraft.

"Like an ungainly, grey-uniformed grouse, a German broke cover and ran across a field. He wasn't fast enough. One of the Havocs swooped. A burst of cannon fire lifted him off his feet, hurling him for several yards before he tumbled head over heels and lay still."

Tracer fire streaked at head height as the men ran "like half shut knives, our bodies bent forward, as if we were forcing our way against a strong wind". *Notes from Theatres of War* observes rather pedantically, "There seems to be some doubt whether this fire was coming from high ground west of Ste MARGUERITE or from the QUIBERVILLE direction or both." Wherever it was coming from it would been intimidating for less experienced troops.

A poker-faced Commando running near to Gilchrist however put it in context when he panted,

"'Jesus Christ, sir, this is as bad as Achnacarry!' At Achnacarry, the Commando Depot, we'd spent half our time shambling along like Charles Laughton in *The Hunchback of Notre Dame* under a hail of live ammunition. This *was* as bad as Achnacarry. With a wrench and twist, I made my trousers fast around my waist. I was dressed, if not properly dressed. To hell with all trousers – I was in the war again."

Gilchrist was not the only man to experience problems with his clothing and equipment as he landed. Brady, who was the third man off the landing craft, was carrying his M1 Garand and ammunition, a Bren magazine, a 2-inch mortar bomb, grenades and a section of scaling ladder. As the ladder was being assembled at the foot of the cliff he discovered that the buckles on his haversack had become detached. By the time he had reinserted them he was number five in the order of ascent for the ladder. The delay was providential as the man in front of him was shot and fell back on the big American. A round creased Brady's buttocks and the man behind him was hit in the mouth.

The main body of men under Lovat crossed the coast road and moved down to the right bank of the flooded River Sâane. After a short run the word was passed to a halt to allow men to close up. Like a demanding Directing Staff (DS) on exercise Lovat appeared and giving the section commanders "a reproachful glance he demanded, 'Why isn't someone up with the recce group giving encouragement?' At Achnacarry too," recalled Gilchrist, "we were frequently expected to be in two places at once".

Lovat spotted Webb with his rifle slung, and unaware that the Captain had been wounded, briskly informed him that he was a disgrace and he would be on a charge when they returned to England.

"From this point everything worked according to plan," wrote Lovat two days later, "We proceeded in close formation in dead ground along the east bank of the River Saane (sic) with all possible speed". Picking up the narrow track on the right bank of the Saâne Group 2 was protected by the steep riverbank and strip woods. The group was headed by B Troop with Lovat and the Force HQ in the centre and F Troop in the rear.

The move did not work entirely to plan. Cook who was in what was designated a liaison group headed by Capt Pat Porteous and composed of Sgts M. Desmond and G. Horne, LCpl A.Diplock, and Fus T. Bramwell recalled that once across the beach, "Everything became silent. The firing had stopped and we were going across these fields, just this little group of us, we'd lost all track of the others, everybody had just melted very quietly away."

However the German troops covering the beach were also confused. Group 2's speed through the defences the fact that some casualties had been left behind, and the continued presence of the craft offshore, led the German defenders to believe that they had repelled a landing. A signal was transmitted to the 15th Army HQ at 05.30 hours stated that bombs had been dropped at 05.05 hours and, "enemy attempted landing in the areas Berneval-Diepe-Pourville and Quiberville".

At 08.40 hours the 15th Army issued its fourth situation report. "Around Quiberville the situation is not clear and it has not yet been established whether Quibverville itself has been attacked or not."

Later the HQ would send the hesitant assessment that, "The position at Quiberville is not clear".

When the fighting was over General Curt Haase would be confident that Orange Beach 2 had been defended against an attack. In his after action report he would assert "The attempt (to land) was frustrated by the concentrated fire of Company 1".

In fact Group 2 had taken just 35 minutes to fight their way through the wire obstacles and run 1,600 metres through long grass and saturated ground. The second bend in the meandering river Saâne marked the point where they would swing east. At 05.15 hours they started to move uphill from sea level to 52 metres along a shallow re-entrant. Careful study of the maps, aerial photograph mosaic and the model had impressed the terrain in Lovat's memory. This route took them across more exposed terrain which they crossed in open formation using tactical bounds between cover.

Earlier as they were setting off to run along the river, Cook had spotted a magnificently Gallic scene. A Frenchwoman was standing in the doorway of a small bungalow, "She was shouting, *bonjour*, *bonjour* and waving a bottle of wine. I would have loved a drink but we had no time."

It may well have been that this hospitable French patriot was not saying, "Good day" but wishing the Commandos, "*Bon chance!*" – Good luck!

Cook recalled, "we just kind of give her a bit of a salute and run on." Porteous[5] remembered her too, a figure in her nightdress, bottle in hand shouting, "*Vive les Anglais*".

After CAULDRON was over the population around Varengeville and Ste Marguerite would be made to pay by the Germans for their active or tacit support for the Commando operation.

As the men ran they could hear the fire from the Group 1 action at the battery. "At Zero + 40 the heavy crump of a 3" Mortar (sic)", wrote Lovat, "added a pleasant note to the barrage, and shortly afterwards a roar of sound supplemented with sheets of flame that rose high into the air increased our confidence that all was going well."

The explosion was big enough to be heard by Peter Scott off the beaches, "One very loud bang was Lord Lovat's 4th Commando blowing up the ammunition dump of the 6-inch battery he had been detailed to destroy."

Back on Orange Beach 2 the two Liverpool born medical orderlies, brothers Ted and Jimmy Pasquale started to check the casualties. One of the Commandos, with a grim stomach wound had still had sufficient strength to shout a soldier's encouragement to his comrades as they raced up the shingle.

"You fuck off and get those guns!"

James Pasquale recalled the casualties. "A few had been hit and a couple were dead on the wire. The numbers one and two on the mortar were kneeling ready to fire and had been killed in that position. I've never seen anything like it. There was a man named Mercer with his eye hanging out and of course he was in a terrible state, so I stayed with him. It had got light by this time and I spotted another chap further along the beach. As I walked towards him someone started firing at us, so I crawled over the shingle towards him, but he had just been knocked unconscious and shocked".

The unconscious man was L Cpl P. Flynn, Lovat's radio operator. He had been unconscious for ten minutes, stunned by the same mortar bomb that had wounded Webb. In the words of *Notes from Theatres of War*, "knowing the plan and, as the only signaller in his section, knowing that he was of major importance, he pulled himself together and rejoined his section, by this time in the wood."

With the quiet bravery that characterises many medical personnel in the front line the young Jimmy Pasquale remained with the wounded in the knowledge that he and they would be captured. His brother, who would later die at D Day, escorted three walking wounded along the coast to Orange Beach 1, two of them were killed on the way to the evacuation beach. Jimmy Pasquale would only learn of the death of his brother when he was released from prisoner of war camp in Germany in 1945.

Tragically, as the group moved along the coast they were seen by the Royal Navy flotilla offshore who mistook them for German troops. "They were thought to be enemy troops," noted Mulleneux, "as our own forces should not have been in this position". Fulfilling their orders to intercept any attempts by the enemy to penetrate the beachhead the crew of MGB 312 opened fire with Oerlikon and .50 machine guns.

Inland Lovat noted, "One of the remarkable things was the speed at which we got around, considering that we might have run into trouble and didn't. Although we went through German infantry on both sides we weren't even shot at once we had left the beach. We ran the whole damned way, just stopping occasionally to regroup but nobody got out of breath and we didn't have to wait for laggards. These chaps were trained like athletes to run the course and, my word, they did."

Lovat set up his Force HQ when he had reached a sunken track junction and cluster of buildings to the south west of Blancmesnil le Bas wood. It was an obvious, but covered location, selected from the aerial photographs and maps before the operation.

The Force HQ was a small flexible group consisting of the CO, his adjutant Captain Michael Dunning-White, two runners, three signallers and four men from the Orderly Room armed with Thompson sub machine guns for local defence. Like all the specialists within the Commando, the Orderly Room clerks were primarily trained fighting men for whom administrative skills were secondary.

Signallers from this Force HQ now made contact with Group 1 and Lovat received an optimistic situation report from Mills-Roberts. A Troop detachment with Group 1 also came up on the air and confirmed that they were covering the west flank of the battery and had suppressed the PINCER Flak position.

Lovat and his HQ party now moved into position between and behind B and F Troops. The terrain and woodland had effectively screened the advance of Group 2 from observation by the battery position. B and F Troops divided according to plan and made their way to their allotted concentration areas but F Troop started to come under fire. They had worked their way forward under cover along the northern edge of Blancmesnil le Bas wood but the final leg of their advance took them up the north/south road running into the battery position. Here they used smoke to cover their advance.

B Troop was more fortunate since it had the best covered approach along the southern edge of the wood. From the corner they made their way north and in sub-sections worked their way through orchards and small enclosures using a sunken track as their left of axis on a route up a shallow re-entrant that led directly into the battery.

There was a brief moment of confusion recorded in *Notes from Theatres of War* when a section of F Troop opened fire on the Force HQ as it moved up behind them, there were no casualties and the shooting was quickly halted by orders over the radio.

In B Troop Gilchrist could see the Flak tower and recalled, "A few Germans were moving about on top of it.

"The troop closed up, and we crawled to the rear of the position. The Germans were unaware they had visitors entering by the back door.

Gordon Webb gave the order to fire. Rifles cracked. We watched, amazed, as a German soldier on top of the tower toppled over the edge and slowly fell to the ground some sixty feet below – like an Indian from a cliff in a Western picture."

Gilchrist watched as the marksman turned to the troop commander and said cheekily, "Now do I get back my bloody proficiency pay, sir?". He remembered the Commando had had his pay reduced by 6d (2½p) for a bad score on the range in Scotland. George Cook recalled, "Somebody shot a bloke out of the ack-ack tower ... he did a lovely swallow dive off the top, I think it was Spearman who actually shot him." Other Commandos remember Spearman as a good shot, but "something of a barrack room lawyer".

Under cover of smoke from their 2-inch Mortars and smoke grenades the two troops had reached a position where Bangalore torpedoes could be pushed beneath the perimeter wire.

B Troop would hit the battery perimeter at its most southern point and split to clear the buildings and occupied houses of le Mesnil. F Troop would work its way along the western edge of the position before hooking right and attacking the gun line. This meant that there was less danger of the two Troops becoming entangled either as they broke into the position or subsequently as they fought through. F Troop however had a more exposed approach along the western perimeter.

"Luckily," recalled Porteous in an interview for the IWM, "we found a spot on the wire ... where obviously the German soldiers had been coming home late from leave or something of the sort and had trampled a passage down through this bit of barbed wire at the back. We managed to get in there without any problem at all."

However F Troop was coming under fire from the PIEFACE Flak position and from troops in buildings in the battery.

Bullets kicked up the dust as Fus. George Cook and Sgt G. "Honk" Horne moved forward to open up the wire. "I was against this tree and I could see little bits of it flying off," recalled Cook. "Then I heard

Horne go "Ugh" and he fell on his side. I cut the wire, went over to him and rolled him over. He had gone very white and I thought he was dead. So I nipped back to report to Capt. Pat Porteous that Horne had been killed."

Cook saw blood spurting from the Sergeant's chest. "It was a bit of a shock to me because he was about the toughest fellow I ever knew, was Geordie Horne. I decided with being in his sub-section … that I would stick pretty close to him because he was a Regular soldier, he'd been on the North West Frontier and in Palestine and knew his stuff. I thought, 'I'll stick by him', but he was the first chap I actually saw shot… The next thing I knew I was hit too."

Remembering the moment he was wounded Cook said, "It might sound daft but I actually felt nothing. It was just as though somebody had shone a big light straight in my eyes. I could feel myself falling. Then I knew no more."

Though Horne had a serious wound, Skerry was able to prop him against a tree and light a cigarette for him before moving forward to the guns.

Within the battery perimeter Porteous recalled it was "typical bocage country with masses of little hedges, cottages and farm buildings … it was very close country."

As they advanced, two scouts working ahead of F Troop spotted 35 German soldiers in a farmyard climbing into a truck ready to be driven to the battery. In *Combined Operations* the paperback published by HMSO in 1943 this force is rather grandly described as *Stosstruppen* – Assault Troops who had been brought forward to roll up the right flank of Group 1. The Germans may have just arrived from their billets in outlying houses for many were unarmed.

F Troop closed up and Lovat recalled, "There is no finer target at point blank range than troops in or out of lorries before they have shaken into any fighting formation. They were liquidated and we moved on to take up our final position." The troop of German artillerymen had been cut down by close range Thompson submachine gun fire.

Once they were through the perimeter the volume of fire increased in intensity. Pte Clifford Leach with F Troop recalled, how in the overgrown garden of a bungalow he was wounded in the temple and TSM William Stockdale lost his foot when two stick grenades came cartwheeling over the roof.

"Trooper Mackvey went behind the house and caught the man who was throwing the grenades and saw him off with his Tommy Gun." The grenade had landed a metre from Leach and he recalled that, "it did not hurt at the time. It was like having a hot dishcloth thrown over my face. It stunned me temporarily and I heard one of my mates say 'Yorky's got hit in the head', but I was all right… I was a bit deafened, like having cotton wool in my ears."

Stockdale, the F Troop TSM, who would later receive the Distinguished Conduct Medal, wrapped his first field dressing around the shattered foot, sat up, shouldered his rifle and continued to engage the enemy.

Sgt Bill Portman hunched under his rucksack of high explosives was lucky when a grenade exploded near him, a fragment lodged in the skin below his eye. " I pulled it out and looked for the guy who had thrown it. Like a fool I was looking towards the gunpits about 300 yards away. My own common sense should have told me nobody could throw that far. Then a second one was thrown. It exploded in a tree behind me and pieces went through my pack of explosives, detonators, charges everything. I could feel the blood from the splinters running down my bottom. If it had hit one of the charges I would just have been a hole in the ground."

In an interview with Dunning many years later he remarked, "They were all primed charges, they had all got detonators and primers".

"Then I saw the bloke who had thrown it. His head was poking up out of the ground eight to ten yards away. I pulled one off at him with my rifle. I was a marksman, a pretty good shot, and I got him plumb centre." The Sergeant worked the bolt of his SMLE rifle, fitted its sword bayonet, and started to walk towards the trench. "When I got there I saw there were two of them, in a dog-leg trench. The one I had shot had half his head blown off, but the other one was looking the other way, his rifle poking through the bushes. He hadn't noticed his pal was dead. He turned and saw me at the same time as I noticed him. I can see his face now, turning. I stabbed him in the neck with my bayonet, then I was so scared I shot him about three times to make sure."

By late August the apples in the orchards near le Mesnil were ripe and despite the fire, the Commandos reverted to childhood habits and stole the odd apple, snatching bites as they moved forward in tactical bounds. Other men found time to stuff the fruit into the capacious fronts of their denim blouses. It was an incident that the Americans attached to A Troop would hear of and retell back in England. Later the "apple story" would almost rival to the "egg story" in the mythology of Operation CAULDRON.

"I want a few of you to go round and knock out the right-hand gun," said Gordon Webb indicating an MG 34 *Kampfstand* and looking at Donald Gilchrist. The young officer stood up and found that Sergeant Watkins and three Commandos, Marshall a Bren gunner, Keeley and Hurd were already on their feet beside him.

"We cut across a hedge, raced through some trees, and darted between buildings. Before us, not seventy yards away, was the battery position, German heads bobbing up and down. We began to stalk – we'd learned how – walking upright, stiff-legged, our weapons at the ready. Suddenly we froze.

"A German soldier appeared, carrying a box of grenades. He must have sensed danger at his back. He stopped, turned cautiously, and looked open-mouthed at us, his face distorted. Then, still holding the box in both hands, he started to jump up and down like a baby in a temper, as he shouted dementedly, '*Kommando, Kommando*!'

"A sarcastic voice said, 'I'll give him flippin' Commando!' A rifle spat, and the German fell over his grenades.

"Our section doubled forward. Close to us the hedge rustled. The Bren leapt in Marshall's hands. I glanced sideways in surprise at a grey form settled in a huddled heap. Up went hand grenades to explode in the right-hand gun pit. Groans were coupled with a Cockney voice, 'Every time a coconut!'"

Interviewed after the war by the IWM Gilchrist remembered that his group initially cleared two buildings to work their way round to attack the machine gun position. "In Scottish Command we had been told to give clear concise orders, but it's difficult to do this with mortars and grenades going off." Using field signals sign he indicated by sign language to a Commando the first building that needed to be cleared. He received a "thumbs up", the man ran forward, tried the door then pulled the pin from a grenade with his teeth, let the handle fly off and pitched the grenade through the open door which he then closed.

Seconds later there was the thump of the explosion – but, "no screams. They were away from home".

As they moved on one of the group spotted a concealed German soldier "There was a rustle in the hedge and I heard a Tommy gun rattle and looked in surprise at a grey uniformed body of a German who was shot. If he had stayed quiet and waited till we passed we would never have noticed him, he was marvellously camouflaged." It was the burst of submachine gun fire that alerted the German soldier carrying the box of grenades.

Eighty-five minutes after landing B Troop reported that they were in position for the final assault. F Troop came on air a minute later to report that they too were ready but had suffered casualties from the PIEFACE Flak tower and rifle fire from Germans in the buildings within the battery perimeter.

Spearman recalled that earlier one Bren gunner had a malfunction with his LMG. All soldiers were trained on this normally reliable weapon and knew the drills to follow if it failed to fire. The barrel on the gun had overheated but to reduce weight the gunner was not carrying the Spare Parts Wallet (SPW) with a spare.

"He piddled down it," said Spearman. "After he finished the machine gun fired alright and then we went on."

Attached to F Troop, Free French Commando Cpl F. Baloche was also approaching the battery. Glancing down he had spotted wild strawberries and picking and eating one recalled his boyhood holidays in Normandy. Now however such nostalgic memories were quickly forgotten.

The tiny French Marine had located a German machine gun position about 45 metres away out of range of his Thompson and too far for an accurate throw with a grenade. The two man crew had not seen Balloche and picking up their machine gun began to move to a better position. They were 20 metres away when Baloche rose from behind cover and raked them with fire. The first man pitched forward and the other his arms spread wide open crashed backwards with a scream.

"Well done!" shouted Pettiward.

"Roger Pettiward who was Troop Commander was later killed by a sniper" recalled Pat Porteous. "John MacDonald the other Section Commander was killed by somebody who threw a stick grenade, I think the chap was hiding in the roof of one of the barns and threw it as he went past underneath ... which left me in command of the troop.

"So we carried on. I was going along a little lane towards the battery with a bank on the left and I suddenly saw a German popping up on the other side of the bank. I threw a Mills grenade at him and he threw a stick grenade at me. As soon as they went off I popped up but unfortunately he popped up a little bit quicker and he shot me through the – I had a rifle in my hand – and he shot me through my left hand so I withdrew a bit and put on a field dressing." The bullet had passed through the palm of his hand and lodged in his upper arm. "We pressed on and there were several other casualties, chaps who'd got sniped or blown up with grenades.

"We lined ourselves along a bank which was giving us a little bit of cover from where the actual guns were, low bank about four feet high... I made contact with Commando Headquarters who were in the centre of the battery area or approaching the battery area and said. 'Come on it's time we went in'."

The start line for the final assault was a ditch by a road running immediately behind the gun emplacements. It was now 06.20 hours and on cue the Spitfires flew in low from east to west in their strafing run across the battery.

It was a spectacular and awesome attack as recalled by Spearman, "You could see the bullets ... hitting the dust just before the wire started. If they'd have been a little bit out and started early they'd have shot us up."

Lovat raised his arm and fired a white Very light, as it soared upwards he flicked the empty cartridge case from the pistol, reloaded it and in quick succession fired two more white signal cartridges.

The final assault was going in.

"So," said Porteous modestly, "we then did a little bayonet charge into the gun pits themselves".

The moment of the assault remained vivid in Gilchrist's memory.

"With fixed bayonets F Troop attacked, yelling like banshees. In too came B Troop, led by Gordon Webb. His right hand was dangling, useless – but he had a revolver in his left. Razor-sharp, Sheffield steel tore the guts out of the Varengeville battery. There is probably nothing more frightening than British troops with the bayonet – Sheffield steel guaranteed".

"It was a stupendous charge which went in, in many cases, over open ground swept by machine-gun fire." wrote Lovat.

The slightly built, dark haired Webb, his rifle slung over his wounded right arm, advanced with his Colt .45 in his left hand. "We were asphyxiated by our own bloody smoke", he recalled, " (I) couldn't see a thing. Fifty of us lined up abreast and went forward, disposing of Germans as we came across them. I only remember one (Commando) casualty. This German came out of a bunker, shot him down and started kicking him in the head. Everyone opened fire on that bugger and he was cut in half. Then we came across a dozen or fifteen Germans all lying in firing positions, all facing the other way. Several of them hadn't even had time to put their trousers on."

In his report Tony Smith noted, "Their methods were typical and a German, who stopped to kick in the face one of our wounded, not only did not live to worry about it, but acted as an incentive to our troops to give as good as they got, which seemed to shake the enemy."

In the mayhem of the attack the incident is remembered, but in a different way by Donald Gilchrist. "A rifle shot from the buildings behind the hedge. Lying in a yard was a wounded commando soldier. From the gloom of a barn emerged the German who had cut him down. He jumped up and crashed his boots on the prone face.

"Our weapons came up. A corporal raised his hand. We held our fire. The corporal took aim and squeezed the trigger. The German clutched the pit of his stomach as if trying to claw the bullet out. He tried to scream, but couldn't. Four pairs of eyes in faces blackened for action stared at his suffering. They were eyes of stone. No gloating, no pity for an enemy who knew no code and had no compassion.

"We doubled across the yard to where the two wounded lay side by side. For our comrade – morphine. For the beast – a bayonet thrust."

"All pandemonium broke loose," recalled Spearman. "It was total confusion really because anyone who wasn't a Commando you recognised, you just killed him. People were running out of buildings, running into buildings. Some were quite brave, they were trying to put up a fight but they really didn't get a chance because there must have been a hundred (sic) finely trained troops attacking them."

To the north of the battery Sgt Lindley with Group 1 could not see the attack going in but recalled that.

"All we could hear was the shooting and the screaming."

The barbed wire fence around the battery that had been constructed to keep enemy forces out, now became the cage that would keep the German soldiers trapped as the Commandos set to work. "Absolutely nobody escaped" said Spearman in an interview by the IWM, "they had nowhere to escape to. They couldn't get out of the wire, it was surrounded by all of us".

As B Troop began to clear the buildings and village to the rear of the gun emplacements, the fighting became fragmented into small scale actions. In an incident described by Eric Maguire in *Dieppe August 19* one German, a veteran NCO, took cover in a wooden shed and armed with an MP38 sub machine gun fought a one man action. A grenade – probably a No 77 was pitched through a window and the building rapidly caught fire. "Out of the door burst a horrid blackened figure, with clothes afire and tommy-gun shooting, to run a few steps and then collapse as a merciful bullet ended his life".

In the fighting Austin reported that the Army boxing champion backed up by a stocky Scots Commando fought his way out of a dangerous situation among the buildings. The Scotsman personally killed four Germans in this tough localised fire fight.

Lovat writing two days after Operation CAULDRON described the B Troop action "The battery positions were over-run in less time than it takes to tell. Considerable numbers of Germans who had hidden in underground tunnels containing stores and ammunition, in the battery office, under tables, in the cook house and out buildings, were either bayoneted or shot at close range by sub-machine guns. Two officers including the Military Commander were also killed after a rousing chase from one house to another".

For *Hauptmann* Schöler the running battle had ended when Gdsm A. Dennis kicked in the door of the battery office and raked the German officer with submachine gun fire. He was left for dead. The Commando recalled the snap decision "I couldn't take him prisoner. It was him or me." In the office he grabbed as many documents as he could find, while Webb who despite his damaged arm was able to do a little looting found two Luger PO8 pistols. The officer would describe them afterwards as modest loot.

"I did much better on the Lofoten Raid, got some fox furs there."

Raymond La Sierra describes an incident in *Le Commando du 6 Juin*. When clearing the bunkers and shelters behind the gun pits a Commando discovered a German officer in one of them attempting to burn confidential documents. The startled officer lunged for his pistol and in a reflex reaction the Commando raked him with submachine gun fire.

"Pity," he said to Webb. "I wanted to take him prisoner. He didn't give me a chance."

As B Troop worked their way around the defences mopping up the *Kampfstände* they suffered further casualties because each position was enfiladed from the next. *Notes From Theatres of War* records, "when one position was stormed and the crews killed, the Commando personnel engaged came under heavy fire from the next position. Isolated snipers continued to resist from cover outside the gun emplacements. It was noted that they picked off single men moving by themselves but appeared unwilling to unmask their position during mopping up operations if two or more men exposed themselves simultaneously."

"The morale of the enemy was good", reported the IO Tony Smith. "They fought well and their discipline was good, at any rate so long as they were fighting from within a building. Once in then open they were inclined to run."

Now Group 1 received radio orders from Lovat to send forward the medical detachment and withdraw to secure the beachhead defensive perimeter. Mills-Roberts had already anticipated these moves and accompanied by his Runner Cpl Smith was moving forward with the

Medical Officer Capt R.J.Walker and three Medical Orderlies. They walked up the road, past La Volière and had a chance to take a closer look at the battery.

"About forty yards further on we heard someone screaming – it appeared to come from a hay field to our right. There was a spasmodic noise of shooting, but otherwise it was a beautiful August day with hot sun.

"I saw a couple of German soldiers in front of a cottage by the edge of the battery, followed by Pat Porteous and two of his men."

Porteous recalled that the final assault was about 80 to 100 metres. "The guns were fully occupied dealing with the chaps on the other side … and we got very little opposition coming in in fact. I got another bullet through my thigh which slowed me up. We got into the gun pits. The first gun pit I came to was the one which had the mortar bomb in it and it was just full of corpses. I staggered on to the next gun pit and then I rather gave up the ghost after that."

It is a modest account of an action that earned the young Royal Artillery officer the Victoria Cross, the highest British and Commonwealth award for gallantry.[6]

"The gun emplacements … were a remarkable sight… Other bodies of men who had been sniped by C and A Troops lay round the area, in and out of bunkers, slit trenches or buildings" records *Notes From Theatres of War*. "Dead Germans were piled high behind the sandbag breastworks which surrounded the guns. Many of them were badly burned when the cordite had been set alight in the early stages of the operation."

In the gun pits Balloche was in action. In *10 Commando* Ian Dear describes how "The British officer in charge of the last assault said he saw a small French Commando – Balloche was only 1 m 60 cm tall – trying to climb up the parapet of the battery with British Commandos all around him. When he got to the top he fell down the other side and apparently came face-to-face with a German and killed him before the man could move."

Lovat noted, "The last survivors had fought it out with 'F' Tp. during their successful attack with the bayonet. Other bodies which had been sniped by Major Mills-Roberts and 'C' Tp, lay in heaps all round the area."

When Portman reached the gun emplacements he knew which gun was his designated target. Talking to Dunning years after the attack he admitted that at that moment,

" I was a bit of a nutcase when I went in." He was determined to be the first man in the group to destroy his target gun. Dunning concurred recalling how the intoxication of the moment could act as a spur.

Portman recalled the close combat in the gun positions "I pitched a 36 Grenade in – there were two Jerries dead, their clothes burnt off them and there were another couple and I sorted them out. Vic Ford jumped in the gun position behind me and I cussed him and said, 'Come here give me a hand', I wanted him to give me a hand putting a shell in the breach." Looking around the gun emplacement that was covered with scattered burning fragments of cordite and the twisted blackened shapes of the bodies of the German artillerymen Ford stared at the Portman and gasped. 'F … you, I'm not going in there'.

"So I threatened him … he was scared and so was I.", recalled Portman. "When I asked him to help I opened the breach and there was a shell there. So I pulled the cordite out and then I didn't know what to do with it, there were little bits of flame all over the site."

On board an LCA on the return journey to England Ford asked Portman if he would have shot him if he had failed to join him in the emplacement to assist with the demolition work. In reply the robust Sapper Sergeant laughed.

Before the guns could be destroyed Captain Porteous had to be carried to safety from the position.

The peacetime safety distance for "cutting steel" with explosives is 1,000 metres. The men of F Troop did not have the luxury of time. Portman recalled the fuses were designed to burn for two minutes but, "to speed things up we cut them down to a minute."

They pulled the pins out of the igniters and ran to the adjoining communications trenches about 20 or 30 metres away where they hunched awaiting the explosions.

The charges had been made up in advance to fit the guns and Portman explained, "All they had to do was open the breach, make sure there was a shell in it to take the blast of the explosives and that would do a real good job." He was so determined to destroy his target that he "stuck a Limpet[7] on the side as well".

Clifford Leach recalled that, "It was quite spectacular when they went off … it was quite earth shaking". The massive overpressure created by the charge detonating the shell in the breach "split the barrels like bananas".

Apart from one officer the men tasked with the destruction of the guns were all NCOs. Gun No 1 was the responsibility of Lt D.B. McKay; No 2 Sgt R.E. Lillicoe; No 3 Sgt I. Portman; No 4 Cpl M. Hinton; No 5 (unknown) and Cpl J.C.Skerry had No 6.

The 23 year old Skerry had lost his battle partner Pte P.H. McGann, fatally wounded as the troop fought through the position. He recalled, "No one else could or would help." The young Corporal plunged off alone through the smoke, explosions and dust towards his gun at the far end of the battery. He inserted the charge, pulled the pins and sprinted clear of the gun pit.

As he emerged from cover an NCO grabbed him and told him to help carry the stretcher on which lay the badly wounded Sgt S. "Fogie" Watkins. Manoeuvring it down the gully to the beach was hard work as Watkins seemed "very heavy". He survived and was recommended for a decoration by Lovat.

After the guns had been demolished McKay said with professional pride of the charges, "They fit like a glove, just like a glove". The guns were comprehensively wrecked including the barrels, breech blocks and instruments. This would prevent parts from different guns being cannibalised for reconstruction.

In the woods to the north Smith remembered, "large chunks of metal began to fly through the air over the tops of the trees. I did not know what it was, but I later discovered that it was the bits of the guns which were being blown up."

Some of the F Troop demolition experts now moved on to destroy the ammunition stores and bunkers on the battery site.

As he went about his work Portman saw three wounded German prisoners lying propped against the wall of a house. As one man had a serious stomach wound Portman went to collect a tin of water for the casualty. Later on the far side of the building searching for anything of intelligence value he found a stack of shells in a lean to shed. That these 155 mm shells were not in the bunkers or gun pits is a further indication of the lax ammunition handling at the battery for which the German gunners had already suffered.

Portman showed them to McKay and said that he intended to blow them up. "You're going to have to wait behind until all the others have gone," said the officer. Portman decided against waiting put two Limpet charges on the shells and moved off towards the evacuation beach. The shells exploded and Portman wondered, "If any of the house fell on these blokes who were on the other side."

While F Troop destroyed the guns, B Troop who had fought through the houses and battery buildings, now moved out to set up all round defence for the site and occupied the captured *Kampfstände*.

About 20 metres beyond the flak tower Mills-Roberts, who had gone forward from Group 1's, position encountered Lovat and his adjutant Dunning-White. "I noticed one very light-haired, blue eyed dead German lying staring up at the sky without a sign of violence upon him," wrote Mills-Roberts. "As I turned him over Lovat said, 'Killed by a grenade', and I saw that a fragment had penetrated his back."

The approach march and attack on the battery had been risky and dangerous. Now with the work of destruction complete Lovat gave the orders to No 4 Commando that were fraught with new dangers – they were to withdraw.

Even with good troops unnecessary casualties can be suffered in a badly handled withdrawal and at worst it can become a rout. The enemy is by now aroused and angry and the attackers who have suffered casualties, may be burdened with wounded. Crucially the attacking troops will have lost the rush of adrenaline that carried them through the assault.

The Commandos would have to make their way through the woods, down the gully, through the gap in the barbed wire and then across a beach now exposed at low tide.

Between them and the LCAs lying offshore were enemy snipers lurking in the woods, patrols making their way towards the battery site and the fighters and bombers of the *Luftwaffe* now in full cry. Operation CAULDRON had so far been a complete success. If the withdrawal did not go to plan, in less than an hour the whole thing could unravel.

Notes

1 The 27 mm *Leuchtpistole* – Light Pistol was a smooth bore single shot signal pistol that was used to fire illumination, smoke and even small HE rounds. It could be fitted with a 23 mm barrel liner and shoulder stock to improve accuracy when firing HE rounds. *Das Heer* (the German Army) made extensive use of signal flares for identification and to call for fire from supporting weapons.

2 At Omaha Beach on D Day June 6, 1944 the Deputy Commander of the US Army's 29th Division, Brigadier General Norman Cota, who like Lovat had favoured a landing before first light, summed up the situation to the GIs lying on the sand. "There are two types of men on this beach, those who are dead and those who are going to die." He then gathered together a scratch force of soldiers and led them off the beach. He chose the Rangers of the 5th Battalion, led by Lieutenant Colonel Max Schneider, to make a way through the murderous fire with the command, "Rangers, lead the way off this beach!"

   The order has become the familiar unit motto, "Rangers lead the way."

3 Returned To Unit (RTU) remains the ultimate ignominy for any Special Forces volunteer, as effective today as a way of maintaining standards and enforcing discipline as it was in 1942. John Skerry recalled that in Scotland he had escorted men from No 4 Commando to the tough Barlinnie gaol in Glasgow to do a stint of 28 days in the cells, a punishment they were happy to accept, rather than suffer the shame of being RTU'd.

4 Douglas Havoc II night fighter/intruder
   Type: Light bomber, three crew
   Power plant: two 1193.12kW (1,600 hp) Wright R-2600-11
   Performance: maximum speed at 3,658 m (12,000 ft) 563 kmh (350 mph)
   cruising speed 447 kmh (278 mph)
   maximum range 3,700 km (2,300 miles)
   service ceiling 8,717 m (28,600 ft)
   Weights: empty 6,727 kg (14,830 lbs)
   loaded 10,795 kg (23,800 lbs)
   Dimensions: wing span 18.69 m (61 ft 4 in)
   length 14.63 m (48 ft 0 in)
   height 5.51 m (18 ft 1 in)

Armament: two fixed .50 in nose guns, .5 in upper gun, twin rearward firing .30 in guns in engine nacelles. Max bomb load 1,179 kg (2,600 lbs)

Though Havocs operated over Dieppe during JUBILEE the German may have been killed by the Spitfires that strafed the battery.

5   Captain Pat Porteous the fair haired 24 year old Royal Artillery officer in No 4 Commando had been tasked with liaison between the two Troops in Group 2. The description of Porteous as a "liaison officer" probably disguised his real role as a back up Troop commander in the event of casualties in B or F Troop. He was familiar with the tasks of both troops and given the strict limit on numbers Lovat would not have spared space or manpower for the luxury of a liaison officer.

Though No 4 Commando had trained and prepared for the eventuality of casualties during Operation CAULDRON it was less brutal to describe the spare officer, NCOs and soldiers as a "liaison group" than as "Battle Casualty Replacements". During the Gulf War of 1990-91 British Battle Casualty Replacements were designated "In Theatre Reinforcements".

6   Long after Operation CAULDRON was over, Porteous, now a Major, was accosted by a crusty senior officer who had glimpsed the single maroon ribbon of the VC on the young Royal Artillery officer's tunic. He failed to notice that it did not have two narrow white bars of the Long Service and Good Conduct Medal, awarded to soldiers who had served for 18 years, and assuming it to be the GCM he growled at the young officer,

"You're an impostor. You're too young to have been awarded that decoration".

"Appearances can be misleading" came the ironic and modest reply.

7   Limpet Mk 2

The Limpet Mine was a demolition charge that consisted of 0.9 kg (2 lb) of Plastic Explosives in a cylindrical brass container 20.9 mm (8½ in) by 6.35 mm (2½ in). It could be fixed to a steel target with three rubber mounted U-shaped magnets on either side of the container that were flexible enough to allow it to be attached to uneven surfaces. A set delay for the fuse was activated after a butterfly nut at the end of the charge had been screwed home, breaking the chemical ampoule. The charge was powerful enough to make a 1.82 metre (6ft) hole in the hull of a merchant ship.

CHAPTER 8

Withdrawal

As the men of No 4 Commando prepared to withdraw, above the crackle of burning buildings and exploding small arms ammunition, they heard the sound of fast approaching aircraft. Suddenly a formation of German Me Bf 109[1] fighters roared low over the battery

Lovat raised his arm and waved at them in what he later recalled was, "a debonair, wholly half-witted gesture". To the German *Jagdflieger* – fighter pilots, the obvious confidence of the men below in the battered coastal artillery position indicated that it must still be in friendly hands.

"Looking back," said Lovat, "I suppose it was the right thing to do."

Mills-Roberts noted, "From the air most troops look alike and so instead of taking cover we waved genially to them, receiving in return a reassuring wave from the German Squadron Leader – their interference would have been an embarrassment. They were flying very low, but they did not tumble to the fact that we were not the rightful occupants of the battery."

Union Jack flags were then spread on the ground around the battery to warn Allied fighters not to attack the position. One was run up the flag pole at the villa that was the battery officers' mess. Those Commando dead that could be found and recovered were brought in and laid beside it.

Among the dead who could not be found that morning was Captain

Roger Pettiward OC of F Troop. Long after the war Lovat would recall this troop commander with affection.

"Older and wiser than the rest … Roger had a delightful sense of humour, illustrated by the drawings he sent to *Punch* under the pseudonym of Paul Crum. Not a tidy soldier in the parade-ground sense, he kept his own council as a leader, which is more important. The men admired him greatly and when the red-haired artist fell fighting hand-to-hand in the gun pits at Varengeville, he led one of the best troops in the Commando."

Though some stretchers had been brought ashore from the LCAs and were in the beachhead, doors were removed from buildings and houses to carry the less badly wounded. Four unwounded German prisoners were drafted in as stretcher bearers.

During the operation standing patrols from A Troop were in position on the west, one blocked access along a track from the lighthouse, the other on a road junction a short distance to the south.

Also on the right flank were the fighting patrol from A Troop commanded by the tall moustachioed Lt Veasey who had landed at Orange Beach 2. After the short action on the beach they had come under sporadic sniper fire as they moved inland through the woods near Ste Marguerite. About ninety minutes after landing they were in position covering the cross roads and junction at Haut de Blancmesnil

Here they could intercept any enemy patrols from a company believed to be billeted in Ste Marguerite and Quiberville on the other side of the River Saâne.

Veasey's patrol could hear the noise of the fight but no enemy reinforcements came up the road from Ste Marguerite. As the firing died down the officer checked his watch, looked at it again and realised that, unwound from the previous evening, it had stopped. He guessed that about two and a quarter hours had passed since the landing and ordered his section to close in from their positions.

There was a strict timetable for the withdrawal and troops arriving late at Orange Beach 1 would find the LCAs gone. He was about to order his patrol to withdraw when Pte G. Kendall spotted an enemy patrol working its way cautiously up the road from Ste Marguerite. The Germans were split into two groups of five, hugging the hedgerows on either side of the road. The Commandos including US Ranger Brady waited until the two lead scouts were within 15 metres, and then opened fire. The first round fired by Kendall from his Thompson passed through one German soldier and the big .45 rounds killed a second behind him and wounded others. Under fire from this unseen enemy the German patrol withdrew rapidly down the hill to the village. Afterwards Lovat described the action robustly saying the section, "let the patrol come through and then shot 'em up the arse".

"The enemy was thrown into confusion and beat a hasty retreat," wrote Veasey, "I took advantage of the confusion and withdrew with all possible speed across country back to Orange 1." He had lost four men in the initial landing, but suffered only two men slightly wounded in the subsequent action.

Adopting the slightly didactic tone of a tactics instructor Martin Lindsay in *Notes from Theatres of War* observes; "As an example of bad training, it is worthy of note that the enemy advanced points were too close together, and that the shot that sprang the ambush passed through the bodies of the two leading Germans."

In *Dieppe 1942 The Jubilee Disaster* Ronald Atkin records yet another version of the "egg story". An elderly Frenchwoman who had witnessed that ambush presented each man with a newly laid egg. She explained it was "for their breakfast" and miraculously some of the Commandos were said to have brought many of the eggs back to England intact. Sapper K. Kennet in the patrol remembered the locals emerging from their homes wondering what was going on and offering food. "They told us they thought we were starving in Britain".

Boucher-Myers has a slightly different story. In it a man cycling with eggs to market who was surprised by the men of A Troop at the crossroads, tumbled off his bicycle and, "I am afraid he lost his eggs".

This may have been the man described in Smith's report as, "A French civilian (who) came across our troops West of LE HAUT village. At first he imagined us to be German and he was very enthusiastic indeed when he discovered we were British. He said he was a greengrocer from Ste Marguerite on his way into market in DIEPPE. The Fighting French personnel with our troops believed him to be genuine. He gave the following information:-

a) A Bty of 75mm guns had moved into Ste MARGUERITE 15 days previously. He thought there were only two guns, although there seemed to be as many men there as there were at the VALENGEVILLE (sic) Bty.

b) There were 80 Germans in the lighthouse (confirming gardener's statement)

c) That "people say" there are Germans in QUIBERVILLE.

d) There was a camp about 2 km inland that held about 200 Germans "as a reserve"."

As Veasey moved back he met the other section of A Troop under Boucher-Myers that had moved to cover the right flank. They occupied two crossroads for forty minutes. Small arms fire had damaged the radio and being out of direct contact Boucher-Myers decided that they should withdraw since he reckoned the demolition of the battery was now complete.

For Szima on flank guard duty there was a heart-stopping moment as, his ears still singing in the aftermath of the fire fight, he heard the sound of a man approaching cautiously on the other side of a wall. He motioned to the Commando with him to remain silent.

"A seasoned Commando would have thrown a grenade because all our people had vacated the area. I shouldered the weapon (M1 Garand) … the door opened … and Koons was never closer to death in his life." Szima ordered the Corporal to join the main party pulling back to the beach.

Koons' close brush with death may have been the result of his earlier encounter with the family of Raymond Boulier. When the battery was secure, accompanied by Corporal Baloche, he appears to have gone forward into le Mesnil. Cadot has identified the site of the encounter as a building in the southwest corner of the hamlet, where the French Commando explained to a family that Koons was an American. Koons' foray was not only a significant propaganda gesture it had some intelligence value since he collected papers and pay books from the German dead.

Szima and Corporal Jessop pulled back and covered the road with a Boys anti-tank rifle. Roughly where their previous position had been a truck pulled up and a German soldier dismounted and looked carefully around. Szima whispered;

"'If they get back in the truck and come this way we'll fire.' Which is exactly what happened. The muzzle blast of the .55 set up a cloud of dust and I stood up and unloaded eight rounds at the truck with soldiers going over the side. Ran over to the gunner ... grabbed the gun ... started running and he decided to pass me on the left ... an impossible move, because we both went down and we started to receive rifle fire."

The curves in the road gave them cover from the fire of the pursuing Germans and when they reached the C Troop perimeter they heard the challenge "Monkey" remembered the correct response "Nuts".

A Section from C Troop under Lt David Style, moved through the woods to the east to cover the minor road from Varengeville that ran past the Parc Floral des Moutiers directly to the coast. In earlier fighting Style had been hit in the leg but insisted that he was fit enough to continue.

Before they pulled back to the beachhead Style's Section destroyed a wooden footbridge across a small minefield laid to block access from Port des Moutiers to the gully leading to the beach.

On the beach Sedgwick and his Phantom signals detachment reported to General Roberts aboard HMS *Calpe*, Lord Mountbatten with the Combined Operations HQ and the Phantom Rear HQ.

0735 0730 hrs. 4 Commando withdrawal delayed. Information later.
0745 Will advise when embarking. Identify now. Identify [This was a provision against any enemy attempt to break in on a British net].

Back at the battery Lovat was standing near Gilchrist and the young officer recalled that,

"Lovat's next words brought me to my feet.

'Set them on fire', he ordered, with a gesture at the surrounding buildings. 'Burn the lot'.

Not the words of a commanding officer in the British Army. They were the order of a Highland Chief bent on the total destruction of the enemy."

Porteous recalled that the demolition teams from F Troop left a Bangalore torpedo with a time fuse in one of the ammunition bunkers. It exploded when the LCAs were offshore and convinced the Germans that the battery position had been booby trapped.

There were survivors among the men of the Battery, Colonel General Zeitzler,[2] the Chief of the General Staff of the *Oberkommando des Herres* (OKH) the Army High Command reported that, "A telephone operator defended his blockhouse until the arrival of reinforcements, and is now in hospital, seriously wounded".

At Vasterival after a strict warning from his mother to take no risks Cadot, and his father crept out to see what was happening. From behind a hedge they watched as the LCAs moved up to the shore, fifteen minutes later the first Commandos appeared. Their camouflaged faces, knit caps and the silence of their rubber soled boots remained a vivid memory for the young French man.

The walking wounded were being supported by their comrades and to Cadot the radio operators appeared heavily laden. Mills-Roberts had informed Lovat that the road was a secure route for withdrawal. Though there was some sniping it would be quicker than pushing through the overgrown woods. Cadot guessed that about one hundred men passed and after a delay, another fifty with four German prisoners carrying two British casualties on doors.

Bill Portman remembers that at the top of the gully one of the Germans attempted to escape, running towards the woods. "He was a BF (bloody fool) if he'd stayed quiet he would have been brought back to Blighty and would have been a prisoner." The reflex reactions of the Commandos were quick and deadly they turned and fired and "He was riddled".

Spearman who was an NCO with F Troop goes further and asserts that prisoners were tied and escorted to the beach, where, because there was insufficient space on the LCAs they were shot. This interview, in the Imperial War Museum collection, is quoted by John Parker in his book *Commandos*.

However the interview contains numerous inconsistencies. In an earlier section Spearman and another Commando Bernard Davies described the Boulogne raid and claimed that one of three LCAs under tow capsized and, "I reckon about 30 men died".

No 4 Commando had suffered two casualties during an earlier training exercise involving towing LCAs off the English coast but there were certainly no accidents or casualties of this magnitude during the raid.

Spearman also says, they attempted to breach the wire at Orange Beach 2 with Bangalore torpedoes, when they failed to explode wire mesh mats were used to cross the barbed wire. All other accounts, including the orders, state that the mesh mats were used – Bangalore torpedoes would have been kept for breaking into the HESS position.

At HESS he says that the fighting on the battery site took place in darkness, there was smoke, but by 06.30 hours in August it is daylight.

Spearman claims the prisoners were tied by the thumbs, which fits with the instructions for prisoner handling in the CAULDRON orders. However secured like this they would have been unable to climb through the gap in the barbed wire and down the gully to the beach without falling or becoming trapped in the wire. And any such efforts would have been noticed and remembered by other Commandos.

There was no shortage of space on landing craft since Mulleneux had requested three extra LCAs to be sent to the beachhead from the boat pool off Dieppe. Moreover casualties among the Commando and the stores and equipment expended during the operation left ample space.

"Men embarked in these craft were later transferred to our own, whilst casualties were transferred to a destroyer." Mulleneux notes "The Commandos had collected three German prisoners, one of which was put in LCA 5, which was commanded by a Polish officer. Apparently this prisoner's main effort at conversation consisted of frantic denials of having anything to do with the fighting in Poland."

Austin unaware that extra LCAs had been added to the flotilla recalled "For some reason that none of us could explain, there was no overcrowding in the boats coming back, though not a great many had been left behind."

Boucher-Myers interviewed by the IWM was asked about the prisoners and stated, "There was always plenty of space on the boats, so we never had a problem with prisoners... The prisoners we had taken in the battery were simply taken off without any problem of fitting them in." He suggested Hitler's reaction to Commando operations and the report that prisoners had been tied and shot during a raid on the Channel Islands was what prompted the notorious "Commando Order".[3]

Clifford Leach with F Troop dismisses the suggestion that prisoners were shot as, "rubbish as far as our particular Commando was concerned. No, pure propaganda. We just took three or four prisoners for interrogation".

Hughie Lindley remembers that as the force withdrew through the C Troop perimeter, "they brought the two or three prisoners with them."

Finally Cadot who watched the evacuation recalls seeing only four prisoners, though albeit not the fatal escape attempt.[4]

It took some time to get the wounded through the gap in the wire in the gully, which, though it had been blasted apart by Bangalore torpedoes, to Lovat's irritation had not been widened with wire cutters by the troops who had held the Orange Beach 1 beachhead. The criticism may have been harsh, they had been busy carrying ammunition and smoke generators up the gully as well messages down to the signallers and had cleared the AP mines.

On the road down to the beach Mills-Roberts watched walking wounded and stretcher cases making their way to the beach. "One man, Sergeant Watkins, was lying on a stretcher. He had been shot in the stomach. His face looked grotesquely ill beneath its covering of camouflage paint, but he was quite cheerful. He asked how the battle had gone and told me that he was all right – the stretcher-bearer silently shook his head." Sgt S. Watkins was safely evacuated to Britain and survived.

The "stretcher" on which he was being carried may in fact have been the door of Mme Bertin's outside lavatory that had been removed by the Commandos.

Kennett did not use a stretcher to carry the exhausted TSM Williams across the beach to the LCAs. He hoisted him on his shoulders. "I was lucky to be able to carry Charley on my back on the way down to the boats to get off. He was bleeding very profusely from his chest, he was in a bad way, but I got him back onto a landing craft and onto a destroyer."

The elderly gentleman who had been disturbed by Group 1 crashing through his vegetable garden now appeared dressed in formal black morning coat and striped trousers and saying goodbye offered Mills-Roberts a glass of wine. He in turn apologised for the damage to the Frenchman's garden, "He and his family appeared impressed by the destruction of the battery, but they were obviously nervous. They no doubt felt that they were still under unseen Nazi observation, which would make trouble when we had departed".

By the time the re-embarkation began at 07.30 hours the LCAs had been waiting in position off Orange Beach 1 for three-quarters of an hour. It was a sheltered area in the lee of the wooded headland where they were only troubled by the occasional sniper. Shells exploded on the beach about 500 metres to the west but they were probably from guns firing blind on what the Germans presumed to be an evacuation beach. Off to the flank a 2 cm Flak gun had been brought up probably from the lighthouse battery it only fired a few bursts before it had a stoppage.

Szima recalled seeing a man watching them through binoculars near the lighthouse. The observer's relaxed demeanour did not suggest that he was a German. "I had no reason to not consider him friendly or it would have been easy to put his lights out, the range was under 150 yards."

The chief worry for the coxswains of the LCAs was the shallow beach. There is a considerable difference between high and low water in the Channel even more marked on a flat beach. To make matters worse the tide was ebbing and the LCAs ran the risk of grounding. The solution was for the Commandos to wade out to the landing craft. This they did in some cases up to their necks.

The German prisoners carrying Porteous also found themselves up to their necks in the sea before they reached an LCA and Porteous recalled "they needed a little encouragement with the bayonet".

The prisoners had already negotiated the top of the gully which Porteous recalled they "didn't like ..at all because they had laid all the mines there and they weren't quite sure where they were".

For Mulleneux, the crew of one of the Goatley boats that was helping in these operations, "provided comic relief being paddled around by a small bucolic Commando clad solely in a Mae West and woolly hat."

This relative tranquillity contrasted with the earlier experiences of the LCAs and LCS off Orange Beach 2. Here reported Mulleneux, "a large volume of enemy fire was drawn which was fairly successfully dodged, and replied to when the source of fire was seen.

"The largest weapon which troubled the landing craft in the early stages was a mortar or howitzer of a calibre of 3 to 4 inches, which was situated just over the high ground to the eastward of Orange Two Beach. A light flak battery and several machine gun posts were also situated in this area which was fairly well plastered by the Oerlikon in the LCS."

The LCS and LCAs 3 and 4 remained off Orange Beach 2 and Mulleneux assessed that they were fired on by rifles and machine guns, a larger .50 inch weapon, light Flak that he compared with the 20 mm Oerlikon. Finally he noted three salvoes of what looked like 4-inch HE that landed at the beach below the lighthouse during the final re-embarkation. Though landing craft were hit, some up to twenty times, none was seriously damaged. Three ratings in the flotilla were wounded.

A wooded headland screened the light Flak battery by the lighthouse from Orange Beach 1 which Mulleneux remembered as a haven.

At 06.10 hours Mulleneux had paid a final visit to Orange Beach 2 "except for once again coming under fire and getting 'near missed' by the mortar or howitzer, saw no activity on the beach or road."

It was on the return trip that he had mistakenly opened fire on the walking wounded making their way along to Orange Beach 1.

As the withdrawal got under way the German 8.1-cm Mortar probably firing blind at the map reference of the two gullies began to drop bombs in the area. The Commando's 3-inch Mortar crew under

Lt Ennis and Cpl J. Nankivell had trained for just this situation but most were busy carrying ammunition back down to the beach. A makeshift crew was scratched together. Ennis grabbed Austin and said:

"Hey, would you mind?" showing him how to unscrew the safety caps on the fuses and prepare the bombs for firing. The IO joined the crew firing at the enemy mortar and a machine gun position at the lighthouse and even a single soldier sniping at the beach.

The shoot against the enemy 8.1-cm Mortar required some quick calculations of the trajectory and bearing of the base plate. That against the lighthouse was an observed shoot. Pte John Price who had landed laden with four 3-inch bombs in a carrier on his chest and four on his back, as well as a haversack with grenades and a Colt .45 pistol, recalled. "There was a sniper and we eventually got him by firing a 3-inch Mortar bomb at the cliff face and he came down along with it."

With the shoot over Austin returned to the beach and, "looked up to see Lord Lovat sitting against a rock beside me. He was bubbling with happiness. 'By God, we did the job all right', he said. 'Went straight in with the bayonet. Cut them to shreds. Not a man left. How glad I wasn't in that battery. But they fought hard'".

At 07.30 hours the men of A Troop passed through the C Troop perimeter around the beachhead, B and F Troop followed. C Troop and the 3-inch Mortar crew forming the rear guard were the last to withdraw at 08.15 hours.

Following a frequently rehearsed drill pairs of Bren gunners had leap frogged back ready to give covering fire should the Germans attempt to counter attack. At the top of the gully were haversacks of Smoke Generators that had been dumped early in the landing. The rear party ignited these to build up a thick grey smoke screen.

Smoke would play an important part in the last phases of Operation CAULDRON. It would blind any enemy forces trying to observe the beach and cover the movements of the landing craft and Commandos.

Lovat waited until two thirds of his force were on board the LCAs and as the volume of enemy fire increased and a mortar bomb exploded on the edge of the cliff turned Austin and said:

"Getting a bit hot. I'm going aboard." Accompanied by Austin the tall Scots chieftain strolled out across the beach until he was up to his knees in the sea and shouted cheerfully to an LCA coxswain, "Come in here, why should I get my knees wet?". It was too shallow and like the rest of his men Lovat had to wade deeper.

Down on the beach the Phantom signallers had transmitted a terse message

> "0800 0744 hrs. Half embarked. Remainder follow. Will open up in boat."

On the beach the Commandos doubled across the shingle, sand and rock pools through a lane of smoke 200 metres wide streaming from pre-positioned No 18 generators. The crews of the landing craft had extended the lane for a further 50 metres with Mk VI smoke floats. Two of the big floats had been landed on the beach others anchored to the west and each landing craft had two floats fixed to its aft deck. After the operation was over the censor, unsure about the function of this drum on the landing craft, deleted them from photographs.

The plan for Operation CAULDRON had seen smoke used both aggressively and defensively. The battery had been blinded by 2-inch and 3-inch Mortar fire and now the smoke generators screened the beach. However smoke can be a two edged weapon. Szima remembered, "we walked until the water was chest high before clearing the smoke ... wondering all along that we might be going parallel to the beach."

Mulleneux was pleased with the way the coxswains of his little flotilla handled their craft on the shallow beach in a fast ebbing tide. Only two craft suffered slight damage to their propeller shafts, LCA 3 grounded on a sandbank and LCA5 grazed a rock while dropping off smoke floats.

When a landing craft was full the coxswains moved to a position about four kilometres offshore and joined MGB 312. It was a slightly hazardous trip since as soon as an LCA emerged from the cover of the wooded headland it came under fire from Flak, machine guns and riflemen near the lighthouse. This continued for a range of about three kilometres. The Commandos on the LCAs returned the fire with rifles and Bren guns.

As the C Troop Bren Gun teams dashed across the beach from the gully, it was obvious that this was the final perimeter defence withdrawing and it was now or never for the men on the beach.

Jones wading out to the LCAs, with his Bren gun held above his head, stumbled into a submerged hollow and dropped the LMG. As he desperately struggled to recover the weapon from the murky water "diving like a duck" he was spotted by Lovat who shouted,

"What are you doing there Jones?"

"Trying to get my Bren."

"Bloody leave it there and go on."

The startled, but relieved Jones eventually had to swim to an LCA, relieved that he was not responsible for the loss of a weapon that in other circumstances would have been a court martial offence.

Szima remembered that by the time an LCA appeared, he was "nose deep" in the water. It was the last LCA to leave Orange Beach 1. Earlier skippers had reassured the waiting men, "All along, they kept repeating 'There'll be another one coming' ".

Aboard an LCA Jones wet and exhausted collapsed at the bottom of the craft on decks that were awash with six inches of seawater.

Recalling the aftermath of the action Lovat wrote, "After standing down, the battle over, some men shake; others turn to stone. One thought blurs the mind: a vast relief steals over the senses, transcending conscious feeling. 'It's over.' In a detached way I felt neither pleased nor sorry to have destroyed the enemy. The sense of elation, a grasp of victory, hunger or thirst, and physical fatigue – these came later. So we returned to England – each to his thoughts, wrapped in a dream."

For Private Michael Faille and Private Paul J Karesa the two radio operators from The South Saskatchewan Rgt the return journey was an agony. As they moved away from the shore they could hear the transmissions from their regimental call signs. They could recognise the voices of the men on the net.

The after action report records:

"The last we heard from them was a burst of M.G. (machine gun) fire at about 1030 hrs."

The South Saskatchewans and Camerons had landed at Green Beach, Pourville with 1,026 officers and men. By the end of the day they had lost 685 killed, captured and wounded. More than 65 per cent of their strength.

The terse reports about Operation CAULDRON in the Phantom Radio Log told a happier story:

> 0840 0835 hrs. Now in MGB with OC 4 Commando and wounded men offshore one mile.
>
> 0859 To CCO from OC 4 Commando. Everyone of gun crews finished with bayonet.

Operation CAULDRON had been successfully completed the men of No 4 Commando were now required to be available as reinforcements for JUBILEE, the larger operation at Dieppe. Within CAULDRON Force only the two Canadian radio operators had an idea that the bigger operation was going horribly wrong.

Notes

1   Messerschmitt BF 109 G "Gustav"
    Type: Single-seat interceptor fighter
    Power plant: One 1099.9kW (1,475 hp) Daimler-Benz DB 605A
    Performance: maximum speed at sea level 510 km/h (317 mph)
    maximum speed 653 km/h (406 mph)
    maximum range 850 km (528 miles)
    service ceiling 12,000 m (39,370 ft)
    Weights: empty 2,253 kg (4,968 lb)
    loaded 3,200 kg (7,055 lb)
    Dimensions: wing span 9.92 m (32 ft 6½ ins)
    length 8.85 m (29 ft 0½ ins)
    height 2.50 m (8ft 2½ ins)
    Armament: one 20 mm MG 151/20 cannon firing through the propeller hub and two 7.92 mm MG 17 machine guns in the upper cowling.

    The fighters were probably from the newly operational 11th *Staffel* (Squadron) of JG 26.

2   Kurt, Zeitzler was a professional soldier whose career would change dramatically after the German victory at Dieppe.
    He had served in the infantry in World War I and as an energetic officer enjoyed

the nickname "Lightning Ball". By 1942 he was a Major General and Chief-of-Staff of Army Group D. Hitler promoted him over the heads of more senior officers to Chief-of-Staff of the OKH in September 1942 because he believed that he had been responsible for the successful defensive plans at Dieppe.

Zeitzler held this post until the Bomb Plot in July 1944. During this time he made a futile effort to convince Hitler that it was necessary to withdraw to stronger positions on the Eastern Front. Hitler refused to accept this advice and Zeitzler then adopted a novel form of resistance. He reported sick and ceased to carry out his duties. He was dismissed in July 1944 and retired from the Army on January 31, 1945. Zeitzler was released from British captivity in 1947 and died at Hohenaschau (Upper Bavaria) on September 25, 1963.

3   This was Operation BASALT, a raid mounted on Sark on October 3/4, 1942 by men of the Small Scale Raiding Force (SSRF).

There were numerous probes by Commando forces against the Channel Islands, but Operation BASALT, undertaken by seven men of the SSRF and five from No 12 Commando led by Captain Geoffrey Appleyard and the Dane Lieutenant Anders Lassen may have prompted the Commando Order. In Peter King's *The Channel Islands War 1940-1945* he explains that five prisoners from a German engineer detachment were captured in bed in the Discart Hotel on Sark. With their trousers around their ankles they were bound with the Commando's toggle ropes. (Six foot long with a wooden toggle spliced in at one end and an eye at the other. They were used for climbing cliffs or building simple rope bridges). Despite these restraints a running fight developed. Two Germans escaped, though one of them was wounded and two soldiers, Esslinger and Bleyer were killed.

Inflamed by this news on October 18 Hitler issued the secret *Kommandobefehl* – The Commando Order.

Der Führer   SECRET
No. 003830/42g.Kdos.OKW/Wst F.H. Qu 18.10.1942
12 Copies
Copy No.12

1. For a long time now our opponents have been employing in their conduct of the war, methods which contravene the International Convention of Geneva. The members of the so-called Commandos behave in a particularly brutal and underhand manner; and it has been established that those units recruit criminals not only from their own country but even former convicts set free in enemy territories. From captured orders it emerges that they are instructed not only to tie up prisoners, but also to kill out-of-hand unarmed captives who they think might prove an encumbrance to them, or hinder them in successfully

carrying out their aims. Orders have indeed been found in which the killing of prisoners has positively been demanded of them.

2. In this connection it has already been notified in an Appendix to Army Orders of 7.10.1942 that in future, Germany will adopt the same methods against these Sabotage units of the British and their Allies; i.e. that, whenever they may appear, they shall be ruthlessly destroyed by the German troops.

3. I order, therefore:-

From now on all men operating against German troops in so-called Commando raids in Europe and Africa, are to be annihilated to the last man. This is to be carried out whether they be soldiers in uniform, or saboteurs, with or without arms; and whether fighting or seeking to escape; and it is equally immaterial whether they come into action from Ships or Aircraft, or whether they land by parachute. Even if these individuals on discovery make obvious their intention of giving themselves up as prisoners, no pardon is on any account to be given. On this matter a report is to be made in each case to Headquarters for the information of Higher Command.

4. Should individual members of these Commandos, such as agents, saboteurs, etc., fall into the hands of the *Wehrmacht* through any other means – as, for example, through the Police in one of the Occupied Territories – they are to be instantly handed over to the SD.

To hold them in military custody – for example in POW camps etc., – even as a temporary measure, is strictly forbidden.

5. This order does not apply to the treatment of those enemy soldiers who are taken prisoner or give themselves up in battle, in the course of normal operations, large scale attacks; or in major assault landings or airborne operations. Neither does it apply to those who fall into our hands after a sea fight, nor to those enemy soldiers who, after air battle, seek to save themselves by parachute.

6. I will hold all Commanders and Officers responsible under Military Law for any omission to carry out this order, whether by failure in their duty to instruct their units accordingly, or if they themselves act contrary to it.

(Sgd) *Adolf Hitler*

Ten days passed in discussion among lawyers and staff and security officers of the *Oberkommando der Wehrmachtführungsstab,* the German Armed Forces High Command Operations Staff (OKW) before it was endorsed by Colonel General Alfred Jodl the chief of the OKW. He added the caveat that "This order is intended for Commandos only and is in no circumstances to fall into Enemy hands". The orders would be the death warrant for many of the men of the Commandos and SAS captured in France and Italy between 1942 and 1945.

At the Nuremberg trial in 1945 Jodl said of the *Kommandobefehl* "it was one of the few – or the only – order I received from the Führer which I, in my own mind, completely rejected".

4 *Hitler's Revenge* Chapter Eight of *Commandos* by John Parker reads "it was alleged in the Berlin newspapers that a number of German soldiers found dead on the beaches at Dieppe had their hands tied behind their backs. It was further claimed that some had been shot in the head. The story got around that this was the result of cold-blooded executions by Lovat's No.4 Commando whose men, it was said, had been instructed not to take prisoners."

Since 1933 German newspapers had been an instrument of political propaganda under the strict control of Dr Joseph Goebbels the *Reichsminister für Volkserklärung und Propaganda* (Reich Minister for Public Enlightenment and Propaganda) and were not a source of accurate news. Even in wartime the British and American press, under far less restrictions than the German, were capable of exaggeration and inaccuracies in their reporting of the Dieppe operation.

Parker quotes Porteous, "There were no prisoners taken in the main part of the Dieppe raid as far as I know; they were too busy saving themselves. We had three or four prisoners on our part of the operation, and they came with us, carried me in fact, and certainly did not have their hands tied. But it (the captured Canadian orders) was of course wonderful ammunition for Hitler, who then kept all the prisoners from Dieppe in shackles for the next six months or so."

Parker dismisses Porteous' recollections writing that he "had been severely wounded (and) ... may not have been fully aware of exactly what was happening around him". Porteous may have collapsed from loss of blood, but had not lost consciousness as is shown in his detailed account of the operation and his subsequent evacuation recorded by the IWM.

Spearman quoted from the IWM interview in the book says, "Lovat called me over with another fellow, Percy Tombs, and asked us to find the safest route but because we had prisoners to take with us and we had wounded to carry. We'd be slowed down by walking wounded and stretcher wounded; people were carried on made up bits of wood. Percy Tombs and I found the best route, and we all made our way back on to the beach to look for the boats."

For an operation that had been carefully planned and rehearsed this seems very haphazard. At about this point Mills-Roberts was in radio communication with Lovat and had stated that the road was clear and that he was coming up it to the battery with the MO.

In his account Spearman uses the evasive language that the American author and historian Stephen Ambrose has identified. In essence the US soldiers recorded by Ambrose for *Citizen Soldiers*, discussing the shooting of prisoners are understandably defensive and say, "Yes it happened but I didn't do it" though some then go on to say that they witnessed it.

Spearman says "There came a point when it was realised there were too many people to get in the available boats. And because there were too many people, a decision had to be made as to what to do with the prisoners. I wasn't, of course, involved in any of this decision-making. I was just a bod there on the beach. But what happened in the event was that they decided the only thing they could do was to shoot some of the prisoners…

Because we were limited with the boats, there were too many (prisoners) and they had to be shot. And they were shot and they were left on the beach. This was unfortunate because there was no way that any of us enjoyed shooting prisoners. I mean, it's not in the nature of an Englishman to do that. Even though the Germans and the Japanese did some terrible things, I don't think that anybody would enjoy shooting a prisoner, especially people like us, because we weren't fighting because we were killers, we were just fighting to complete an operation".

Circumstantial evidence as well as the memories of many of the participants in the raid suggest that there was enough space on the boats for prisoners and no orders were given on the beach to shoot prisoners who had been tied up by the thumbs.

Mills-Roberts noted, "Several of our more badly wounded men had been left to surrender, in the care of a medical orderly," and Lovat, "sadly the dead and dying, with some fine medical orderlies stayed behind in France". Though it is unclear in these accounts whether these were the men on Orange Beach 2, Szima remembers wounded men on Orange Beach 1 when he withdrew. He was convinced that they could have been carried to the LCAs but Mills-Roberts asserts:

"These were the cases where the movement of a sea passage would have meant inevitable death and an enemy hospital was the only alternative. The medical orderlies knew before the raid began that in certain circumstances some of their number would have to remain in this way to look after the wounded and plans had been made accordingly."

If orderlies and Commando wounded were left on the beach, it was tantamount to signing their death warrant to shoot prisoners and leave their bound bodies only a few hundred metres away.

Significantly the detailed and analytical after action report by Haase the CO 302nd Inf Div gives the numbers of killed and wounded in the No 813 Battery position and states:

"It was probably 08.00 hours when the British Commandos re-embarked, taking with them 4 prisoners."

Further up the chain of command Zeitzler, reported that the battery had suffered "30 dead, 21 wounded who were got away, amongst them the Commander of the battery seriously wounded, and up to now 10 missing, the greater part of whom were presumably brought to safety by the troops. It seems two of the men of the battery were taken prisoner, but it is doubtful whether they were taken on board the enemy's ships".

Neither of the officers makes any reference to German prisoners being shot, or to the discovery of bodies of men with their hands tied.

Even if Spearman's statement is taken as true, it still begs many questions.

Who said the boats were overcrowded and gave the order to shoot the prisoners?

How many prisoners were shot?

Were they shot inland or on the beach by the cliffs? If inland how did Spearman or others know that the boats, that were several hundreds of metres away shrouded in smoke, were overcrowded?

If out on the open beach, even allowing for the smoke screen, why was the shooting not witnessed and remembered by other Commandos?

Spearman is the only person in any account who asserts that three or four German prisoners made their way to the beach. Where did the other PoWs he asserts were shot come from?

One can only surmise why these assertions were made in the interview.

Spearman may have wanted to tell a dramatic tale to shock or impress the interviewer.

He or others may have shot Germans in the heat of action attempting to surrender or who had surrendered among the buildings in the battery position. There was no question that in Lord Lovat's words the fight had been "a rough party".

It is however typical of a revisionist approach to history to take a specific and from it draw a general conclusion. War is full of stories of men who, in the immediate aftermath of fighting, angry and on edge after seeing friends killed and wounded, have shot prisoners. If Spearman witnessed this, it does not mean it was done on the basis of a general instruction to No 4 Commando, nor that it was a policy of taking no prisoners by Commandos.

CHAPTER 9

Homecoming

The LCAs carrying the Commando moved off towards the larger force standing off Dieppe. Mulleneux who had transferred to MGB 312 led the flotilla and observing the destroyers and landing craft felt "from a distance (they) looked more like a regatta day at Cowes than part of a warlike operation".

In the morning sunshine aboard an LCA, Austin felt a tap on his shoulder and a voice asking hesitantly:

"Vous correspondent? Parlez française?"

He initially wondered if the speaker was a French Commando and then realised that he was being addressed by one of the German prisoners. It is likely that the man Austin found himself talking to was the 24 year old *Unteroffizier* Leo Marsiniak. To Austin, he seemed "a little too anxious to ingratiate himself" and revealed that he had been in the army for two years and had a brother on the Eastern Front, "The Russian war" he said "was *schrecklich* (frightful)."

"Later he saw me reading a pamphlet that had been captured, one of those Nazi publications designed to prove that the German race is superior to every other kind of human being. He shook his head at me, made a grimace, and waved his hands palm downwards to show that he did not think much of such stuff.

"One of the prisoners who had been captured in his trousers, braces, socks and one carpet slipper, was a typical old sweat.

"He sat down at the side of the boat, and dozed off. A Commando soldier winked at me.

'We caught him in the cookhouse' he said."

Leach remembered that the German prisoners who had initially been scared, "were quite pleased to be treated as normal human beings, they were offered cigarettes". Austin watched as one of the Commandos found a blanket for the prisoner with no shirt and Germans were passed the water container and a tin of soup.

"The prisoners, he explained, had been caught before breakfast."

The MGB was carrying the more serious casualties and in a merciful flat calm seven of them were transferred to HMS *Calpe*, the Hunt Class destroyer, that festooned with radio antennae, was the floating HQ for General Roberts. It was already full of wounded and Lovat observed afterwards that as the German air attacks increased in intensity, "it was lucky not to be sunk".

During the short journey to the *Calpe* Pte J. Price of F Troop watched the patient tenderness of a Medical Orderly as he worked to sustain life in a wounded Commando on a stretcher in the LCA. The soldier, who would not live to see England, stared up at the sky with glazed eyes.

Even with excellent training, good equipment and a sound plan there would inevitably be casualties in Operation CAULDRON. Lovat's aim had been to fulfil the mission while keeping them to a minimum. Still the young Commando, like soldiers in history before and in conflicts that were as yet undreamed of, looked down at his comrade on the stretcher and found himself wondering.

"Why him, why not me?"

Earlier Austin had watched as two casualties were loaded onto an LCA. "Both were hardly conscious, their lips just moving, the whites of their eyes rolled back. In their filthy uniforms, with the blood still soaking them, and the dirt and sweat of battle on their faces, they looked very different from the hospital wounded we visit and think, 'Looks quite comfortable. Must have been a bit of a shock, but I suppose you soon forget these things' ".

In an annotation at the end of his personal account of CAULDRON Tony Smith the No 4 Commando IO, added in his tidy handwriting.

"Holding dying man's hand."

The Commando remains an unknown warrior, but he was one who did not die alone.

Following CAULDRON the Commandos were to be available as a floating reserve for the larger JUBILEE operation. "We then circled the ship, taking avoiding action for the Luftwaffe were starting to buzz, waiting for General Roberts to give further orders but there was no sign of him." recalled Lovat.

"After what seemed an interminable delay – but probably no more than ten minutes – we were told by an unidentified and hesitant staff officer on the loud hailers "that we might as well go home". A bad order of which I took full advantage."

The hesitancy of the officer was understandable. It was becoming increasingly clear to the HQ staff aboard *Calpe* that the main landings had gone disastrously wrong. Lovat's Commando had arrived alongside the *Calpe* at the exact moment when General Roberts was considering whether to issue the order "Vanquish", the tragically inappropriate code name for the withdrawal from Dieppe.

Among the wounded transferred to the *Calpe* was Pat Porteous. He had been given initial treatment by a medical orderly on the MGB and he recalled:

" The destroyer I was on went on trying to pick up all the awful mess that was going on outside Dieppe, the wounded and landing craft being sunk, absolutely appalling shambles. We were loaded with wounded, we had one bomb very near us from a Junkers. I was on a stretcher in the wardroom and all the lights went out and it was all rather frightening. However it didn't seem to do any serious damage to the destroyer and we eventually returned to Portsmouth at about one o'clock the following morning having started off about 24 hours before."

HMS *Calpe* was fortunate to survive Operation JUBILEE. As the landing craft and warships formed up to begin the return journey, German fighters strafed her bridge causing several casualties including Air Commodore Cole, the senior RAF officer on board. When *Calpe*'s Captain Lt. Cdr J.H. Wallace left the protective AA cover of the convoy to pick up a downed fighter pilot the destroyer was subject to two dive bombing attacks by the Luftwaffe. The ship was damaged and suffered casualties from near misses – it was these attacks that plunged Porteous into darkness.

Meanwhile Mills-Walker recalled that the flotilla of LCAs carrying the Commando, "made its way across the calm, glassy sea through gaps in the mine-fields marked by numbers of small floating platform buoys from which diminutive flags flew."

Mulleneux noted that the first enemy aircraft were seen soon after 06.00 hours. "From then on a large number of FW 190s and Me 109s were seen at all ranges. A few enemy bombs were seen in the distance, but no bombs were dropped on any of our boats. Only one boat, LCA 3, was machine-gunned, but a number of enemy aircraft were engaged and LCA 4 claims to have shot down one Me 109 with her Lewis gun."

With a more literary turn of phrase Austin wrote, "All through the afternoon I watched fighters scribbling their quarrels across the sky." However even he had to admit, "After many hours, even watching one of the most significant air battles of the war palled and we huddled slackly down in the boat, dead tired, filthy-looking, ragged, happy men – happy because we knew the Commandos had made the Battle of Dieppe possible."

Some of the dogfights were fought so close to sea level that Boucher-Myers remembers ejected cannon and machine gun cartridge cases clattering onto the LCA.

Mills-Roberts recalled that after the casualties had been transferred to HMS *Calpe*, "a more light-hearted atmosphere prevailed and we opened tins of self-heating soup – a circular tin with a candle-like substance in the middle. When the wick was lit the soup quickly heated and was excellent."

Though the orders for Operation CAULDRON had stated that troops would not carry water bottles or even rations ashore, some Commandos had been given cheese sandwiches wrapped in greaseproof paper by the crew of HMS *Prince Albert*. Clifford Leach recalled that they now began to eat them along with the French apples picked during the raid.

"The Navy boys produced some self heating tins of soup, they were absolutely delicious. It was a hot day, but I had certainly worked up an appetite for those tins of soup."

Szima was one of about a dozen men who managed to board the MGB using a scramble net from their crowded LCA.

"(I) laid on the deck and found myself staring up at Lovat and a navy person on the bridge. Someone said there was tea downstairs. I found tea, biscuits, a large tin of bully beef and Sgt. Maj. Williams lying bandaged in a bunk." Like many of the men on the raid Szima fell asleep on the return journey.

The flotilla was now moving at about seven knots with LCAs 3 and 5 under tow from MGB 312. "The remaining LCAs and the LCS formed a loose formation on the starboard quarter."

At 09.30 hours a Spitfire crashed into the sea close to the flotilla. "The pilot," observed Mulleneux, "followed down more sedately by parachute; I detached one of the LCAs to pick him up. He was a Canadian, wounded in the shoulder, who had been shot down by a FW 190. Later MGB 312 collected two more fighter pilots, a Canadian and an American, from the ML on duty at the minefield".

Mills-Roberts recalled that it was difficult to tell friend from foe. "Suddenly there was a whine of a plane out of control and we saw a parachutist dropping less than a hundred yards away from us: then down came another plane plunging into the sea near us, and the landing craft behind us turned back and picked up the American pilot almost as he touched the water."

It was a moment captured as a blurry photograph by Langland with the Commando's German Leica and later worked up as a picture by Mullen. The Spitfire pilot was believed to be an American from one of the RAF Eagle Squadrons[1].

"The Yank pilot hit the sea alongside our boat," remembered Gilchrist, "and was hauled aboard by his parachute simultaneously. The commandos sat him down. Somebody stuck a tin of self-heating soup in his hand. The American gazed at it incredulously. A voice enquired, 'How's that for service bud?'"

On Mills-Roberts' LCA a signaller tuned to the BBC Home Service and though reception was poor they heard the report of the success of their part in Operation JUBILEE. The Second-in-Command of the Commando took out his field glasses and looked at the occupants of the other landing craft.

"Most of them seemed to relapsed into a mild coma. I had in my rucksack a paper-backed novel which I had been reading on the ship:

I finished this and then lay down with my head on my rucksack under the gunwale."

Aboard another LCA a Commando looked up at Austin and with a chuckle summarised the two emotions that many of the men had felt during the day:

"God! I've had fun. Scared! I'll never need to use cascara [a powerful laxative] again as long as I live."

In the stern of the craft the small Scots soldier, who had killed the four Germans in the battery, "sat erect, humming to himself and smiling." To Austin "He was the raiding islesman coming home triumphant in his long boat."

At about 11.00 hours the LCA coxswains spotted the distinctive outline of the white chalk cliffs near Newhaven. To Lovat, "the cliffs along the Sussex coast, bathed in sunshine, looked warm and welcoming...'In Sussex by the sea.' How good it looked! Over the red roofs of the town, huddled round the gap in the chalk cliffs, a scatter of fan-tailed pigeons wheeled and tumbled in a happy display of aerobatics."

The LCA crews put on their caps and straightened their uniforms and the exhausted Commandos woke up and gathered their weapons and equipment together.

At their relatively slow speed the flotilla did not reach Newhaven until 17.45 hours where a large silent crowd lined the harbour, but at the sight of the landing craft they broke into cheers that lasted until they tied up alongside the harbour wall.

Austin remembered that after a day of blue skies and summer sunshine, a fine rain was falling and one of the Commando officers, "turning his face up to the wet for a moment, grinned at me and said ironically:

'Back to England.'"

Lovat remembered the, "anxious crowd – civilians, general staff, auxiliary services and ambulance drivers – who lined the harbour wall neither knew our identity nor were aware which side had won; the battle had petered out across the Channel and the assembly gazed down at troops in silence... Time stood still that August evening as boats were made fast below and commando soldiers climbed stiffly up the iron ladders."

Journalists, an official photographer and a film crew were waiting at Newhaven and the pictures capture the moment described by Lovat in his autobiography *March Past*. "The sprinkling of bandaged commandos, patched up on the crossing, climbed nimbly enough on to the dock: for reasons now forgotten, the prisoners had been blindfolded on sight of land." Ironically Marsiniak who wore spectacles was not blindfolded. The prisoners were handed over to the Canadian Forces Provost at the Control Point at Newhaven.

The Commandos clambered ashore with a selection of trophies from the operation, German rifles, steel helmets, caps and amazingly, one man, held the wooden signboard bearing the warning *Achtung Minen!* that had greeted Group 1 at the top of the gully on Orange Beach 1. Along with the prisoners these objects were tangible evidence of the success of the raid.

"Our appearance could not have been reassuring," recalled Lovat. "We were soaked to the skin (men had waded up to the armpits to re-embark), and war-painted faces, streaked with sweat and powder burns, clashed strangely with starched aprons and pretty VADs. The green beret was not yet issued: we raided in stocking caps, few of which remained in place: I lost mine on the wire, early on…

"All identification badges were removed before a raid, but it didn't take long for a whisper to turn into a buzz; then a shout went up, 'It's the commandos, God bless them, and they've knocked out the German guns!'"

Among the Commando assembling on the harbour were the Phantoms signals team. They had donned cap comforters, hooked their helmets over their small packs and blended with the men of No 4 Commando. However though the Commandos had removed the titles from the denim blouses Capt Sedgwick had his Royal Tank Regiment titles and coloured flashes prominent on his shoulders.

The photographer spotted Gunner Len Ruskin of B Troop a young fair hared Commando standing on the deck of an LCA. He was holding his Thompson SMG and smiling slightly nervously, with his denim trousers ripped and one bandaged bare leg exposed from ankle to upper thigh. Lovat remembered the public reaction, "At once a rush of girls found this hero a blanket; blushing, he wound it round his waist into a kilt. Tension immediately relaxed: 'Hasn't he got lovely legs'! chanted the back-slapping crowd."

The sight of a camera caused Heggarty, Szima's battle partner, to duck out of sight. He explained that as a citizen of the Irish Republic serving in the British Army would not be popular at home in Dublin.

Also present on shore, immaculate in service dress, was Brigadier Bob Laycock. He was accompanied by Walter Knickerbocker an American journalist. Before Laycock introduced him to Lovat and Mills-Roberts he warned both officers that there were indications that the Canadians had taken heavy casualties at Dieppe.

"As you'll be questioned by many of the people here, and as we know nothing definite, you'd better be careful what you say." he instructed Mills-Roberts to Lovat. "Go easy with the press. The Canadians have taken losses."[2] However the Commanding officer of No 4 Commando then received crisp instructions "You're for London and Mountbatten: we start immediately".

Lovat and Mills-Roberts remember Knickerbocker as wearing civilian clothes, perhaps the cut and style of his US Army summer weight khaki cotton chino uniform and garrison cap looked like civilian clothes to British eyes.

Both Commando officers showed that they were in modern parlance – media savvy. Lovat introduced Knickerbocker to MacKinnon the senior boat officer "who had landed us with distinction twelve hours before and brought us safely home".

In *Clash by Night* Mills-Roberts describes how he deflected the journalist deftly saying, "I'm sure that he'd prefer to hear the story from one of his own countrymen". Soon the American journalist, accompanied by a Press Officer from the Cameron Highlanders of Canada, was surrounded by the tall US Army Rangers.

The photographer captured one of the classic images of World War II, which in 1942 encapsulated Anglo American collaboration in the fight against Nazi Germany.

He had initially wanted to take a group picture of Rangers and Commandos. Szima however, aware that his scarred face would not be acceptable to the US Army public relations officers explained to him, "…fella you won't get this scar to ever be printed in our army, now take one with him lighting my cigarette".

Wading nose deep had saturated Szima's cigarettes. Now safely ashore he was more than ready to light up.

A slightly bewildered Sgt A. "Bunny" Austin produced cigarettes and matches. Whether from fatigue or nerves at becoming the centre of attention, his hands shook as he positioned the cigarette. Through his pursed lips Szima muttered,

"Hurry up and light this bloody fukin' cigarette."

Grins appeared on the faces of the men of A Troop around him, including Brady towering above the group, and the photographer tripped the shutter. It was an image that would go round the world.

Robert Black perceptively observes in *Rangers in World War II* that because the landings had been a disaster, the press in Britain were not discouraged from playing up those aspects of the Dieppe operation that had been a success. Some of the initial coverage was pure invention. The *Daily Mail* under an eight column headline "Dieppe Victors Come Back Singing", asserted that Commandos had seized Dieppe racecourse and held it as an emergency airstrip for Allied pilots.

General Eisenhower had insisted that the American involvement be kept secret and be referred to only as "a detachment from a United States Ranger battalion". However seeing the success of the British propaganda blitz the US public relations staff, "saw the event as the opportunity to blow the American trumpet and proceeded to do so with a flurry of releases".

Despite the media coverage of the US involvement Szima remembers that in subsequent US network radio interviews a sanitised version of the action was recorded in which they were told to say they shot at the Germans but there was no reference to killing any enemy soldiers. The interview would be broadcast to audiences in the USA on Sunday afternoon and at this early stage in the war with men being drafted into the forces American censors in London were still concerned about public sensibilities.

In the United States the newspapers gave the raid the biggest headlines since Pearl Harbor stressing the role of the US Rangers in the operation.

Headlines included "US and British Invade France" – *New York Journal-American*, "Yanks in 9-hr Raid on Nazis, Rangers Join Commandos" – *Daily News* and "We Land in France" – *New York Post*. The opening paragraphs of the *Post* coverage began, "Not all the eloquence of Goebbels is going to be able to gloss over for the German people one nightmare fact – the Americans are landing in France again."

One London based American journalist went further. He claimed to have landed with the Rangers and to have been standing by the side of a Ranger who shot a sniper and thus became the first American to kill a German on land in World War II. Even the experienced US correspondent Quentin Reynolds who had been aboard the *Calpe* during the operation was guilty of embroidering his account. In *Dress Rehearsal: The Story of Dieppe* he describes meeting men from No 4 Commando as they boarded the destroyer. Among the group he mentions two Rangers.

"It was bad on shore, but my God, how those Commandos can fight! We were after a six-inch battery, and there was an orchard before we came to it. Know what those Commandos did? They lay down and fired; then stood up, grabbed an apple off a tree and fired again". The two wounded men helped aboard the warship were indeed Rangers, Sgts Marcell Swank and Kenneth Kenyon and it is to Kenyon that the "apple" quote is attributed.

Neither were with No 4 Commando and the "apple story" was in fact picked up later by Reynolds back in Great Britain and added to the account. The error and the anecdote reappeared in 1980 in *Darby's Rangers* by General William H. Baumer. Alex Szima recalled that the apples that he grabbed were very sharp – they may have been destined to become the French apple brandy Calvados or cider.

Not all the US media coverage was extravagant. Knickerbocker who had met the Rangers at Newhaven filed an accurate story that, though cut about by the censors, was syndicated in the US appearing in *The Chicago Sun*. When *The Dayton Herald* published the photograph of Szima with the men of No 4 Commando his mother recognised her son and contacted the paper. The picture had been wired without a detailed caption and the *The Dayton Herald* could not resist one that began ""My Baby!" cried Mrs Alex Szima..."

Interviewed by Knickerbocker Szima summed up the feelings of any soldier in the moments before he goes into action:

"You've got a kind of knot in your stomach until you get into action, and then it gets untied and from then on it's fine. I was all tied up until the nose of our boat pushed up the beach and we jumped out." Indicating Lovat as they stood on the harbour at Newhaven he said to Knickerbocker, "He's the best officer I ever saw – he never got as excited as you would in a game of tennis."

The veteran US journalist Drew Middleton who was able to draw on Knickerbocker's story and included a photograph of the four Rangers enjoying a drink in a London pub close to the US Embassy during their post operation leave.

Professional and principled Austin came ashore at Newhaven and quickly filed the story that appeared in the British newspapers the following day. Mills-Roberts remembered "a fair-minded and not exaggerated report".

Some of the papers featured a picture of a Commando with a rueful smile and a first field dressing on a head wound and the headline, "I was at Dieppe".

Among the journalists waiting at Newhaven was a reporter for the popular newspaper the *Daily Sketch*. With little material he wrote a colourful but basically honest account of the disembarkation.

"They may have been tired but they sang all the time… On their faces were the remains of black, green or yellow paint. All wore Balaclava hats. One man walked barefooted carrying his boots in his hands. There was little delay while the men were loaded into lorries and coaches, but it was long enough for some of the cottagers to run indoors and reappear with cups of tea, matches and cigarettes. One coach went off so quickly that a Commando had no time to return a cup. The woman looked glum for a while, then cheerfully said, 'Well, he's worth it'".

Mills-Roberts was offered "a cup of coffee by a very nice Canadian woman who asked me how things were going 'over there' – I was suitably non-committal."

As Kennett stepped onto the quay at Newhaven a doctor from the Royal Army Medical Corps picked him out and said, "'You go over there to the ambulance'. This was because I had a lot of blood over me and he thought I was badly wounded. It was Charlie's blood". The badly wounded Williams like Porteous had been transferred to HMS *Calpe* off Dieppe.

Williams survived his wounds and in post war reunions would greet Kennett as his 'blood brother'. Williams would be among the Commando veterans who would make the pilgrimage back to Dieppe in 1992 for the 50th Anniversary of the operation.

Among the other casualties who had been evacuated Sgt Watkins fully recovered and returned to join the Holding Operations Command in Wrexham in North Wales.

The men of No 4 Commando with their French and American comrades were given a meal at a tented cook house and then moved to a transit camp in the grounds of a country house near Newhaven. At the camp the men were allowed to send a telegram home,

"Faced with this uncensored opportunity," Gilchrist recalled, "I was at a loss for words."

"The people of Newhaven seemed to be waiting for the result of a lottery," wrote Mills-Roberts. "One could not relax properly in the atmosphere of worry and apprehension as the Canadians strove to get information about the Raid. I was not sorry that we left the scene before the full impact of the disaster became apparent."

At the transit camp the men were debriefed, by Intelligence staff. The next morning the Commando had a pay parade and were issued a seven-day leave pass, ration coupons and the rail warrant for Weymouth. Dunning managed to hitch a ride in a 3-ton truck to his family home in Southampton taking Carr and one or two other Hampshire lads with him. Some of the officers departed for London.

On the train up to London Mills-Roberts found himself sharing a compartment with a gloomy looking business man who showed him a very depressing account of the main Dieppe raid. In a world in which security was constantly emphasised and posters warned that Careless Talk Costs Lives Mills-Roberts was not drawn into conversation about Dieppe and the talk soon drifted to more mundane matters.

The newspaper coverage of the return of No 4 Commando yielded some unpredictable benefits. Scotsman Gordon Webb who had been wounded in the landing on Orange Beach 2 decided to have the injury treated at the Victoria Infirmary in Glasgow. During training some months earlier he had been injured by a faulty grenade and he had been well looked after at the Glasgow hospital.

"I got to London, bought an *Evening News* and there was my picture all over the front page. While waiting for the train to Scotland I got a bit tight in the station buffet. Nobody would let me buy."

The picture showed a slightly bedraggled grinning Webb with his arm in a rudimentary sling smiling as he talked to Len Coulson who, with his grinning face still smeared with camouflage and Thompson sub machine gun crooked in his arm, towered over the Scots officer. In the background Lovat could be seen pointing and clearly issuing instructions.

For the more seriously wounded Porteous recovery would take longer. "I was carted off to a Canadian hospital at a place called Bramshott ... where I spent the next six weeks or so." He made a full recovery and after a month's sick leave returned to duty with the Commando.

London drew the four US Rangers, who had been given free transport up to the capital.

Alex Szima had retained his stock of British currency and so became the de facto leader of the foursome. Spotting the Stars and Stripes flying from a distant building he asked the driver to drop them off and they discovered that they had stumbled on the US Embassy. At about the same time they noticed British papers on newstands featuring the cigarette lighting scene at Newhaven. Emboldened by his new celebrity status Szima walked into the Embassy and requested that the US Marine on guard fetch someone in authority. Accompanied by two Sergeants a man in shirt sleeve order appeared and seated himself at a desk displaying the name plate of a USMC Captain.

He picked up a copy of the newspaper and asked Szima,

"Is this you?"

"Yes Sir."

Szima then "made a concrete effort (with the officer) to at least allow us to leave our weapons and bags to lighten our load. To this the officer replied,

'The Marine Corps is not expected to handle Army equipment' and went on to dress me down for even considering it."

There has never been a history of cordial relations between the US Army and the US Marine Corps. This unhelpful reply, reinforced this hostility, Szima snapped the officer a salute, and with an equally crisp:

"Fuck you, Sir" he about turned and marched out of the building. "Expecting to be hauled down by the two Sergeants, in which case I'd be back with the Army … in gaol."

Far from arresting him the "Marine spy network had alerted a photographer who was hanging in there for a group picture. (I) told him 'Not outside, but inside that pub and you give us whiskey'.

I probably made it sound like an Indian in a Western movie trading for a blanket. Anyway it worked and we inhaled a gallon jar of pickled sausages and drank two Vat 69s before the Army stormed in and put an end to the party.

We are sitting at the bar, (we couldn't stand) and I said 'We owe this guy a picture'

Present was Douglas Fairbanks Junior[3] the Hollywood actor, or his double, dressed in Navy uniform. He took charge and insisted that the picture be taken seated at a table, toasting our return."

Szima confesses this was the only time that a press photographer took a picture that showed his damaged cheek "only because I was too drunk to react to it".

The surreal day grew more bizarre as the Ranger NCOs accompanied by Fairbanks, an Army Colonel and a squad of Military Police were moved through London in staff cars to the London HQ of the US European Theater of Operations. Here introduced as Bill Darby's boys they were faced by a group of Generals. Szima confessed "not knowing one general from another, reported to the loudest and first to address us". He guessed afterwards the man might have been General Hartle.

"I weaved a salute at him and reported to him as 1st American Commandos." His first remark was,

'Tell me Sergeant, did you shit in your pants?'

'No Sir.'

Then for the benefit of the lesser three or four generals present he said:

'I carried a turd in my pants for three days in the Argonne.'[4]

Turning to a Colonel he said, 'These boys look like they need a drink.'

This broke the ice in many ways and we drew maps, outlined and traced our assignments."

After being billeted overnight near Green Park, under guidance from Douglas Fairbanks Jr, the four NCOs went to the Combined Operations HQ. At the "Hive" that Lovat so disliked, they were ushered into the presence of Lord Mountbatten, "the same guy who gave us that encouraging send off aboard the *Albert* ... the night before the raid."

The sanitised radio interviews for NBC and CBS for the audiences in the United States followed, and then the four NCOs returned to their parent unit the 1st Ranger Battalion, "Where nobody believed a third of what had happened".

Mills-Roberts and Dunning-White had escaped to London and arriving at Victoria station hailed a cab and went to a well known hotel that had been an old pre-war haunt. The character had completely changed, it was crowded and becoming more congested. Mills-Roberts, "reached for (his) drink over the head of a dwarf-like lady who was engrossed in conversation. As an involuntary eavesdropper, I gathered that she was being subjected to a realm of terror in the WAAF [Women's Auxiliary Air Force] – Hitler in female guise was her persecutor."

The No 4 Commando Second-in-Command and adjutant escaped and "moved to less constricted surroundings".

London also attracted George Jones and some of his fellow Commandos who recalled that its citizens "gave us a marvellous reception. We were scruffy, some of us had ripped our clothes, but we just went down there as we were."

For Lovat in the immediate aftermath of Operation CAULDRON there was neither rest nor refreshment in London.

He had orders to report to the War Office almost as soon as he landed at Newhaven. He handed his rifle and pistol to Guardsman Jim Mellis his batman, a soldier whom he would recall as "a gold nugget" who would remain with him for 20 years, and climbed into a waiting staff car. Mellis was instructed to find the quickest route to Weymouth and somehow send a change of clothes to London for the morning. The adjutant was to ring the CO from the transit camp with a full casualty list. Lovat may have seen preliminary casualty figures before he departed.

The staff car carrying the CO of No 4 Commando stopped at East Grinstead to pick up more news of Operation JUBILEE. When they reached London at about 21.00 hours Lovat realised the last food that he had eaten was "a stale rock cake, that sat uneasily on a pint of beer, shared with Derek (Mills-Roberts) the previous afternoon". Unlike the other participants in CAULDRON Lovat, with the concerns of the impending operation, seems to have skipped the two main meals served aboard HMS *Prince Albert*.

He went straight into a meeting that began in the Combined Operations HQ in Richmond Terrace and then moved across to the War Office. It ended late.

He was still dressed in the muddy, salt stained cord trousers and denim blouse that he had worn on the raid. With no money on him he knew that the only place he could stay was the Guards' Club. It was only a short walk away across St James's Park but was locked up for the night by the time he arrived and it was only with some difficulty that he roused the elderly night porter.

The club was full, but the porter produced a new bar of soap, "a wartime luxury – that did not lather, and, shaking his head, sorrowfully removed various garments to clean and dry them." Lovat fell asleep in the bath. Later wrapped in towels in the library he had a fitful sleep tormented by nightmares of tracer fire and desperate beach landings.

"Something troubled and hurt me more than the chilling dreams. With the false dawn came the realisation that I must break the news to the families of the men who had died at Varengeville."

Notes

1   The three Eagle Squadrons were RAF Squadrons formed from US volunteer pilots before the United States entered the war. No 71 Sqn was formed in September 1940, No 121 Sqn became operational in July and No 133 Sqn in August 1941. Of

the 73 enemy aircraft destroyed by Eagle Squadrons 41 were claimed by No 71 based at Gravesend. In the course of their short existence out of the 244 pilots who flew with the RAF, the squadrons lost 77 US and five British pilots killed in action. The British officers assigned from the RAF served as squadron and flight commanders.

Flying Spitfires all three squadrons were in action over Dieppe during Operation JUBILEE. On August 19 No 121 Sqn operating from Southend flew three sorties and claimed one Fw 190 destroyed, two probables and one damaged. No 133 Sqn across the Thames estuary at Eastchurch claimed six enemy aircraft destroyed, two probables and eight damaged. The air battles over the port and the Channel would be their operational swan song since on September 29 that year they were absorbed into the Fourth Fighter Group USAAF.

The United States Army Air Force was keen to spread their experience through their fighter squadrons but the pilots pressed to remain as formed squadrons and so became the 334th (71) Sqn, 335th (121) Sqn and 336th (133) Sqn USAAF.

2   In the immediate aftermath of JUBILEE the Germans were convinced that they had repulsed an attempted invasion. To them the scale of the attack, nearly 5,000 men of the 2nd Canadian Division with armour and about 1,000 British Commandos as well as the lack of an obvious tactical *raison d'etre* could only indicate an invasion.

Out of all the attacks only that by No 4 Commando achieved its objective. On the left flank No 3 Commando had been disrupted by the encounter with the German convoy at 03.47 hours. Only a small number managed to land, those at Yellow Beach 1 led by Captain Richard Wills fought a fierce action as they attempted to penetrate inland. Among the casualties was America's first soldier to be killed in Europe in World War II, US Ranger Lt. Edwin V. Loustalot.

At Yellow Beach 2 only one landing craft with 18 men under Major Peter Young the Second-in-Command of No 3 Commando made a landfall. Under Young's energetic leadership they went ashore and managed to get within 200 metres of the battery and by accurate sniping prevented the guns from firing on the assault ships for two-and-one-half vital hours before they were safely evacuated.

At Blue Beach, the Royal Regiment of Canada landed at 05.07 hours and were unable to move off the beach. German troops in machine gun nests on the cliffs above were throwing grenades down onto the beach. Michael Boultbee, a young naval rating saw the slaughter.

"I wouldn't know how many survived more than a matter of minutes, because by this time everything was happening. The noise of gunfire was all around. I can't imagine they would have got more than a few yards from the beach."

After a few minutes, a German officer appeared and shouted to the surviving Royals that their CO had surrendered. Only three men of the Royal Regiment of Canada return to England that day 225 were dead and 264 had been taken prisoner.

At Green Beach, the South Saskatchewan Regiment achieved surprise and local successes advancing until they reached a defended bridge over the River Scie. Here they were halted by machine gun fire. Their CO, Col. Cecil Merritt, stood up, walked out onto the bridge, and called back to his men:

"What's the matter with you fellows? You're not frightened, are you? Come out here." Swinging his helmet in the forefinger of his left hand he shouted, "You see? There's no fire out here!" The men, rallied and charged across the bridge. Merritt survived the war and was awarded the VC.

The Cameron Highlanders of Canada landed at Green Beach at 05.50 hours with Piper Alex Graham standing on the bow of his landing craft, playing "One Hundred Pipers". The Highlanders got ashore, but though they did not reach their objectives made some of the deepest penetrations inland during JUBILEE. Out of 503 men in the Winnipeg regiment, 346 were killed.

The Canadian action at Green Beach probably allowed No 4 Commando to complete their mission and withdraw without suffering from undue attention from German forces in the vicinity.

The main assault of JUBILEE went in at 05.10 hours on Red and White Beach, led by the Royal Hamilton Light Infantry and the Essex Scottish. The smoke screens laid by aircraft proved ineffective and the Germans had enough time to recover from the attacks by Hurricanes and bombardment by destroyers. The RHLI were pinned down in front of the Casino under intense artillery and mortar fire. Herbert Titzman a German machine gunner at Dieppe recalled:

"I knew as an infantryman I wouldn't have wanted to be in the place of those Canadians, lying on those damned stones, not only having the fire come at them but with fragments of stone flying everywhere."

The Royal Hamilton Light Infantry were able to clear this strongly-held Casino and the nearby bunkers and some men of the battalion got across the bullet-swept boulevard and into the town, where they were engaged in vicious street fighting.

The RHLI were followed by two waves of LCTs carrying the Churchill tanks of the Calgary Regiment. "I think I would have to say at that point I felt sheer terror," recalled Archie Anderson one of the tank crewmen. Of the tanks that landed only 15 out of 27 managed to cross the seawall but were prevented from penetrating into the town by road blocks in the narrow streets. The German 3.7 cm anti-tank gun crews were unable to penetrate the armour, but cut the tracks. Nevertheless, the immobilised tanks continued to fight, supporting the infantry and contributing greatly to the withdrawal; the tank crews became prisoners or died in battle.

The Essex Scottish landed on Red Beach, and a dozen men led by CSM Cornelius Stapleton charged across the fire swept promenade and into town. After a brief action they returned to the beach. A signal to force headquarters on HMS *Calpe* reported that "12 Essex Scottish" were in the town. The message however was garbled and General Roberts believed that his men had broken through and at 07.00 hours committed the Royal Marines, and the French-speaking *Fusiliers*

Mont-Royal, under Col. Dollard Menard. The Fusiliers landed as the tide was falling and were immediately caught in fire from the positions in the cliffs.

Menard ran up the beach and saw soldiers lying on the ground, "with their heads pointed towards the wall as if they were getting ready for something. So I waited for them to do something – but they didn't move. So I crawled over to one of them, turned him over, spoke to him – he was dead. I checked a few more. They were all dead.

We had no cover. We couldn't dig in the pebbles – it was just like trying to make a hole in the water. You just can't do it. We were in a crossfire from the two high sides of the beach and a frontal fire that covered the whole area. We couldn't walk back, we couldn't get forward, we couldn't go on the sides. We were dead, really, before dying." The *Fusiliers* lost 513 out of 584 men.

The Royal Marines were only saved from an equal disaster by their CO Colonel J.P. Phillips who realising that that the beach was effectively a killing ground stood on the foredeck and using white gauntlets signalled other approaching landing craft to turn back. They put about just before the Colonel was killed, but his bravery had saved the lives of over 200 men.

At 11.00 hours Roberts issued the withdrawal order and by 14.00 hours the last landing craft pulled away. Some men were picked up in the sea including a Royal Marine who was seen swimming towards England with his rifle resting on his Mae West.

"Eight or ten hours and it was all over," a Canadian veteran recalled, "That was my war." One of the Canadians left behind was Maj. John Foote, the RHLI chaplain who had refused to be evacuated, and cared for the wounded on the beach under heavy fire, later joining them as a PoW. Foote was awarded the VC.

The Germans picked Foote at random for detailed interrogation along with the regiment's MO Capt Claire. After a few minutes of questions, one of the German interrogators said,

"Well, this is certainly the army. Out of all the people at Dieppe, we chose at random two people who know nothing about the military situation. One is the chaplain and the other is a medical officer!"

Meanwhile, exhausted and wounded Canadians trickled back under guard into captivity. On the other side of the channel, Menard was the only battalion commander to fight on the beaches and return to England.

The 2nd Canadian Division lost 3,164 men and 215 officers as casualties or PoWs as well as all its tanks and other vehicles.

Some of the 45 US Rangers and six officers led by Captain Roy Murray were captured. Interrogated by his captors one tall Ranger was asked how many Rangers were based in Great Britain.

" Three million, all as tall as I am", came the reply.

The Royal Navy suffered 550 casualties, lost 33 landing craft and the destroyer HMS *Berkley* torpedoed after she had been severely bomb damaged. The RAF which had hoped to draw the *Luftwaffe* into an air battle lost 106 aircraft, while the *Luftwaffe* which had committed 945 aircraft to attacking the beachhead, lost only 48.

With some justification the Germans could claim Dieppe as a victory, their casualties on land were 345 killed and 268 wounded.

The results of the raid have been disputed for decades. Canadian veterans take positions ranging from saying they were "sold out" to the raid being a "necessary sacrifice".

Mountbatten asserted that the lessons learned at Dieppe were important for the successful invasion of Normandy in June 1944.

"The Duke of Wellington said that the battle of Waterloo was won on the playing fields of Eton. I say the Battle of Normandy was won on the beaches of Dieppe."

Field Marshal Montgomery, who commanded the D Day assault at Normandy, argued that these lessons could have been learned without expending so many lives.

After the war, the British Commonwealth War Graves Commission established the Dieppe Canadian War Cemetery at Hautot-sur-Mer, two miles south of Dieppe. It contains more than 700 Canadian and 200 British graves.

The 40 Canadians who died, returning to Britain were buried in the Brookwood Military Cemetery in Surrey where there is a memorial for those who died and have no known graves.

3 Hollywood actor Douglas Fairbanks Jr, an Anglophile was an active fundraiser for British charities in the United States before Pearl Harbor. It was typical of Mountbatten to arrange that the high profile Fairbanks should be assigned to the Combined Operations HQ when the United States entered the war. The swashbuckling actor, now a US Navy officer, trained with the Commandos at Achnacarry. He would go on to serve with distinction in the US Navy in World War II developing ideas for deception and tactical cover for amphibious operations. He returned to Hollywood after the war and enjoyed a diverse career in TV and films including production as well as acting. He died on May 7, 2000 aged 90.

4 In World War I between September and November 1918 most of the 22 Divisions of the American Expeditionary Force (AEF) fought in the Meuse-Argonne sector and the area between the regions of Champagne and Lorraine in France. Commanded by General John 'Black Jack' Pershing they captured nearly 51.5 kilometres (32 miles) of territory before the Armistice on November 11, 1918. Like many men who would later hold senior rank in World War II Hartle was probably a platoon commander in the AEF.

CHAPTER 10

Aftermath

Smoke drifted across the now silent battery as severely wounded Commandos, some left for dead by their comrades or whose injuries had precluded them from evacuation, began to revive in the warmth of the midday sun.

George Cook drifted into consciousness, lying on his back staring up at the sun became aware of the buzzing flies clustered around his smashed and bloody jaw. He lay for a few minutes gathering his thoughts and considering his next moves.

" I thought I would try to hide under a hedge but I just couldn't move. While I was debating what to do and wondering what the hell had happened three Germans came along the path. One of them stuck a bayonet at the side of my throat. They went through my pockets, took my watch, cigarettes, money and ammunition off me.

I said to one, 'Can I have a drink?'. One who spoke English said yes and shouted to two women nearby." The English speaking German soldier had established that Cook could not move and told him, "We'll be back for you".

Despite the fact that Cook was grievously injured and surrounded by his enemies a young man's instincts had not deserted him and he sized up his two female helpers.

"One was youngish and the other was quite old. The old one sat down and put my head on her knee and the young one came back with a cup and tried to give me a drink. I couldn't manage it, so she ran off and came back again with a beautiful red glass with a bit of white moulding round it, an old Victorian-type glass. She had a spoon with her, and kept dipping the spoon into the glass and tipping it down my throat. It was wine. All the time the old woman was crying." Her distress is understandable for in Cook's words recorded years later by the IWM, "All this part of my face had gone, just a big hole there."

Later young Cadot would talk to one of Cook's helpers Madam Tanquerel who explained that the British soldier's jaw had been smashed by a grenade. "He did not speak French. She made him a dressing and gave him something to drink. She saw in the afternoon that he had a bayonet wound in the side."

Cook's next memories were of a crowded cattle truck filled with other casualties from JUBILEE. They were transported to Rouen and once again he passed out as he and many others lay on the floor of a hospital. After about a month he would become partially conscious and discover that he was in a Paris hospital.

"Then, when I came round ... they put a plaster cast on me because all my shoulder was smashed. A bullet had gone through there ... and they wired what was left of my jaw up, to my top teeth and they made like a splint. It was all screwed together. I actually kept passing out for days on end. It would be October before when I woke up and I could stay awake."

Following European orthopaedic practice Cook's arm and shoulder was immobilised in a plaster cast that had his arm raised at an angle "like a Hitler salute". The curious angle ensured that shattered bones were best positioned to knit together or for the growth of tissue to assist in the reconstruction of the joint. Complex bone grafts followed for most of next year and even when he returned to Britain Cook required a further hospital treatment.

Another survivor was "Honk" Horne, whom Cook had taken for dead. In *Dieppe 1942 The Jubilee Disaster* Ronald Atkin notes that Horne "also owed his life to German doctors, though he wondered if he was being preserved for a worse fate."

The tough and canny pre-war Regular sergeant had decided he would avoid compulsory church parades by stating Judaism as his religion. This denomination was duly entered in his documents and along with his blood group, service number and date of birth was stamped on the two identity discs worn around his neck.

Though the Allies were not aware of the full extent of the Nazis "Final Solution of the Jewish problem" with its extermination camps in eastern Poland, the persecution of the Jews and the existence of concentration camps were public knowledge.

Back on Orange Beach 2 Jimmy Pasquale tending the wounded watched as armed German soldiers approached warily. He too wondered about his fate.

"I must admit the Germans were very good then. They sent stretchers down," but then events took a frightening turn for the worse. "After a while six of us were lined up against a ditch. They never said anything but it was obvious what was going to happen.

"Just then a marvellously dressed officer who spoke English came over and stopped them. They were very good after that, gave us a meal later on, but I think the intention had been to shoot us because, after all, our lads hadn't left one bloke alive on that gunsight."

The Commando lost a total of seven men as prisoners, Sgt G. Horne, L Cpl G. Vowles and Pte G. Cook from F Troop, L Cpl A. Diplock and Pte C.A. Doublair from A, Gnr G.H. Iverson from B and Pte J. Pasquale from HQ Troop.

Though they were confident that the landings to the east and at Dieppe had been defeated, at 14.45 hours the German Corps HQ reported cautiously that, "Some of the forces landed are still in Varengeville wood".

The main fighting in Operation JUBILEE had been confined to the beaches and the Dieppe seafront and the local population had not become involved. Early in the landings RAF aircraft had dropped leaflets in French that explained,

"This is a raid and not an invasion," a message backed up by BBC French language broadcasts.

Consequently only a limited number of French men and women had either welcomed or assisted the raiders. Hitler was reported to be so pleased with these reactions that he praised the "perfect discipline and calm" of the citizens of Dieppe. Ten million francs were placed at the disposal of Mayor Levasseur for reconstruction work. The shrewd

Frenchman decided to capitalise on the German feelings of generosity and requested that French PoWs from the Dieppe area, captured in 1940, should be released.

The Germans complied. They explained that their humanity was based on that fact that, "The behaviour of the French people has been more than correct ... they aided the German troops in their combat, rendering services of all kinds, put out fires, tended the wounded and provided the combatants with food and drink."

In Berlin General Jodl was informed in a report that, "The behaviour of the civil population during the battle has been correct. No cases of sabotage or interference with military measures. Shops re-opened as early as midday on the day of the attack."

On September 12 a train carrying 1,500 French ex-PoWs pulled into the station at Serquex away from Dieppe. It was decorated with garlands and slogans like *Vive Dieppe*, *Vive la France* and *Vive le Maréchal* – a reference to Marshal Pétain. After the German victory at Dieppe the Anglophobe Pétain had sent congratulations to the garrison for their gallant defence.

The Marshal's portrait was prominently displayed at the station festooned with red, white and blue bunting and *Tricolour* flags. A large number of German and French functionaries including the *Feldkommandant* of Rouen General von Zitzewitz, the *Préfét* of Seine-Inferior Rene Bouffet and representatives of the Civil Defence, Red Cross and Police had assembled at the station. Mayor Levasseur was also present with officials and mayors from adjoining towns.

The men were ordered off the train and assembled to hear, with growing frustration, long speeches of thanks and congratulations.

The train finally pulled into Dieppe station close to the Basin Duquesne. The return of the first 984 soldiers was a subdued occasion because the German authorities had forbidden any official welcome. The crowds were kept back by a cordon of German soldiers several hundred metres from the station and only when a small girl spotted her father slipped past the soldiers and ran across the road did the heartless control collapse. Many men holding their wives, mothers and children broke down and wept with relief and happiness.

A second train arrived in Dieppe on October 22 carrying a further

316 men. However no conscripts from the areas around Varengeville-sur-Mer or Berneval-le-Grand were on these trains. In these locations the Germans felt the population had actively assisted or tacitly supported the Commando raiders, and so deserved to be punished.

Fourteen year old Cadot ran the risk of punishment or worse when he set out at 08.00 hours on the morning of August 20. Accompanied by his father he began to explore the battery position. Emyr Jones's translation of Cadot's account conveys the chaos of the fighting and the snap shot character of people's memories.

The first things the Cadot's saw were, "grenades and khaki-coloured cardboard packages," while the latter were probably discarded ammunition boxes the former may have been the expended smoke generators.

The destructive effect of small arms and anti-aircraft gun fire on the southern side of La Volière was dramatic. It had ripped out most of the southern side of the building and wall. As father and son approached they saw the body of a Commando. There was no weapon near him which suggests that he may have been L Cpl W.D. Garthwaite the medical orderly of C Troop who had been killed by mortar fire. Closer to the battery, 70 metres in front of the guns and 50 metres from the road were the bodies of three Commandos caught on the perimeter barbed wire. The day before Szima had seen them draped with a Union Jack – it had probably been taken as a trophy by the Germans as they began to check the area.

Walking into the village the Cadots then saw a German *Kampfstand* with three of the machine gun crew lying dead. They reached the junction of the roads from Vasterival and le Mesnil and at the corner of a house saw the body of Captain Pettiward. The F Troop Commander was dead in a sitting position with his back against the wall of the house. In his left hand he held his Thompson SMG, a Colt .45 pistol was in the holster of his webbing and binoculars slung around his neck. His right hand had been torn off by a grenade explosion.[1]

Though his body was seen by Cadot, along with Lt MacDonald and four other Commandos, Pettiward he has no known grave.

As the villagers gathered and shared their experiences the Boulliers and Operes chatted with the Cadots at Madame Bertin's house. She had lost her lavatory door as an improvised stretcher and said that a German soldier, wounded in the foot had lain in her yard and feigning death had survived.

In the middle of the village the Cadot's found two dead German soldiers in the *Kampfstand* opposite the house that later in the war would become their home.

Madame Tanquerel, who had assisted George Cook, described how German soldiers had taken up positions in her yard as she went into her air raid shelter. Unlike the Boulliers and Operes who remained in their shelters and only caught brief glimpses of Commandos and German soldiers curiosity must have been too much for her. She had seen the men of B Troop engaging the Flak tower. When she emerged to assist Cook she also saw another wounded Commando near the well in her back garden.

Initially the Germans forbade her from approaching him but after she had pressed them they returned later in the day with a ladder as an improvised stretcher. She packed straw under the British soldier's head to prevent it falling through the rungs.

After talking to Mme Tanquerel father and son turned left and began to walk along the road to Varengeville. Later when the older Cadot returned to Mme Tanquerel he discovered two SMLE rifles hidden in the nettles.

Passing the Flak tower they saw four dead Germans, killed by the Commando's accurate fire. Further along the road were two more German dead lying on the grass. In the house next to the villa that had been commandeered as an Officers' Mess they discovered that Mme Lefevre had been hit in the arm by a stray round. The severity of the wound was such that surgeons were later obliged to amputate her arm. She was the only civilian to be injured.

Around 07.00 hours Mme Lefevre had watched Commandos running up the Union Jack on the flag pole outside the officers Mess. It flew defiantly until 09.00 hours.

Monsieur Gueudin had felt the explosions, as men from B Troop pitched grenades at a German soldier concealed behind a well. Later in the morning when Gueudin attempted to emerge from his shelter to collect food for his children he was fired on by German soldiers and forced back into cover.

The Cadots glimpsed severed wires protruding from the smashed junction box for the battery telephone system and watched as two German soldiers moved around the position locating the dead gunners and preparing a casualty list.

Leaving his father the French boy walked over to No 6 Gun, the most easterly in the battery. It appeared to be intact to him and in front of it lay the body of a Commando, close to him a box of large headed matches and "a bar 5 cm long and 3 cm in diameter".

Cadot's observation appears to tally with reports that one gun was not destroyed and that it was later used by the Germans to fire a salute to their fallen comrades following their interment at Varengeville Church at 11.00 hours on August 22.[2]

The second gun that Cadot inspected had obviously been destroyed, with a dead German gunner lying by the breach. The third was the gun that had suffered the cataclysmic explosion of the ready use cordite and it was "completely broken up. The embankment which surrounded it no longer exists. Three English soldiers are dead, and two Germans." The terrible effects of the detonation of high explosive are evident since the bodies were "completely torn to pieces".

The camouflage nets concealing the gun position had caught fire and burned and 155 mm shells littered the gun pits.

As Cadot wandered through the position he was spotted by a German NCO, who with a blast on his whistle gestured that he should leave the site. Even as he was making his exit the young Cadot quickly noted that the fourth gun had been destroyed and the bodies of three Germans in shirtsleeves and steel helmets lay crumpled in the pit.

At 11.00 hours father and son linked up again and compared notes. As they walked back home they encountered German soldiers carrying two red painted extending ladders. The distinctly untactical colour suggests that they had been provided by a Fire Brigade in Great Britain and brought over by the Commandos. Back at the gully the Cadots saw that four AP mines had been lifted and put on one side and the barbed wire had been flattened by the explosion of the two Bangalore torpedoes.

After lunch the acutely observant 14 year old set off again and this time made his way towards Ste Marguerite. Cutting off the main road he picked up the final leg of the route taken by Group 2 and found a cap comforter and a spare radio battery in its haversack.

At the wood at Blancmesnil-le-bas he discovered that Mme Dumont, the young wife of a French Army PoW, had encountered Group 2 as she was putting her horse out to pasture. She saw them arrive in single file "They asked if they were going the right way for the blockhouse. In reply she showed them the way through the wood."

At Ste Marguerite Paul Rosay told Cadot he was awakened by the sound of rifle and machine gun fire.

"By the tracer bullets I realised that the fire was directed towards the beach. That will last about ten minutes. A bit later, crossing my garden to see better I find myself nose to nose with three soldiers dressed in khaki.

One of the soldiers asked me if they were going the right way for the batteries. I tell him yes, that they have a wood to cross, a road (the road that leads to the lighthouse), that they will pass near the Hotel des Sapins and continue along the path."

Taking this route Cadot found a webbing belt dropped by one of the Commandos.

Given the extent of the victory on the other beaches along the Dieppe front, even at Varengeville the Germans could afford to be relaxed. On August 21 Cadot and his father had permission to go down to Orange Beach 2. Here they saw the rabbit wire that had been placed across the barbed wire and the ladders erected by the raiders. The four men from A Troop who had been killed still lay on the beach, two more were in a field inland and one further to the west on the beach.

The Germans later instructed a local man, M. Govel to bring his horse and cart down to recover the Commando dead. The priest at Ste Marguerite was instructed that the British dead were to be buried in his churchyard. While this was acceptable, the German proposal to bury them wrapped in groundsheets, was not. He insisted they have coffins and Lucien Benoit, a cabinet maker in le Mesnil was given the task.

On August 22 the German dead were buried and at midday twenty survivors of the battery paraded to receive decorations for bravery. It was a rash move, two low flying RAF fighters on a roving patrol strafed the position as the troops were forming up.

The British and Allied soldiers who fought at the HESS battery were also to receive decorations. Whatever his faults as a tactician Mountbatten had an acute sense of PR and its effect on morale. He was insistent that if servicemen had been recommended for decorations following an operation, they should be awarded as promptly as possible.

Within the Commando Captain Porteous received the Victoria Cross, the British and Commonwealth's highest award for gallantry.[3]

The citation published on October 2, 1942 in the *London Gazette*, the official publication in which citations for decorations and awards are announced, reads:

Captain (temporary Major) Patrick Anthony Porteous, Royal Regiment of Artillery (Fleet, Hants)

At Dieppe on the 19th August, 1942, Major Porteous was detailed to act as Liaison Officer between the two detachments whose task was to assault the heavy coast defence guns.

In the initial assault Major Porteous, working with the smaller of the two detachments, was shot at close range through the hand, the bullet passing through his palm and entering his upper arm. Undaunted, Major Porteous closed with his assailant, succeeded in disarming him and killed him with his own bayonet thereby saving the life of a British Sergeant on whom the German had turned his aim.

In the meantime the larger detachment was held up, and the officer leading this detachment was killed and the Troop Sergeant-Major fell seriously wounded. Almost immediately afterwards the only other officer of the detachment was also killed.

Major Porteous, without hesitation and in the face of a withering fire, dashed across the open ground to take over command of this detachment. Rallying them, he led them in a charge which carried the German position at the point of the bayonet, and was severely wounded for the second time. Though shot through the thigh he continued to the final objective where he eventually collapsed from loss of blood after the last of the guns had been destroyed.

Major Porteous's most gallant conduct, his brilliant leadership and tenacious devotion to a duty which was supplementary to the role originally assigned to him, was an inspiration to the whole detachment

After he had recovered from his wounds he was invested with his VC by King George VI on October 28, 1942. With characteristic modesty he told reporters gathered outside Buckingham Palace

"It was just luck I got the award."

Following CAULDRON Lord Lovat was awarded the Distinguished Service Order (DSO) and his Second-in-Command Major D. Mills Roberts received the Military Cross (MC) as did Lt D.C.W. Style. A bar was added to the Captain G.G.H. Webb's existing MC.

The Military Medal was awarded to Sgt I. Portman, Sgt F. McCarthy, Cpl G. Blunden, L Cpl R. Mann and Tpr W. Finney. Talking about Mann's MM, Sgt Hugh Lindley recalled the performance of the young sniper, "I put the lad's name forward for recognition. The fact was I saw him drop a few while I was there."

The boyish Cpl Franklin "Zip" Koons became the representative soldier from the US Rangers to be decorated. All had fought with distinction, but he received the Military Medal from the British.

Lovat wrote of him:

"During the action Cpl Koons displayed conspicuous gallantry and admirable leadership. In charge of a small sniping detachment he continued to carry out his duties with very marked success under heavy fire which eventually caused the almost total destruction of the building from which he and his men were sniping. Cpl. Koons is probably the first American N.C.O. to account for a number of Germans in this war". For the same operation Koons would later be awarded the Silver Star by the US Army.

Of the diminutive Corporal F. Balloche of No 10 Commando who had been with Group 2 and who was also awarded the Military Medal Lovat wrote:

"He was attached to one of my Troops and played a conspicuous part in the searching and occupation of the village of Le Haut, which lies in close proximity to the German Heavy battery at Varengeville. He proved of great assistance to the Troop Leader, who could not speak French, and having gained the information required, he subsequently went into action and, with the rest of the Troop, inflicted heavy casualties on the enemy".[4]

Troop Sergeant Major W.R. Stockdale received the Distinguished Conduct Medal (DCM).

Captain B.W.S. Boucher-Myers received a Mentioned in Dispatches (MID) a distinction that also went to Lt J. Ennis, L Cpl J.C. Skerry, Pte F.J. Horne and Pte J. Dale.

At the close of his report on Operation CAULDRON Hugh Mulleneux paid tribute to the officers and ratings under his orders whom he said had;

"carried out their respective duties very well. The Commanding Officers of MGB 312 and SGB 9 handling their craft with skill and provided valuable help and support, and the Commanding Officer of HMS *Prince Albert* has every reason to be proud of his flotilla of landing craft."

It is a common practice in military history to sum up a battle or action with the comparative losses suffered in dead and wounded by both sides. Listing these dry statistics can demean the memory of friends and comrades who sacrificed their lives and runs the risk of reducing the outcome of a fire fight or a campaign to something akin to score card of a sports meeting. Casualty figures can also be misleading.

For the record, within the battery perimeter the German gunners of No 813 Battery lost 28 dead, 33 wounded and four prisoners. Lovat estimates that an additional 30 men may have been killed in the ambushes and actions in the surrounding area. Of the remaining men in the battery, a total of 97 on duty that morning, some may have managed to hide or escape into the surrounding countryside.

Gerard Cadot was told that some men based at Longueil, a small village to the south, well outside the area of Operation CAULDRON hearing the small arms fire and explosions had run away to hide on

August 19. This may however have been wishful thinking by the local population, for most of the indicators are that reinforcements for the Dieppe garrison were closing in on the port throughout the day. Individual German soldiers appear to have shown considerable initiative sniping at the Commandos during the operation and even earned a tribute from Lovat after the CAULDRON was over.

"For their songs and their sniping I give them top marks."

In the course of the operation the Commando lost two officers killed and three wounded, 14 other ranks killed and 17 wounded.[5]

Of the 20 wounded who returned to Britain, 12 were back on duty within two months. Some 13 men were left behind in France posted as missing. As the tide rose later on that hot August day the bodies of some of the men killed on Orange Beach 2 may have been washed out to sea for there are a number of Commandos who have no known grave.

The balance of casualties appears to favour the Commandos, however killing Germans was not the purpose of Operation CAULDRON. The aim was the destruction of the guns at the battery at Varengeville-sur-Mer and this was achieved with singular success.

Compared to the grim losses suffered by the Canadians on the beaches to the east No 4 Commando had come off very lightly. In the following weeks for all of the Next of Kin of the 29 men there was the grim prospect of the official telegram with words like "killed in action", "missing" or "missing presumed dead". Letters from Lord Lovat and Troop Commanders that followed would help to ease some the pain.

When back in Weymouth John Skerry learned of the death of his friend Fred Gooch it came as a double blow. He knew that when he returned to Scotland and his lodgings with the Campbells in Troon he would have to break the news to Fred's girlfriend Ray.

For the families of the German gunners killed at Dieppe there would be a visit by one the Nazi Party functionaries who delivered the news of the death of soldiers killed in action. These grim messengers had been nicknamed by civilians *Totenvögel* – Bird of Death.

The next of kin might also have received a gold *Verwundeten-Abzeichen* – Wound Badge with a document expressing respect and gratitude for loyal service sacrifice for *Führer/Volk und Vaterland*.

German families would place a black bordered announcement in the local paper and circulate remembrance cards with a photograph and details of the soldier.

Colonel General Curt Haase, CO 302nd Infantry Division, Dieppe paid a personal tribute to the men who had fought and died at No 813 Battery.

"(The) enemy force, about 300 men (sic), attacked the battery from two sides with hand grenades, machine guns and revolvers and mortars, while air bombardment neutralised the defences of the battery with continuous diving raids. Tracer bullets ignited the cartridges that were stored in the battery. The battery defended itself bravely right up to the end as is proved by the 28 dead and 29 wounded, including the Commanding Officer who directed the fire and did his best to hold out. When at last the battery had passed into British hands practically all the guns had been rendered unserviceable by the ignition of the ammunition."

Cadot noted that the battery was dismantled following the success of Operation CAULDRON. The bunkers were filled up with concrete and a month later work began to make the two beaches more secure. At Orange Beach 1 the two gullies were blocked with large tree trunks which were then tied into a dense barbed wire entanglement.

On the spurs on either side of the gorges slit trenches with machine gun positions were dug. Fifty metre deep minefields were laid along areas of the coast and trees felled to give better fields of fire.

In Fundamental Remarks of Army HQ No 8 the Germans stated:

"(9) CLIFFS
The enemy climbed the cliffs by the help of various means, even places considered impracticable. The valleys having been mined he approached them from the side.

Lessons deduced – No point is "inviolable", every possibility must be reckoned with."

At Orange Beach 2 seaside villas were demolished and bunkers were constructed giving interlocking fire to cover the shingle beach. On the beach steel beams were concreted in placed and remotely detonated heavy calibre artillery shells dug in along the cliff. The mouth of the Saâne was blocked to create a man made lake behind the beach. A French fishing boat was commandeered, armed and turned into an offshore patrol vessel covering the approaches to the Point d'Ailly.

These precautions reflected the assessment of the skills and capability of the Commandos. The German LXXXI Army Corps after action report of August 22, 1942 stated:

"In the first landing waves the mass of men and materiel landed will not be considered so important as choosing an unexpected locality and the fighting value of the troops who will first touch land. This is proved by the fact that the action of No 4 Commando of 200 men (sic) succeeded, while the action at Dieppe in which 10 times as many men landed supported by tanks, was a complete failure…

"The combat efficiency of the Commandos was very high. They are well trained and fought with real spirit. It is reported that they showed great skill in climbing the steep coastal cliffs".

A.B. Austin's assessment of the character and motives of Lovat as CO explains in many ways why the attack on August 19 was a success.

"As with most fine soldiers, I think there was a little of the poet or artist in him. He had the marauding chief's satisfaction (Lovat is head of the Clan Fraser) at having destroyed his enemies, but his main pleasure was at having completed a perfect, rounded, neatly finished and timed little operation, a tactical model of amphibious warfare."

In Great Britain Martin Lindsay, then a young officer with 1st Bn Gordon Highlanders, was due a week's leave when the Commando returned to Troon. He was fascinated to know how the Commandos had destroyed the battery. "So I visited the appropriate Military Training Branch, then in the Horseguards, and asked them to send me to the Commando to write a paper about the raid."

The result of his interviews was *Notes from Theatres of War, No 11*.

Writing after the war, having commanded his regiment in Europe from 1944-45 and been awarded a knighthood and the DSO, Lindsay remarked that his excellent little manual was;

"ill-received by many regimental officers who considered that they and their battalions could have carried out this action no less successfully...

Those who took part stress Lord Lovat's leadership both in mounting the operation and on the day. But the key to No 4 Commando's success was that the CO had an even more important quality than leadership: the brains to plan so difficult an operation as well...

A CO with the necessary competence for such a specialised operation was much more likely to emerge, and to be a more confident choice, from units which had been continually training in assault techniques, including those from landing craft, and which had already taken part in raids on the enemy coast. Such units could themselves have been expected to be ready at fairly short notice...

The standard of No 4 Commando officers can be measured by the fact that when the war ended two VCs had been won by those who had served in it and five DSOs, while eight of them had risen to the rank of Lieutenant-Colonel or above. The soldiers were of comparable quality."

After their leave the men returned to Troon and paraded on September 5, 1942 to hear messages of congratulations from HM King George VI and wear for the first time their distinctive green Commando berets.

Troon would be remembered with affection by many men in No 4 Commando. Thirty six years later Bill Boucher-Myers, retired from the Army and living in Scotland would as Captain of the Troon Golf Club see it receive Royal status on its centenary in 1978.

Napoleon Bonaparte is reported to have said that what he wanted of his Marshals was that they should be lucky. By this he explained that he wanted leaders with initiative, men who could see opportunities and seize them – however good luck has always been an advantage in an operation of any scale.

The conduct of operations on August 19, 1942 exemplified Napoleon's maxim – the Commandos were blessed with good fortune, but they were skilled and experienced enough to make use of all these opportunities.

In his planning for Operation CAULDRON Lovat made every

effort to insure against "bad luck". The aim of the operation was to destroy or at a minimum neutralise the HESS battery during the duration of Operation JUBILEE. If Group 2 had been stopped on Orange Beach 2, Mills-Roberts was prepared to go it alone and assault the battery. The demolition team from F Troop were equipped with tailor made charges fitted with two igniters but also Limpet mines that were effectively back up charges that could have been used to disable the guns.

However even before either Group had landed they enjoyed their first piece of good fortune when Mulleneux skilfully navigated the flotilla around the darkened German convoy that later encountered No 3 Commando.

The lighthouse at Vasterival continued to operate and allowed Group 1 to land very close to the gullies on Orange Beach 1. There were no German soldiers on the cliff top close enough to intercept the landing.

The attack by low flying aircraft and cliffs covered the detonation of the Bangalore torpedoes used to clear the barbed wire. In fact the landing here was so well concealed that initially the Germans were unaware that it had happened, even at the end of the day.

The C Troop 2-inch Mortar bomb that hit the ready use ammunition at No 813 Battery marks the climax of the Commando's good fortune. Yet even here they exploited this considerable advantage, sniping at the soldiers attempting to put out the fire.

The disaster on the main beaches at Dieppe effectively focussed German attention away from Vasterival. The German troops who were beginning to probe towards the battery were hesitant and so allowed the evacuation to be completed successfully.

Though the Luftwaffe was in action in the area, their pilots were not tasked with attacking the LCAs grouped off Orange Beach 1.

These were all incidents in the operation where luck went with the Commando. However these breaks do not detract from the fact that the attack succeeded because it was a bold plan carried out by well led, highly motivated and trained men.

Victory, as well as defeat, can be the result of the interaction of events and conditions many of which are beyond the control of the combatants.

On August 19, 1942 at Varengeville No 4 Commando enjoyed its share of good fortune, which it exploited to the full. However good fortune will only win battles when joined with skill and bravery.

Fortis fortuna adiuvat – Fortune favours the bold.

Notes

1 The injury may have been caused by a malfunction with a No 36 Grenade or perhaps a misjudged moment in the heat of the action when Captain Pettiward attempted to throw back a German stick grenade. If the friction cord on a stick grenade or pin on a No 36 Grenade was pulled and the grenade was thrown immediately, there was a few seconds delay before it exploded in the target area. A soldier on the receiving end with quick reactions might be able to throw the grenade back or clear of the position. To prevent this happening, and at considerable risk some men would delay throwing the grenade for a couple of seconds. The No 36 Grenade was generally reliable but damage to the gunpowder core of the safety fuse could sometimes cause it to burn slightly faster after the percussion cap had been truck by the plunger and so cause a premature explosion.

2 JUBILEE was clearly a German victory, but the fight for No 813 Battery stands out as their only defeat in the larger operation. The gunners and the HQ staff would have been keen to minimise their losses and the destruction.

German reports about the action at the battery at the time are conflicting. At 09.00 hours on August 19 from the 15th Army HQ reported "Battery 813 near Ste Marguerite had fallen into enemy hands, but has been retaken. It is again firing with two guns". Later a summary at 17.15 signed by Field Marshal von Rundstedt stated that the battery "has held on to its defences in hand-to-hand fighting, but blew up its guns".

Of the guns, No 6 may have been effectively neutralised by an explosion that rendered it unsafe to fire but did not show the spectacular damage visible on the other pieces.

If it was not destroyed, the confusion is understandable. The charge could have been slightly damaged during the action in a way that was not obvious. The detonators could have been over crimped damaging the gunpowder core in the safety fuse or the fuse could have shifted so that the .22 caps would not ignite it. In either case when the pins were pulled the caps would have exploded and it would be time to close the breech on the gun and exit double quick.

It should be remembered that the F Troop demolition crews were working on their targets under pressure, in smoke and dust, with strict time constraints and with explosions in the vicinity. This was not a demolition range in Great Britain with unlimited time to prepare the target and the leisure to return to assess the damage after the explosion.

Given that the mission for No 4 Commando had been completed and the battery had been neutralised and played no part in JUBILEE, whether one gun may not have been destroyed is academic.

3 Born into an Army family in India at Abbotabad on the North West Frontier ten months before the end of World War I, Pat Porteous was educated at Wellington College and the Royal Military Academy Woolwich. He was commissioned into the Royal Artillery in 1937. He served with the British Expeditionary Force in France in 1940 and was evacuated at Dunkirk. He joined No 4 Commando in late 1940 and by D Day was Second-in-Command.

His post war career included a period as Battery Commander with the Royal Artillery. He was clearly a good instructor since two of his happiest times were as a Company Commander at the Royal Military Academy Sandhurst and as commanding officer of the Junior Leaders' Regiment RA. Staff appointments included work with the directorate of Land/Air Warfare.

On retirement a great deal of his time and energy was spent supporting and raising money for the Commando Association and the Army Benevolent Fund. From 1993 he was vice chairman (UK) of the Victoria Cross and George Cross Association.

At his home in Funtington, West Sussex he enjoyed gardening and it was here that he died on October 10, 2000.

4 As decorations for bravery the elegant Military Cross instituted in 1914 with its distinctive blue and white ribbon and the Military Medal instituted in 1916, were awarded for similar acts of gallantry. The former went to officers and warrant officers and the latter to NCOs and other ranks. The MM with a blue, white and red ribbon had on its reverse the words "For BRAVERY in the FIELD" and was held in as much respect as the MC in the British and Commonwealth armies. The medals were awarded throughout World War I and II and during post war campaigns. It was not until the 1990s that British Prime Minister John Major discontinued this distinction and all ranks now receive the MC.

5 The casualty list for No 4 Commando reflects a force in which junior NCOs who had volunteered from Infantry regiments were leading from the front in the attack.

Captain R.G. Pettiward	Beds and Herts
Lt J.A. MacDonald	1st Royal Dragoons
L Cpl L. Bishop	Somerset Light Infantry
F.M. Gooch	The East Surreys
E.P.H. Heckman	The Royal Berks

J. Keenan	Royal Ulster Rifles
D.T. Mercer	The Kings (Liverpool) Rgt
A. Mills	The South Lancashire Rgt
J. Moss	The Loyal Rgt
J. Whately	Oxfordshire and Buckinghamshire Light Infantry
Gdsmn J. Whittaker	Grenadier Guards
Pte W.D. Garthwaite	The Loyal Rgt
S. McGann	The South Lancashire Rgt
G.H. Sutton	East Yorkshire Rgt
Rfn J. Watters	Royal Ulster Rifles
Sigmn G. A. Tucker	Royal Signals

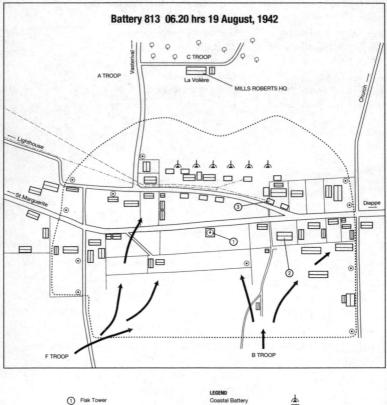

Battery 813 06.20 hrs 19 August, 1942

A TROOP

Vasterival

C TROOP

La Volière

MILLS ROBERTS HQ

Church

Lighthouse

St Marguerite

Dieppe

3

1

2

F TROOP

B TROOP

1 Flak Tower

2 House where German Officers lived

3 Command Bunkers

LEGEND
Coastal Battery
A.A. flak tower
Machine gun
Blockhouse
Building
Barbed wire
Surface telephone line
Subterranean telephone line
British attack

N

1/2 mile

APPENDIX 1

No 4 Commando after CAULDRON

On April 2, 1943 Lt Col Robert Dawson, the same Dawson who had climbed the gully at Vasterival, became the commanding officer of No 4 Commando when Lord Lovat was promoted to Brigadier to command the Commando Brigade.

In May 1943 the Commando moved to Falmouth in Cornwall and in Exercise BRANDYBALL near St Ives on June 7, proved the impossible to the Royal Navy. They showed that men could land from small craft, albeit with some difficulty, on a steep rocky coast that the enemy would imagine to be impassable and so consequently would leave undefended.

It was then back to Braemar in Scotland to the Commando Camp of Mountain Warfare where they were instructed by Wing Commander Smythe and Major (later Lord) Hunt – men who would be part of the successful Everest ascent in 1953.

On April 16, 1944 No 4 Commando returned to England where they were joined by French Commandos under Commandant Phillippe Kieffer. They were held at Camp 18, near Southampton in preparation for D Day and the liberation of Europe.

On June 6, 1944 they landed from HMS *Princess Astrid* (like the assault ship that took them to France in 1942, a former Belgian Channel ferry) and HMS *Maid of Orleans*. Their initial objective was Ouistreham Riva Bella on the right flank of Sword Beach at Normandy.

The rest of the Commando Brigade under Lovat fought its way inland to link up with men of the 6th Airborne Division who had captured key bridges and secured the east flank of the Normandy beachhead.

In conjunction with the paratroops they held the area around Le Plein, Hauger/Amfreville/Breville/Ranville. In the weeks that followed they suffered heavy casualties. On June 10 Kieffer was wounded and evacuated and two days later Lovat suffered the same fate.

Lt Col Derek Mills-Roberts, who at the time was CO of No 6 Commando, took his place as commanding officer of the Commando Brigade.

On August 19 the Commando fought its way into the outskirts of Beuzeville and there on August 26 they were withdrawn from the fighting having been in continuous action for 82 days.

After a period of rest and reinforcement in Britain they returned to the line at Den Haan, Belgium in October as part of the 4th Special Service (SS) Brigade.

On November 1, 1944 the Brigade which consisted of No 4 Commando and three Royal Marine Commandos under command of Brigadier BW Leicester, attacked the fortified island of Walcheren on the Dutch coast. This heavily defended feature dominated the approaches to the key port of Antwerp.

No 4 Commando was tasked with a frontal assault on the port of Flushing on the island. In a bold assault, that was acclaimed as classic example of amphibious warfare, it seized the greater part of Flushing.

Following the landings No 4 remained in the line in Holland until the end of the war. It returned to Britain after VE Day and like all the Army Commandos No 4 Commando was disbanded on March 1, 1946.

The battle honours for No 4 Commando are:

Lofoten Islands 1941, Boulogne 1942, Dieppe 1942, Normandy Landings, D.Day 1944, Dives Crossing, Flushing, N.W. Europe 1944-45.

No 4 Commando order of battle at CAULDRON

Commanding Officer
Lt Col The Lord Lovat MC
Second-in-Command
Major D. Mills-Roberts
Adjutant
Capt J. Dunning-White
Intelligence Officer
Lt A.D.C. Smith,
Signals officer
Lt M.C. Ackernley
Medical Officer
Capt R.J. Walker
Mortar Officer
Lt J.F. Ennis
Regimental Sergeant Major
RSM W. Morris

A Troop
Capt B.W.S. Boucher-Myers
Lt A.F.S. Veasey

Lt L. Coulson
TSM Williams

B Troop
Capt G.H. Webb
Lt D. Gilchrist
TSM Chattaway

C Troop
Capt R.W.P. Dawson
Lt D. Style
Lt K. Carr
TSM Dunning

F Troop
Captain G.P. Pettiward
Lt J.MacDonald
Lt McKay
TSM Stockdale

Liaison Group
Capt P. Porteous
Sgt Desmond
Sgt Horne

For Operation CAULDRON No 4 Commando was split into two groups. Group 1 under Mills-Roberts and Group 2 under Lovat, each group had a self contained headquarters. Group 1 consisted of a section from A Troop and C Troop, while Group 2 had B and F Troop with a section from A Troop. If pressed either group could have attacked the guns if the other had been destroyed. Interestingly it appears that one of the sections in B Troop may have been commanded by a senior NCO or by Webb.

Regiments and Corps represented in Operation CAULDRON

An indication of the diverse origins of the soldiers who served in No 4 Commando is indicated by the list that appears at the end of *Notes from Theatres of War No 11*.

The Royal Hussars
VIII Hussars
The Lovat Scouts
The Royal Armoured Corps (and Royal Tank Regiment)
The Royal Regiment of Artillery
   (Field)
   (HAA)
   (Coast)
   (Searchlights)
Corps of Royal Engineers
Grenadier Guards
Coldstream Guards
Irish Guards
Welsh Guards
The Royal Scots
The Buffs

The Royal Warwickshire Regiment
The Royal Fusiliers
The King's Regiment (including the King's Liverpool Irish)
The Royal Norfolk Regiment
The Devonshire Regiment
The Suffolk Regiment
The Somerset Light Infantry
The West Yorkshire Regiment
The East Yorkshire Regiment
The Bedfordshire and Hertfordshire Regiment
The Green Howards
The Lancashire Fusiliers
The Royal Welch Fusiliers
The King's Own Scottish Borderers
The Cameronians
The Royal Inniskilling Fusiliers
The Gloucestershire Regiment
The Worcestershire Regiment
The East Lancashire Regiment
The East Surrey Regiment
The Duke of Cornwall's Light Infantry
The Border Regiment
The Hampshire Regiment
The South Staffordshire Regiment
The Dorsetshire Regiment
The South Lancashire Regiment
The Welch Regiment
The Black Watch
The Oxfordshire and Buckinghamshire Light Infantry
The Essex Regiment
The Sherwood Foresters
The Loyal Regiment
The Royal Berkshire Regiment
The Queen's Own Royal West Kent Regiment
The King's Own Yorkshire Light Infantry
The King's Shropshire Light Infantry

The King's Royal Rifle Corps
The Durham Light Infantry
The Highland Light Infantry
The Liverpool Scottish (Queen's Own Cameron Highlanders)
The Royal Ulster Rifles
The Rifle Brigade
The Royal Army Service Corps
The Royal Army Medical Corps
The Royal Army Ordnance Corps
The Honourable Artillery Company
The Liaison Regiment
The South Saskatchewan Regiment
1er Bataillon Fusilier Marine
The US Rangers

Bibliography

Atkin Ronald, *Dieppe 1942 The Jubilee Disaster*, MacMillan, London, 1980.

Austin, A.B. *We Landed at Dawn*, Victor Gollanz, London, 1943.

Bellocq, Jean, *Dieppe at sa region face a l'occupation Nazi*, France, 1979

Black, Robert W., *Rangers in World War II*, Ivy Books, New York

Caldwell, Donald L., *JG 26 Top Guns of the Luftwaffe*, Orion Books, New York, 1991.

Darby, William O. with Baumer William H. *Darby's Rangers,* Presidio Press, California, USA, 1980

Dear, Ian, *Ten Commando 1942 – 1945*, Leo Cooper, London, 1987

Dunning, James, *"It Had To Be Tough"*, The Pentland Press, Edinburgh, 2000

Franks, Norman, *The Greatest Air Battle*, Grub Street, London, 1992

HMSO *Combined Operations*, HMSO, London, 1943

Ladd, James, *Commandos and Rangers of World War II*, MacDonald and Jane's, London, 1978

Lovat, Lord, *March Past A Memoir*, Weidenfeld and Nicolson, London, 1977

Maguire, Eric, *Dieppe: August 19*, Jonathan Cape, London, 1963

Messenger, Charles, *The Commandos 1940 – 1946*, William Kimber, London, 1985

Mills-Roberts, Brigadier Derek, *Clash by Night*, William Kimber, London, 1956

Naval Staff History, *Raid on Dieppe, Battle Summary No 33*, London, 1959

Parker, John, *Commandos*, Headline, London, 2000.

Reynolds, Quentin, *Dress Rehearsal the Story of Dieppe*, Angus & Robertson, London, 1943

Robertson, Terence, *Dieppe The Shame and The Glory*, Hutchinson, London, 1963

Saunders, St George, Hilary, *The Green Beret*, Michael Joseph Ltd, London, 1949

Scott, Lt Cdr, Peter, *The Battle of the Narrow Seas*, Country Life, London, 1945.

Sierra, La, Raymond, *Le Commando du 6 Juin*. Presses de la Cité, Paris, 1983

Swift, Michael and Sharpe, Michael, *Historical Maps of World War II Europe*, PRC Publishing, London 2000

Taylor Hills, Reginald, John, *Phantom Was There*, Edward Arnold, London, 1951

Truscott Jr, Lt Gen L.K, *Command Missions*, E.P. Dutton and Co, Washington, 1954

Villa, Brian Loring *Unauthorised Action. Mountbatten and the Dieppe Raid 1942*, Oxford University Press, Canada, 1989.

Wyndham, Joan, *Love is Blue*, Heinemann, London, 1986

Manuals

Notes from Theatres of War No 11, Destruction of a German Battery by No. 4 Commando during the Dieppe Raid, HMSO, 1943

Small Arms Training, Volume 1, Pamphlet No. 3, Rifle 1937, HMSO, 1938

Small Arms Training, Volume 1, Pamphlet No. 4, Light Machine Gun 1939, HMSO, 1939

Small Arms Training, Volume 1, Pamphlet No. 13, Grenade 1942, HMSO, 1942

TM 31-200-1 Unconventional Warfare Devices and Techniques References, HQ Department of the Army, 1966

Imperial War Museum Sound Archive

Boucher-Myers. ID No 10785/3

Cook, George. ID No 9977/3

Davies, Bernard, K. ID No 10783/2

Fussell, Peter. ID No 10242/4
Kennett, Kenneth. ID No 10790/3
Leach, Clifford. ID No 9865/2
Lindley, Hugh. ID No 10909 (Interview by E.W. Jones)
Porteous, Patrick. ID 10060/2
Portman, Irving. ID No 9766/5
Spearman, William. ID No 9796/8

Unpublished sources
Cadot, Gerard, memoir of August 19, 1942 translated by Emyr Jones
Dunning, James, interviews, personal archives
Jones, Emyr, correspondence
Jones, George, interview
Skerry, John, interviews, personal archives and correspondence
Szima, Alex, interviews, personal archives and correspondence

Operation CAULDRON
Operation Order No 1 "Cauldron"
Report on Orange Beach 2 Landing by Lt.Col. The Lord Lovat, MC
Report on Orange Beach 1 Landing by Major D. Mills-Roberts
Report on 'A' Tp. Orange Beach 1 from Capt. Boucher-Myers
Report on Fighting Patrol from Orange Beach 2 by Lt. A.F.S. Veasey
Report on 'C' Tp. during Operation "Cauldron" by Capt. R. Dawson
Report on working of Signals by Lt. M.C. Ackernley
Report by Lieut. A.D.C. Smith, Intelligence Officer No 4 Commando
Personal Account of Lieut. A.D.C. Smith
Journal and extract of report by Lt.Cdr. H.H.H. Mulleneux, RN

Picture credits
AP – Associated Press
BM – Brian Mullen
EJ – Emyr Jones
IWM – Imperial War Museum
JD – James Dunning
WF – William Fowler

Index